DATE			

ANSWERS

Richard J. Taffler, Ph.D., is a lecturer in Operational Research in Accounting and Finance at the City University Business School, London.

Robert Russell is Associate Professor of Management Science and Chairman, Management and Marketing, at the University of Tulsa College of Business Administration.

ANSWERS

Decision-Making Techniques
for Managers

Richard Taffler
revised by Robert Russell

A SPECTRUM BOOK

Prentice-Hall, Inc., Englewood Cliffs, New Jersey 07632

Library of Congress Cataloging in Publication Data

Taffler, Richard J
  Answers, decision-making techniques for
  managers.

  (A Spectrum Book)
  Originally published in 1979 under title:
  Using operational research.
  Includes bibliographic references and index.
    1. Management—Mathematical models.   2. Decision-
  making—Mathematical models.   3. Operations re-
  search.   I. Russell, Robert A.   (date).
  II. Title.
  HD30.25.T33   1981   658.4'034   80-27759

ISBN 0-13-037861-5

ISBN 0-13-037853-4 {PBK.}

This Spectrum Book can be made available to businesses
and organizations at a special discount when ordered in
large quantities. For more information, contact:
        Prentice-Hall, Inc.
        General Book Marketing
        Special Sales Division
        Englewood Cliffs, New Jersey 07632

10   9   8   7   6   5   4   3   2   1

Editorial/production supervision by Eric Newman
Cover design by Honi Werner
Manufacturing buyer: Barbara A. Frick

Originally published as *Using Operational Research:
A Practical Introduction* by Prentice-Hall International,
Inc., London. © 1979 by Academic Services Company.

Prentice-Hall International, Inc., *London*
Prentice-Hall of Australia Pty. Limited, *Sydney*
Prentice-Hall of Canada, Ltd., *Toronto*
Prentice-Hall of India Private Limited, *New Delhi*
Prentice-Hall of Japan, Inc., *Tokyo*
Prentice-Hall of Southeast Asia Pte. Ltd., *Singapore*
Whitehall Books Limited, *Wellington, New Zealand*

CONTENTS

FOREWORD

This book is for present and future managers—for practicing businessmen and accountants, and for students of business management and accounting. It is designed to enable them, with their own resources, to learn about the use of quantitative methods in management, and the extent to which some of these approaches can help them to make decisions.

To serve this purpose such a book has to meet two basic requirements. First, its use of mathematics has to be tailored to the capacities of the people likely to be using it. It must recognize the fact that mathematics is a form of language (a means of communicating or expressing ideas) as well as a tool for performing calculations, and that you cannot communicate with people by using terms that they do not understand. For this reason the mathematical knowledge that is assumed of the potential reader, whatever his background, is restricted to a level that he (or she) almost certainly covered early in secondary school.

Second, the book has to be genuinely self-instructional. It must be written in such a way that the reader can understand the contents on his own without having to depend on any other form of explanation. In practice this is an even more difficult specification to meet than the first.

Although it is not aimed at turning you into an 'instant expert', if you carefully work through the book and complete the examples you should at the very least be able to do three things:

(i) identify problems within your own organization amenable to solution by the appropriate Quantitative Management techniques;
(ii) apply some of the more straightforward techniques described in this book yourself; and
(iii) communicate with the appropriate specialists

In addition, you will possess a sufficiently thorough grounding in the subject to provide a basis for more advanced study.

In the preparation of a truly self-instructional textbook it is necessary to combine three separate ingredients:

(i) knowledge of the subject,
(ii) textbook preparation skills, and

(iii) ignorance of the subject — for the purpose of ensuring that the book really meets the needs of its potential users.

It may be possible to combine ingredients (i) and (ii) in a single author, or (ii) and (iii), but never (i) and (iii). By its nature, therefore, a self-instructional course must be prepared by a team of at least two people who, in some working combination or another, are able to contribute all three ingredients between them.

In this text the knowledge input came primarily from Richard Taffler and the other two ingredients primarily from me. Robert Russell subsequently 'Americanized' the original British version of the book for the American market. In addition, we were both much helped and encouraged by the ideas and suggestions of Dr. Taffler's colleague Al Russell, Senior Lecturer in Operational Research at the City University Business School. On behalf of both of us I would like to take this opportunity to acknowledge and thank him for his contribution to this book.

Dr. Taffler's qualifications as an authority on the subject speak clearly enough for themselves. Robert Russell is an associate professor of management science at the University of Tulsa. He has published numerous research articles, as well as books on operations research and operations management. My qualifications, which require a little more explaining, consisted first of a total ignorance of operations research; second, of a personal background of administration and general management in business, industry and government; and third of the experience developed over several years in preparing a number of earlier courses of the same general type (though in different subjects).

I also wish to thank Judith Neiva, who drew all the diagrams for this book.

Brian Platt

ANSWERS

1

MODELS FOR DECISION MAKING

A — The Model-Building Approach

The manager's prime function is the making of decisions. Until relatively recently however he has tended to handle problems on the basis of his intuition and experience alone. Nevertheless more recently, and associated with the development of the computer with its capacity to revolutionize the processing of information, has come the recognition of the value of a more formal approach to problem solution and the acceptance of a generally more scientific approach to management.

The name given to the application of the scientific method to problems of management decision-making is **operations research** (often termed **OR** for short). Its basic tool is the **model**, which is a representation in mathematical terms of a real-life problem, in the context of certain clearly defined assumptions. It is mathematical because it deals with quantities and measurements, for which mathematics is the most appropriate medium. The model is used to describe the relationship between parts of the problem or system and the effects of changes to one part on other parts of the whole system.

This concept of the model may not be easy to grasp at first for those who lack a scientific or mathematical background, though in itself it is quite simple. Everybody is familiar, for example, with **iconic** models (pictures, sculpted objects, etc.) which reproduce the visual appearance only of the thing being modelled. Most people will also accept that, in order to be a good representation, this type of model does not necessarily have to imitate exactly all the features of the original: indeed, a very simplified or even somewhat distorted version may still be entirely recognisable for what it seeks to represent or may emphasize certain important features of the original which in real life do not stand out from among all the surrounding detail.

By contrast a mathematical model (also termed analytic model) is concerned not with the visual appearance of the thing being modelled but with certain aspects of its behavior. This also is a familiar device, even though it is one which most people tend to use without being aware of having done so. For example, if you watch an airplane fly into a small cloud you will anticipate the time and place at which it emerges from the other side: you have mentally constructed a mathematical model in which, on the assumption that the aircraft's speed and direction and altitude

1

remain constant (or approximately so) you are able to deduce certain conclusions about its behavior.

The analytic model is used in management in two principal ways. One way, with which any manager will already be familiar from his own experience, takes the form of a forecast of future behavior. The other way of using a model, perhaps less familiar to managers, is to reproduce certain aspects of a continuing situation (such as stock control or production planning) so as to study the possible ways in which that job can be done more efficiently.

Like the iconic model, the mathematical model does not have to be an exact representation of the original; there may even be advantages in trying to simplify it. To the basic framework of a simple model, which has been used to identify the main features of the problem and its solution, it may be possible to add progressive refinements which bring it successively closer to the complexities of the real-life situation.

Designing models is skilled work. However, there exist in management a number of basically similar types of problem for which basic models have been designed and tested by experience. Fitting the facts of a real problem into the framework of such a standardized model may actually be less difficult than any other, less systematic way of trying to evaluate the main components of a situation. There are other advantages of the formalized approach, some of which can be listed as follows.

1. It applies a discipline which helps to ensure that the important elements of a problem are identified and considered in a systematic manner.

2. Where a choice has to be made between alternative proposals, the use of a standard form of model offers a consistent basis of comparison between them.

3. For problems which are continuous or repetitive in their nature, the lessons learned can be built into the basic model and are preserved in this way as a form of accumulated experience.

4. A model can be a valuable tool of communication which ensures that those who take and implement the decision all have the same frame of reference, as far as the model at least is concerned.

The ways in which a model achieves these things may not yet be clear to you, but they will become so as you work through this book and gain familiarity with the models themselves. At this stage it is worth making one further point; that the exercise itself can sometimes be more valuable than the answer it was intended to find. For example, the actual exercise of making a forecast of what is expected to arise from a certain course of action, in order to calculate its profitability, may suggest better courses of action which would not otherwise have been considered.

B — Limitations of the Model-Building Approach

However realistic it may be within its own terms of reference, a model deals only with certain aspects of a real-life situation which is likely to have many other aspects. In reaching a decision as to whether and where to construct a new factory, for example, a management team may conclude that on the basis of certain assumptions plan A will offer a better rate of return on capital invested than plans B or C. However, these assumptions can be upset by all sorts of factors of which the effect can only be guessed at: the behavior of the market, the activities of competitors, the possibility of new technical developments which could outdate the process being proposed, political changes, changes in taxation policy, industrial relations problems — any one of which could convert seemingly impeccable plans for success into actual disasters. Again, there could be other factors which fall right outside the model's terms of reference (e.g. possible effects on the environment) while being relevant to the final decision. Having arrived at the answer given above, therefore, the conclusion to be drawn may well be: plan B has been shown to be less profitable than plan A on the basis of curtain assumptions which seem to be reasonable in themselves, but . . .

This point needs to be stressed (even at the risk of belaboring it) because quantitative techniques sometimes have a dangerous appeal of their own; especially to managers who see in them a means of avoiding personal responsibility for decisions which might go wrong. The techniques are aids to management decision-making, not substitutes for it, and as aids they have certain strict limitations. In order to be able to use them effectively it is necessary to understand exactly what they can do; which means understanding the limits of what they can do.

The techniques themselves are mathematically based, and mathematics has been described as an axiomatic science. An **axiom** is, broadly speaking, a statement which is assumed to be true for the purpose of the exercise; whether it is actually true or not. If certain axioms are held to be true, then certain conclusions can be proved to follow from them. Clearly, therefore, a mathematical solution can only be as 'true' as the assumptions on which it has been based. For some management problems the OR model may fit the real-life situation quite closely; for others it may be only a very crude approximation of the real world — while still, perhaps, being the best guideline available.

A manager who is working on a problem in conjunction with an OR specialist may not have the time or the expertise to check for himself the correctness of the mathematical solution. He may have to take this on trust or have it checked by another specialist. What he can and must do, however, is to check and understand the assumptions on which the calculation has been based. This in itself requires no mathematical knowledge, though it is helped by an understanding of the analytic approach. It does require a knowledge of the realities of the situation which the manager should be more likely to possess than anybody else. It is from his understanding of the relationship between the model and the real-life situation that the manager can decide how to make the best use of the solutions that he is being offered.

C — The Objectives of this Book

This book has been designed to give managers and students of management, accounting and business generally, a practical insight into the ways in which operations research actually works. It begins by describing the concept of a model because this amount of background knowledge is essential to an understanding of the approach, but the book does not deal with model-building as such. Its purpose is, rather, to demonstrate the application to management decision-making of a range of analytic techniques. To this end it uses standardized types of model, sometimes in a deliberately simplified form, though in such a way that their relationship to real-life management problems will be obvious.

The particular techniques demonstrated in this book have been selected according to the following criteria:

1. They are relatively well-known and their potential value for a wide range of situations has been demonstrated by repeated experience.
2. They are capable of being understood by a person who has no more than a very basic knowledge of arithmetic and algebra.
3. They can be handled computationally with a simple pocket calculator, although two of the chapters contain appendices in which the use of the computer is briefly illustrated for purposes of comparison.

It should be stressed that not all the techniques described here are likely to be useful to all managers, whose needs are different. However, every manager is likely to find something here which is directly relevant to his own problems and the other techniques are at least worth knowing about for their potential application to other circumstances. Similarly, whereas the level of basic mathematical understanding which has been specified is enough to permit these techniques to be demonstrated in a book, it is not always enough to enable them to be applied to the more complicated conditions which *actually* exist on the ground. What this book aims to do, in such cases, is to describe the technique in enough detail to enable the manager to evaluate its relevance to his own problems or to communicate effectively with an OR specialist for the purpose of applying it.

Because of the variety of needs that it covers, this book has been organized in as flexible a manner as possible. Each chapter starts with a summary of the purpose of the techniques which it describes, of the basic mathematical background required and of the relationship of that chapter to any which have preceded it; and it concludes with an annotated bibliography to more advanced readings for the reader who wishes to explore the techniques and their applications in practice further. The sequence in which the chapters have been arranged is a logical one in itself, but not mandatory. If, for example, you have a current application for critical path planning you may feel free to start with chapter 7.

In general, chapters 2, 3 and 4 should be taken as a whole in so far as they all deal with complementary aspects of investment appraisal, and in sequence in so far as the understanding of each chapter depends to some extent on knowledge covered by the preceding ones. The others are capable of being taken independently and in any sequence.

D — The Conventions Used

An exceptional amount of trouble has been taken to ensure that this book really can function as a self-instructional course. Whether it actually does so in your case is, however, up to you and it will help you to use the book properly if you have begun by understanding the general way in which each chapter has been laid out and the sense in which the different conventions are being applied.

Each chapter is divided into sections. The section has been designed to handle a single idea or concept, reduced to the smallest reasonable limits within which it can be identifiable as a whole concept. In this way the individual concepts which form parts of the technique as a whole are successively built up and brought together through the course of the chapter.

To accompany each section of the text there are a number of questions (20 per chapter). These questions have a very close and specific relationship to the section, such that the purpose of the text is to enable the reader to answer the questions and the purpose of the questions is to ensure that the text is being properly understood: so much so, in fact, that the reader who is new to the subject and hopes to master it without undertaking the questions may well not get all that much from the book.

In a conventional textbook the questions are inserted mainly to give practice. The questions in this book will serve that purpose to some extent, but it is purely incidental to their main purpose, which is to serve as a tool of understanding. They have not been designed to drum a technique home by repeated application until it has been memorized, basically because that is not the philosophy behind this particular book. If a manager has occasion to put into effect some of the techniques that he learns from this book, he will be getting his practice in the best possible way. As for those techniques that he cannot immediately see a case for applying, there is little point in his trying to memorize them in detail. It is enough to know that they exist and to be able to refer back to the book if a problem arises for which a particular technique might be relevant.

To help you refer back, when needed, there is an index of terms at the end of this book. When a technical term is introduced for the first time it is printed in **bold type** and defined at that stage of the text. In effect, the index provides a glossary of technical terms which works by referring back to the stage in the text at which the term was defined and first used.

The remaining conventions of this book are straightforward. Where *italic* is used, this is either for emphasis or for some special purpose (e.g. the statement of a computational rule) which justifies differentiation from the rest of the text, as the context will make clear in each case. Diagrams are numbered in sequence within each chapter. The text rarely requires you to refer back to a diagram that has been printed on an earlier page; the practice is, rather, to reprint the diagram, usually with modifications to suit the current context.

Appendix – The Computer

The computer plays a very significant role in present day OR practice, since many of the problems met by the operations researchers require its use for solution. This may be because their scale prohibits manual calculation or because the mathematical techniques to solve certain types of model are not yet known and their solutions have to be approximated by computer. In this book we focus on some of the more straightforward techniques which, at least in terms of the size of example used, do not need to be solved by computer. Nevertheless to illustrate how it is used in practice chapters 8 and 9 contain appendices in which problems solved by hand in the text are also solved by computer for comparison purposes.

Most large, many medium and even quite a percentage of small companies now own or lease a computer. However these are frequently designed for administrative and clerical tasks such as invoicing, customer accounting and payroll etc., which are characterized by much data input and printed output but little calculation, and are carried out on a routine basis. The OR man, however, uses a computer to meet very different needs, which are characterized by little data input and output but much calculation. Such use tends to be non-routine. As a result he may often resort to a computer outside his company which he accesses on a **time-sharing** basis.

There are many commercial computer centers now that provide such a service whereby a single computer simultaneously meets the needs of a large number of different users in different locations who communicate with it through typewriter-like terminals in their offices linked to the computer via the normal Post Office telephone system. Because of the power of the central computer, users can work on an **interactive** basis in that they obtain a very rapid and frequently virtually immediate response from the computer to the commands they type into their terminal.

Although it is frequently necessary to write specific **computer programs** (sets of instructions directing the computer to process data in the required manner) to solve a particular problem, in many situations there are programs already written and available 'off the shelf' to do the necessary calculations. These are known as **computer packages** and have the additional advantage that their use requires no knowledge of computer programming. This is because the user has only to input the data for his particular problem into the computer in the manner required by the package, which does the rest. Appendices to the last two chapters of this book illustrate the use of a typical computer package which is used on an interactive basis via a time-sharing system.

A basic introduction to computers and their applications is provided in 'Computer Data Processing', by Gordon Davis, second edition, McGraw Hill, 1973.

Further Reading

1. The History of Operations Research
Operations research originated during the 1939—45 war in application to a line of specialized studies relating to the planning and conduct of military operations, and then evolved into a general management aid. A good non-technical review of the history of operations research is provided by S.L. Cook in chapter 1 of 'Operational Research for Managers', edited by S.C. Littlechild, Philip Allan 1977, and a fascinating account of wartime operations research by C.H. Waddington in 'OR in World War II: Operational Research Against the U-Boat', Paul Elek 1973.

2. What Operations Research is
Most operations research textbooks contain extensive descriptions of what operations research is although in many cases such discussions are rather confusing and technical for a non-specialist. The second chapter by M. Pidd in 'Operational Research for Managers', entitled 'The operations research method', however, provides a good summary in a non-technical manner and chapter 19 of the same book entitled 'Putting operational research to work', by S.L. Cook, discusses the role of the operations researcher in an organization. The first chapter of 'Fundamentals of Operations Research' by R.L. Ackoff and M. Sasieni, Wiley 1968, and chapters 1 and 17 of 'Introduction to Management Science' by Thomas Cook and Robert Russell, Prentice-Hall, 1981 cover related ground to the previous two references in a more comprehensive manner.

3. Operations Research in Practice
Well written non-technical surveys of the results from practical application

of the operational research method are relatively scarce although some specific references will be made in the bibliographies to the following chapters. The reader may, however, find the scenarios of real companies using operations research in Cook and Russell's 'Introduction to Management Science', second edition, to be interesting. Further cases and applications can be found in 'Management Science and the Manager: A Casebook' by E.F. Peter Newson, Prentice-Hall, 1980; 'Management Science—Cases and Applications', by Aggarwal and Khera, Holden-Day, 1979; and 'Cases in Operations Research' by Christoph Haehling von Lanzenauer, University of Western Ontario Press, 1975.

2

INTRODUCTION TO INVESTMENT APPRAISAL

Money is a medium for buying other things; among them, things which are capable of being used to earn income. A person can use his own money directly in this way or he can find people who are prepared to pay him for the use of it. Money, therefore, has two entirely different types of value: a value in terms of what it can buy or, alternatively, a value in terms of what it can earn.

Money which is allocated (or capable of being allocated) for the purpose of earning income is called **capital**; the process of allocating that capital is called **investment**, although in this book we sometimes use the word **project** in a way that is interchangeable with 'investment'. This chapter is concerned with ways of measuring the earning power of capital and of comparing the **return** (i.e. the income) obtainable from different types of investment. This is one aspect of the process of evaluating investments which goes under the general name of 'investment appraisal'.

This chapter calls for a sound understanding (albeit to a fairly elementary level) of basic arithmetic; in particular, it requires a prior understanding of the theory of simple progressions. Some of the computations required in working through the examples and questions are laborious and the use of a simple hand calculator is strongly recommended.

Although they may not be the easiest parts of this book mathematically, the techniques of investment appraisal have been introduced first because they have the widest application. Any project requires an injection of capital to start it off. This capital may not actually be in the form of money; it may be in the form, for example, of equipment or effort or 'know-how', but all of these are capable of being assigned a value in terms of money at the time they are contributed. The procedures described in this chapter (and in the two chapters which follow) are therefore as valid in principle for the man deciding whether to buy his house instead of renting it, as for the ship-owner deciding whether to order a new multi-million-pound tanker. Nor are they confined to the type of decision that we conventionally accept as being commercial. The approach can be applied equally to such situations as a local authority's decision to build a road or playground. Because of the fundamental importance of getting investment decisions correct the area of investment appraisal has been one where much OR work is undertaken. However, it is interesting to note that in many organizations the OR specialist is not directly involved, and that the accountant or finance man undertakes the whole analysis himself.

A — Interest (question 1)

We assume that you are already familiar with the concept of interest and the simpler mathematical operations involved in interest calculations. However, we will recapitulate these, in this section, as a preparation for what follows.

Interest is the payment made by a borrower to a lender in return for the use of his money during a certain period of time. The sum of money borrowed is called the **principal** and the rate at which interest is paid is usually expressed as a percentage of the principal. The term **per cent** (which derives from the Latin *per centum* meaning approximately 'for each hundred') is expressed mathematically by the sign % which means, in effect, ÷ 100. Hence 5% = 5/100 = 0.05.

Suppose that a person borrows a certain sum of money, say £1000, at a certain agreed rate of interest, say 12%/annum. (The oblique stroke / means 'per', i.e. 'for each'.) One year after the loan has been made the borrower owes the lender the principal plus the interest accumulated by that date, i.e.

$$\$1000 + (12\% \text{ of } \$1000) = \$1120$$

That part of the debt which is due to interest alone is normally treated in one of two ways: either it remains separate from the principal or it is added to the principal and starts to incur interest at the same rate, the combined sum at any given time being termed the **amount**. The former arrangement is called **simple interest** and usually implies that the interest is payable separately at the end of each time period. The latter arrangement is called **compound interest**.

$1000 + (12% of $1000) is the same as $1000 × 1.12, which is a rather more convenient method of calculation. As we have seen, if *compound* interest is due on $1000 at a rate of 12%/annum, the amount at the end of the first year is

$$\$1000 \times 1.12 = \$1120$$

At the end of the second year, the amount is

$$\$1120 \times 1.12 = \$1254.4 \text{ (i.e. } 1000 \times 1.12^2)$$

At the end of the third year the amount is

$$\$1254.4 \times 1.12 = \$1404.9 \text{ (i.e. } 1000 \times 1.12^3)$$

Thus it can be seen that at the end of 5 years the amount will be

$$\$1000 \times 1.12^5$$

At the end of 12 years it will be

$$\$1000 \times 1.12^{12}$$

and so on.

This general rule can be expressed as a formula

$$A = P(1 + i)^n$$

where A represents the amount, P the principal, n the number of time periods for which interest is paid, and i the rate of interest in % per time period.

Example 1

Give the amount at the end of 12 years on a loan of $3500 bearing compound interest at the rate of 7%/annum.

Solution:

$$\begin{aligned} A &= P(1 + i)^n = 3500 \times (1 + 7.5/100)^{12} \\ &= 3500 \times 1.075^{12} = 3500 \times 2.382 \\ &= \$8337 \end{aligned}$$

Example 2

A loan of $500 bearing monthly compound interest will cost $597.5 to repay at the end of 18 months. What is the rate of interest?

Solution:

$$\begin{aligned} A &= P(1 + i)^n \\ (1 + i)^n &= A/P \\ (1 + i)^{18} &= 597.5/500 = 1.195 \end{aligned}$$

Let $(1 + i) = m$

$$\begin{aligned} m &= \sqrt[18]{1.195} = 1.01 = 1 + i \\ i &= 1.01 - 1 = 0.01 \\ \text{rate of interest} &= 0.01 \times 100 = 1\%/\text{month} \end{aligned}$$

The rate (expressed as a percentage of the principal) at which an investment yields interest is usually referred to as the **rate of return** of the investment.

B — The Time Value of Money (questions 2–5)

It follows from the preceding section that a sum of money which is available *now* is clearly worth more than the same sum of money at some time in the future, because the money which is available now and is loaned at compound interest will have grown to a larger amount at a later date.

Assume that a person has a sum of money, say $100, that he wishes to invest. Of all the alternatives open to him, the one which offers the highest rate of interest yields 10%/annum compound. Logically, then he may value the $100 that he has now as being worth $100 × (1.1) in one year's time, $100 × (1.1)² in two years' time and so on.

Conversely, it can be seen that $100 accruing to him in one year's time should be valued today at

$$\$100/1.1 = \$90.91$$

since $90.91 invested today at 10%/annum will be worth $100 in a year's time. Effectively all that we have done, of course, is to transpose the compound interest formula. The figure of $100, instead of being the principal, is the amount in this calculation. Therefore, if

$$A = P(1 + i)^n, A = 100, n = 1 \text{ and } i = 0.1, \text{ then}$$
$$100 = 1.1P$$
$$100/1.1 = P$$
$$P = 90.91$$

Similarly, $100 due in two years' time should be valued today at only

$$\$100/(1.1)^2 = \$82.64 \text{ and so on.}$$

The equivalent value, if it were available *now*, of money due at a later date, is called its **present value**, abbreviated to **PV**. The process of assessing payments or receipts due in the future in terms of their present value is called **discounting** and the percentage rate at which these should be discounted is called the **discount rate**. This naturally varies for different investors, depending on the range of investment opportunities open to them.

The general mathematical relationship can be expressed as a formula in the following terms:

$$PV = \frac{x}{(1 + i)^n}$$

where x represents the amount due, i the discount rate (expressed as a percentage) and n the number of interest periods before repayment becomes due. Normally, the 'interest period' unit is 1 year, and the discount rate is expressed as a percentage/annum. In this book an annual rate is implied wherever no time period has been specified. The formula itself is applicable to any interest period.

Example 3

Assume that a person's discount rate is 8%/annum.

(i) What is the present value to him of payments due over the next three years, amounting to $400 at the end of the first year, $300 at the end of the second year and $100 at the end of the third year?

(ii) If somebody offers him these future payments in exchange for $600 in cash now, should he accept? (Assume that there is no risk of default.)

Solution: (i) In this example, $i = 8/100 = 0.08$

$$PV = 400/1.08 + 300/(1.08)^2 + 100/(1.08)^3$$
$$= 370.4 + 257.2 + 79.4 = \$707$$

(ii) Obviously the transaction will be worth his while as the present value of the receipts is worth, to him $107 more than he would have to pay to acquire them.

It should be obvious that no method of calculating the return on an investment can be realistic if it does not take account of the time value of money. Traditional methods (one of the best known of which, the pay-back method, will be discussed more fully in chapter 4) did not take this into account and hence led to conclusions that were misleading or even entirely wrong.

C — Present Value Tables (questions 6—8)

Most of the labor of converting to present values can be eliminated by the use of tables of discount factors. The present value formula demonstrated in the previous section may also be written in the form

$$PV = x \times \frac{1}{(1 + i)^n}$$

The **discount factor** in this case is that part of the formula represented by

$$\frac{1}{(1 + i)^n}$$

Thus, when $i = 6\%$/annum and $n = 5$ years, the discount factor is

$$\frac{1}{(1 + 0.06)^5} = 0.7473$$

and therefore to calculate the present value of, say, $4000 due in five years' time at a discount rate of 6%, we have

$$PV = 4000 \times 0.7473 = \$2989.2$$

In table 1 at the end of this book you will find a sufficient range, for our purposes, of present value discount factors that have been calculated to four places of decimals for successive whole number values of i and n. In the text we shall refer to these, for brevity, as **present value tables**. In this table you will find (heading the columns) values of n from 1 to 16 and (heading the rows) values of i from 1% to 25%. To find the present value factor for a sum of money due in, say, 12 years' time at a discount rate of 8%, turn to table 1 and look down the column headed 12 and across the row headed 8%. You will find the figure 0.3971. This is the appropriate PV factor.

Example 4

Give the present value of $1000 due in 8 years' time at a discount rate of 11%.

Solution: The appropriate discount factor is 0.4339 (table 1, column 8, row 11)

$$PV = \$1000 \times 0.4339 = \$433.9$$

Example 5

What is the total present value, at a discount rate of 9%/annum, of a cash income received in the following instalments: $250 after 1 year, $400 after 3 years, $100 after 4 years and $600 after 7 years?

Solution: This is exactly the same type of problem as that of example 4 except that it involves a number of payments (receipts) made at different times. By tabulating the data in an orderly fashion it is easy to keep track of the different components of the problem. The treatment shown below should be self-explanatory.

(1) Year	(2) Payment in $	(3) Discount factor $i = 9\%$	(4) Present value (2) × (3)
1	250	0.9174	229.4
3	400	0.7722	308.9
4	100	0.7084	70.8
7	600	0.5470	328.2
	1350		937.3

Total present value = $937.3

D — Annuities (question 9)

A constant income over a number of years is called an **annuity**. Suppose that a regular income of $1000 per annum is anticipated over the next 9 years. The present value of the annuity as a whole at any specific discount rate can be worked out by calculating the PV of $1000 due in one year's time, the PV of $1000 due in 2 years' time and so on until the 9th year; then adding them all together. However, the present value factors for annuities have also been tabulated. In this text we will refer to such tables, for brevity, as **annuity tables**. A range of PV factors may be found in table 2. To find the present value factor at a discount rate of, say, 8% for an annuity which starts now and continues regularly for 9 years, turn to this table and look down the column headed 9 and across the row headed 8%. You will find the figure 6.2469, which is the appropriate discount factor.

In effect, each factor represents the sum of a geometric progression of n terms with first term $\frac{1}{1+i}$ and common ratio $\frac{1}{1+i}$: i.e.

$$\frac{1}{1+i} + \frac{1}{(1+i)^2} + \cdots \frac{1}{(1+i)^n}$$

The sum is given by

$$S = \frac{1}{i}\left[1 - \frac{1}{(1+i)^n}\right] = \left[\frac{1-(1+i)^{-n}}{i}\right]$$

Example 6

What is the present value of an annuity of \$600 which starts this year and continues for five years, when $i = 10\%$?

Solution: The appropriate discount factor is 3.7908 (table 2, column 5, row 10).

$$PV = \$600 \times 3.7908 = \$2274.5$$

E — Deferred Annuities (question 10)

Now let us consider, for example, the case of an annuity of \$400 for a period of 2 years, to commence in 3 years' time. How can the annuity tables be used to find the present value of this annuity discounted at, say, 8%/annum? Let us begin by taking a look at how the annuity table for $i = 8\%$ is constructed (refer, if necessary, to the preceding section).

Number of years	Progression	Present value factor
1	$\dfrac{1}{1.08} =$	0.9259
2	$\dfrac{1}{1.08} + \dfrac{1}{(1.08)^2} =$	1.7833
3	$\dfrac{1}{1.08} + \dfrac{1}{(1.08)^2} + \dfrac{1}{(1.08)^3} =$	2.5771
4	$\dfrac{1}{1.08} + \dfrac{1}{(1.08)^2} + \dfrac{1}{(1.08)^3} + \dfrac{1}{(1.08)^4} =$	3.3121

and so on.

In this case the annuity is said to be paid at the end of years 3 and 4 only. The appropriate discount factor is therefore

$$\frac{1}{(1.08)^3} + \frac{1}{(1.08)^4}$$

which is the sum of the progression for a 4 year annuity minus the sum of its first 2 terms, i.e.

$$3.3121 - 1.7833 = 1.5288$$

The present value, discounted at 8%, of a 2 year annuity of $400, due to commence in 3 years' time, is therefore

$$\$400 \times 1.5288 = \$611.5$$

Example 7

Suppose a person anticipates an income over the next 5 years which will be paid in instalments of $600 at the end of the first year, $800 at the end of the second year and $400 at the end of each succeeding year. What is the present value of the total income discounted at 11% per annum?

Solution:

(1) Year	(2) Payment in £	(3) Discount factor $i = 11\%$	(4) Present value (2) × (3)
1	600	0.9009	540.5
2	800	0.8116	649.3
3	400 ⎫	3.6959	
4	400 ⎬	− 1.7125	
5	400 ⎭	1.9834	793.4
Total	2600		1983.2

F — Cash Flow (questions 11–12)

To **evaluate a project** is to relate what has been paid into it to what is received from it, and thus to determine its profitability. What is spent on an investment is usually referred to as an **input** (i.e. what has been put into the project) and a yield from the investment is called an **output** (i.e., what comes out of the project). Notice that in conventional usage these terms are related to the investment itself as an entity, not to the person who is making it.

It will be obvious from what has gone before that the time when payments are made or received is very relevant to their value. Furthermore, the only times which matter for our purpose are the times when payments are made or received *in cash*.

Clearly cash has a special value to a business in so far as it is immediately available for reinvestment or other use as distinct from money tied up in machinery, stock or credit to customers. The reason for taking account only of cash here, however, is so that we can relate inputs and outputs directly to each other and measure them by means of a common standard. Expenses or profits as shown by the accountant that do not take a cash form (e.g. depreciation or revaluation) are therefore ignored in this type of approach which, when dealing with capital in the shape of machinery, buildings, stock and so on, is concerned only with the time and amount in cash at which the item is purchased (an input) and the time and amount in cash at which it is sold (an output).

The first step in evaluating a project is therefore to prepare a forecast or summary of what is called its **cash flow**. This means, literally, the flow of payments of cash and receipts of cash in defined amounts and at defined times, arising (or expected to arise, in the case of a forecast) directly from the project itself.

Conventionally, a cash flow summary or forecast is laid out in the form of a table of amounts against time, with inputs (i.e. payments, also known as expenses) shown as negative values and outputs (i.e. receipts, also known as revenues) shown as positive values. Each such payment or receipt is often referred to as an **element** of the cash flow.

Example 8

A company buys a machine for $27,000. It has an estimated life of 3 years and one man is to be employed to operate it at a wage rate of $13,500/annum. Other costs of operating the machine are expected to amount to $4500/annum. The company expects to manufacture with this machine and sell (at $9 each) 5000 items in the first year, 8000 in the second and 7000 in the third. The cost of raw materials for each item is $4.5.

Assuming, for convenience, that all payments and receipts occur at the beginning or end of a year, tabulate the cash flow of the project.

Solution:

Time (in years)		0	1	2	3
Receipts:	sales revenue		+ 45,000	+ 72,000	+ 63,000
Payments:	machine cost	− 27,000			
	labor		− 13,500	− 13,500	− 13,500
	raw materials		− 22,500	36,000	− 31,500
	other costs		− 4500	− 4500	− 4500
net cash flow		− 27,000	+ 4500	− 18,000	+ 13,500

Notice that the bottom row has been headed **net cash flow** (which can be abbreviated to **NCF**) which represents the sum of positive and negative cash payments *at each point in time*. The interval between successive points in time is a year in this particular model but in other models it could be a week, a month, a quarter or any other unit of time convenient to the circumstances.

The NCF of a project can be expressed in mathematical symbols as a series $a_0, a_1, a_2 \ldots a_n$, with the $_{0,1,2}$ and $_n$ known as **subscripts**, where a_0 represents the **element of the NCF** at point of time 0, a_1 represents the element at point of time 1 (and so on) and n is the total number of time periods for which the project lasts. In the preceding example the time period is one year and $n = 3$. The series can therefore be written out in full as

$$a_0 = -27,000$$
$$a_1 = + \quad 4500$$
$$a_2 = + 18,000$$
$$a_3 \; (\text{i.e., } a_n) = + 13,500$$

G — Net Present Value (questions 13—18)

In this chapter we are not concerned with where the money comes from to pay for a proposed investment (e.g. by means of a bank loan or debenture, by the use of retained earnings, by the issue of new share capital, etc.), as this has no bearing on the mathematics of the techniques we are discussing here.

We need only consider in very general terms what is called the **cost of capital** of the proposed project. This, if the project is to be financed with borrowed money, may be defined as the rate at which interest has to be paid on the loan. If the investor has funds of his own to finance the project the cost of capital may be defined as the best rate of return that he is able to get on his money when it is put to work by, say, investing it or ploughing it back into current operations.

In deciding whether an individual investment is worth his while, the investor often compares the return that he expects to get from it with a target rate such that the investment is potentially attractive to him if its rate of return equals or exceeds the target rate and potentially unattractive if it falls short of it. This is often also called the **cut-off rate**; a term that implies the cutting-off or abandonment of projects that fail to meet the target.

The actual choice of cut-off rate and the method of arriving at it are policy decisions peculiar to the individual investor. Obviously, however, an investment is unprofitable if its rate of return is less than its cost of capital.

The first step is to convert the cash flow to its present value at the chosen discount rate, arriving in this way at what is called the **discounted cash flow** (commonly abbreviated to **DCF**) of the project. The associated term **DCF method** incidentally is applied generally to this type of approach to investment appraisal, of which different aspects are covered in this chapter and the two which follow.

By summing all the elements, both positive and negative, of the discounted cash flow, one arrives at what is called the **net present value** (commonly abbreviated to **NPV**) of the project. If the sum of the positive elements exceeds that of the negative elements – i.e. if the NPV is *positive* – this means that the investment yields a rate of return *greater* than the discount rate which was applied to it. Conversely, if the sum of the negative elements exceeds that of the positive elements – i.e. if the NPV is *negative* – this means that the rate of return is *less than* the discount rate.

The NPV can be expressed as a formula in the following manner:

$$NPV = a_0 + \frac{a_1}{(1+i)} + \frac{a_2}{(1+i)^2} + \ldots + \frac{a_n}{(1+i)^n}$$

where n represents the number of time periods, $a_0 \ldots a_n$ the NCF and i the discount rate or cost of capital in %.

It follows that the NPV calculation has to be related to a definite period of time. At the end of that period of time it must either be assumed that the investment has no further value or it may be assigned a **residual value** (i.e. a figure representing its recoverable value in cash at that time) which is treated as a positive element in the final time period.

Example 9

Taking the example in the preceding section, give the NPV of the project if $i = 7\%$.

Solution: In this case

$$NPV = -27,000 + \frac{4500}{1.07} + \frac{18,000}{(1.07)^2} + \frac{13,500}{(1.07)^3}$$

and the problem can be solved by working this out in full. Alternatively, we may use present value tables in which case it is usual to calculate the answer in tabular form, as indicated below.

(1) Year	(2) NCF in $	(3) Discount factor $i = 7\%$	(4) Present value (2) × (3)
0	− 27,000	1.0000	− 27,000
1	4500	0.9346	+ 4205.7
2	18,000	0.8734	+ 15,721.2
3	13,500	0.8163	+ 11,020.05
Total = + 9000		NPV = + 3946.95	

In this example, the NPV of the investment is positive, which shows that the rate of return exceeds the discount rate (i.e. rate of return $> 7\%$).

In this and the subsequent models we have made a number of concessions to mathematical simplicity.

1. We have ignored tax. Obviously taxes and subsidies, where these apply, are very relevant to the final result and must be included in the data of any real-life problem, but they introduce no special complications from a mathematical viewpoint. Taxes are simply expenses or negative elements and subsidies are revenues or positive elements, to be entered as such in the cash flow, in their appropriate amounts and times, like any other revenue or expense.

2. We have assumed that i is constant over time. In practice the cost of money is liable to fluctuate like most other costs. If it declines, projects which were previously rejected as unprofitable may become worthwhile: if it increases, projects which appeared profitable may become unprofitable. In the next chapter we shall show how to calculate the actual rate of return on an investment, which can then be directly compared with the cost of capital so as to assess very quickly, at any time, the investment's relative unprofitability. By contrast, using the methods described hitherto, the only way to check the profitability of an investment in face of a change in the cost of capital, or target rate, is by discounting the NCF at the new rate: i.e. a repetition of the earlier process with a new value of *i*.

3. We have ignored problems of risk or uncertainty. The possibility of variations in the cost of capital has been mentioned. Similarly, in real-life problems the forecasts of expenses and revenues are unlikely to be as reliable as we have perhaps made them appear in our examples. There are a number of methods for taking such uncertainties into account but they cannot be treated adequately within the scope of this particular book as they require a previous understanding of probability theory. One very simple intuitive approach, which requires no mathematical explanation, is that by which an investor assesses the return he expects from a project according to the degree of risk that he considers it to involve. Thus, a person who may be content with a return of 10% from a comparatively risk-free investment may require a return two or three times larger to tempt him into a project involving greater risk.

4. We have disregarded inflation. The argument for evaluating investments in terms of cash flow only was based on the premise that cash provides a single and constant standard for measuring value. This is not strictly true and, in present-day conditions, a state of continuing inflation (i.e. a continuing reduction in the purchasing value of money) has to be accepted as a fact of life. A full treatment of inflation in this context would exceed the scope of this book, but a few simple points can be made. One effect of inflation is to reinforce the general argument implied in the DCF approach; namely, that a return which arises sooner is worth more than one which arises later. In practice, most projects of the type being discussed here call for an initial capital investment which is paid for by a cash return spread over a number of subsequent years. In some cases the method of obtaining this return is such that it rises with inflation — for example, if the investment is being made in a manufacturing or service industry that can raise its prices. In this type of situation it is not unreasonable to ignore the diminishing value of money in the model on the grounds that it will be approximately cancelled out by inflated returns. For other types of investment, however, such as fixed-interest securities, the income in money is constant through the life of the project but the real value (i.e. the purchasing power) of the income is not constant. One fairly simple way of taking this into account (though we do not use it in the examples and problems set in this book) is to devalue the return for each year so as to equate it with its purchasing power in present day terms. Consider an investment of $1000 at 9%/annum simple interest for a period of six years where the rate of inflation is estimated at 10%/annum. The cash flow can be tabulated as follows, using the present value tables, so as to record real values:

Time (in years)	0	1	2	3	4	5	6	Total
Net cash flow in money terms	−1000	90	90	90	90	90	1090	540
Net cash flow in real terms	−1000	81.82	74.38	67.62	61.47	55.88	615.31	−43.52

As expected, a loss results of $43.52 in present day terms.

A cash flow in real terms can be discounted in the normal way so as to give present real values, using a value of i net of the expected rate of inflation. For example, if the cost of capital for a project net of the effects of inflation is 4%/annum and the rate of inflation 12%/annum, then the discount rate is:

$$(1.04 \times 1.12) - 1 = 0.165 \text{ or } 16.5\%/\text{annum}$$

Although in practice many projects have an indefinite duration, the assumption made here of a fixed term is inherently not an unreasonable one to make in terms of a real-life investment decision. A new project should be forecasted only as far as it is realistic to do so: a project which cannot be shown to justify itself within the reasonably foreseeable future is probably not worth undertaking. In the case of many projects, of course, it can be assumed that at the end of the period of time specified for the purposes of the model (i.e. the period of time for which it is reasonable to look ahead) some of the capital equipment such as land, buildings or machinery will still have a resale value. The procedure is to make as realistic an assessment as possible of what the equipment would be likely to realize if sold at that time for cash, and enter this amount as the final output of the series. This is also the way to take account of any potential profits or losses arising from changes in the value of the capital equipment itself. Needless to say, the preparation of a model which has a duration of 5 years does not have to imply any serious intention of winding up the project itself after that period of time if it is still doing well; it is simply a procedure for trying to evaluate realistically the potential return on the investment.

H — Continuous Cash Flows (questions 19—20)

In actual practice the cash outlays and receipts of the project may not all occur neatly at the beginning or end of each time period, but may arise at different times during that period. In such circumstances it may be convenient to average these out by treating them as though they are all paid or received in the middle of their respective time periods. This technique is sometimes referred to as **mid-pointing**.

Example 10

A person invests $600 in developing and patenting a new invention. During the next 3 years he receives royalty payments amounting to $400 in the first year, $300 in the second year and $100 in the third year. These payments are received on a continuous basis.

    (i) Prepare a net cash flow table.
    (ii) Use the table to calculate the NPV of the project, where $i = 8\%$.

Solution:

(i)

Time	0	0.5	1	1.5	2	2.5	3
NCF	−600	+400		+300		+100	

$$\text{(ii)} \quad \text{NPV} = -600 + \frac{400}{(1.08)^{0.5}} + \frac{300}{(1.08)^{1.5}} + \frac{100}{(1.08)^{2.5}}$$

The calculation can be completed in this form by pocket calculator or alternatively by using the present value tables (table 1) by bearing in mind their mathematical construction: i.e. the first number in the column headed 8 is

$$1/1.08 = 0.9259$$

the second number is

$$1/(1.08)^2 = 0.8573$$

and so on.

    To use these tables we must begin by eliminating the fractional indices. This can be done (in part, at least) by rearranging as follows [note that $(1.08)^0 = 1$]:

$$NPV = -600 + \frac{1}{(1.08)^{0.5}} \left[\frac{400}{(1.08)^0} + \frac{300}{(1.08)^1} + \frac{100}{(1.08)^2} \right]$$

The portion enclosed in square brackets can then be tabulated and calculated separately. Thus,

(1) Index number	(2) NCF in $	(3) Discount factor $i = 8\%$	(4) Present value (2) × (3)
0	400	1.0000	400.0
1	300	0.9259	277.8
2	100	0.8573	85.7
	800		763.5

$$NPV = -600 + \frac{763.5}{(1.08)^{0.5}} = -600 + 734.7 = \$134.7$$

Questions

2.1 If I invest $250 now in a building society which pays 5%/annum compound, to how much will it have grown after 5 years?

2.2 What sum of money would a person have to invest now at 7%/annum compound in order to receive $500 after 7 years?

2.3 What is a person's discount rate if he values $100 now as being worth $150 in 5 years' time?

2.4 If a rich uncle, who does not understand that money has a time value, promises his newborn nephew $1000 on his 21st birthday and the relevant discount rate is 9%/annum, what is the present value of his offer?

2.5 What is the sum the uncle in the preceding question should promise his nephew at 21, as the equivalent of $1000 now with relevant discount rate of 9%/annum?

2.6 A person expects to receive payments of $700 in one year's time, $300 in 2 years' time and $200 in 3 years' time. Tabulate this information in the manner of example 5, and keep a note of the answer for question 7.

2.7 (i) Taking the data of question 6, use present value factors to complete the table and to calculate the total present value of the expected income discounted at 8%. Keep a note of your answer for use in question 8.
   (ii) If you can normally expect to earn 8% on the money that you invest, would it be worth your while to make a payment of $1000 now in order to obtain this future income? Justify your answer.

2.8 (i) Calculate the present value, discounted at 8%, of receipts of $200 after 1 year, $300 after 2 years and $700 after 3 years.
   (ii) Why is the result different from that of question 7?

2.9 (i) Use your annuity tables to determine the present value of $100 a year for 10 years with discount rate 10%.
   (ii) If this annuity were to be purchased for $750, what would the discount rate then be (to the nearest ½%)?

(iii) If your own discount rate is 10%, would it be good policy to sell or buy this annuity for $750?

2.10 Give the present value, discounted at 5%, of an annuity of $300 for a period of 4 years commencing: (i) in 1 year's time; (ii) in 4 years' time; (iii) in 7 years' time.

2.11 (i) What is the definition of 'cash flow'?

(ii) In one company the practice is to depreciate the value of machinery in its accounts at the rate of 20%/annum. In what way should this practice be taken into account, when making up the cash flow forecast for a proposed purchase of new machinery?

2.12 A company can undertake a project that will require $10,000 immediately and will have operating costs at the rate of $5000/annum. Cash receipts are expected at the rate of $3000 in the first year of operations, increasing by $2000/annum in each subsequent year. Prepare a cash flow table for the first 4 years of operation. Assume all cash payments are made at the end of each year.

2.13 A man can normally expect a return of 7% compound on any money that he invests. He is offered an opportunity to invest $1500 now for a return of $600 in a year's time, $300 in 2 years' time and $800 in 3 years' time. (i) Calculate the NPV. (ii) Is it positive or negative? (iii) Should he accept the offer, or not?

2.14 A company can purchase a machine now for $25,000 that has an operational life of 4 years. The expected increase in cash profits directly due to the installation of the machine is $10,000 at the end of the first year and $7000 at the end of the remaining 3 years of life. Tabulate this information for the purpose of calculating the NPV of the project, and keep a note of your answer for use in question 15.

2.15 (i) Given the data of question 14, calculate the NPV of the project if the company's cost of capital is 10%/annum.

(ii) Is the investment likely to be profitable, or not? Justify your answer.

2.16 A company is considering whether to enter a new market. Recruitment and training of the new salesmen required will cost $65,000, payable immediately. The salesmen will receive a basic salary totalling $40,000 per annum and a commission of $0.25 on each item sold. The cost of each item will be $1 and the selling price $2. Expected sales are 50,000 items in the first year and 100,000 in each succeeding year. Take all annual payments and receipts as occurring at the end of the year and, by tabulating the cash flow for the first 4 years, show the NCF. Keep a note of the answer for question 17.

2.17 If $i = 12\%$, calculate the NPV of the project of question 16 over a period of 4 years. Is the project likely to be profitable if it lasts no longer than 4 years?

2.18 In response to a tender a shipbuilding company has made a bid of $1.5m payable on completion for the construction of a ship which will take 3 years to build. The net cash payments for labor, materials, directly attributable overheads, etc. are expected to be $0.5m at the end of the first year, $0.4m at the end of the second and $0.3m at the end of the third. If the bid is accepted, $i = 11\%$ and the construction is to start immediately, is this a worthwhile project for the company?

2.19 A man who wants to borrow $3000 is offered the opportunity to pay back the sum plus $600 in equal weekly installments over the next

3 years. Prepare a net cash flow table and keep a note of the result for use in question 20.

2.20 The man in question 19 can also borrow the sum from his bank at a rate of interest of 12%/annum. Calculate the NPV of the project with $i = 12\%$ and hence determine which method would be the more advantageous to him.

Further Reading

The 'bibles' of investment appraisal are the related books by A.J. Merrett and Allen Sykes, 'The Finance and Analysis of Capital Projects', Longman 1976 and 'Capital Budgeting and Company Finance', Longman 1973, both of which are well written. The former is written more for the specialist whereas the latter is aimed more at the non-specialist and is probably easier to follow as a result. Both take an elementary mathematical treatment of the subject. Another good book is 'Analysis for Investment Decisions' by Bryan Carsberg, Accountancy Age Books/Prentice-Hall International 1974.

The basic principles of discounting, cost of capital and the NPV approach are well covered in all three books with the computational aspects described in chapters 1 and 2 of 'Finance and Analysis'; chapters 1 to 3 of 'Capital Budgeting', and chapter 1 of 'Analysis for Investment Decisions'. However, since the authors discuss the topics we discuss separately in the next chapter simultaneously with the NPV approach the reader may well find it more helpful to read through chapter 3 of this book before referring to them. Chapters 3, 4 and 7 respectively discuss the cost of capital in some detail.

In this chapter and those that follow we make four concessions to mathematical simplicity, viz: we ignore tax, we assume i is constant over time, we ignore the problems of risk and uncertainty, and we largely disregard the effects of inflation. Each of the above books covers these issues in some depth with the treatment of 'Finance and Analysis' more detailed than that of 'Capital Budgeting' or 'Analysis for Investment Decisions'. The introduction of tax calculations into the discounting model taking into account the various allowances available is handled by the use of tax tables in chapter 2 of 'Finance and Analysis' and chapter 3 of 'Capital Budgeting', with a more general (and mathematical) treatment given in chapter 9 of 'Analysis for Investment Decisions'. The effects of inflation are discussed in chapters 6, 4 and 8 respectively. The problems of risk and uncertainty including the relaxation of the assumption of constant i are discussed in detail in chapters 6 and 7 of 'Finance and Analysis' and chapter 5 of 'Capital Budgeting'. Chapter 7 of 'Finance and Analysis', which describes some advanced methods, requires an understanding of probability theory and elementary statistics. Chapter 6 of 'Analysis for Investment Decisions' provides a brief review taking a somewhat different approach to that of the other two books.

3

DISCOUNTED CASH FLOW

This chapter continues with and develops further the concepts described in chapter 2. The requirements of basic mathematical understanding are no greater for this chapter than for the preceding one. The process of calculating the **DCF rate,** which is the main subject of this chapter, is somewhat more laborious than the NPV calculation even when undertaken with a pocket calculator. For this reason, DCF rate calculations are often carried out in practice by computer. Nevertheless the basic principles still apply.

A — The DCF Rate (questions 1–2)

It is possible, by use of the discounting method, to calculate the return on a project expressed as a *rate*: i.e. as a percentage of the principal initially invested. The percentage figure so calculated is referred to as the DCF rate.

Suppose a bank agrees to lend a man $3000, repayable over 3 years in equal instalments of $1000 paid at the end of each successive year; the lending rate to be 10%/annum compound and all interest to be paid, with the final instalment of the loan, at the end of the third year.

Thus, interest for year 1 will be 10% of $3000 = $300. Interest for year 2 will be 10% of $2300 = $230. Interest for year 3 will be 10% of $1530 = $153. The sum to be repaid at the end of year 3 is therefore 1000 + 300 + 230 + 153 = $1683 and we know in advance that the bank's rate of return is 10%/annum as the whole transaction has been calculated to that end.

It follows that if we discount the cash flow of this transaction at 10%, which was its rate of return, the NPV will be zero. This can be demonstrated, as follows:

Year	NCF ($)	Discount factor $i = 10\%$	Present value ($)
0	−3000	1.0000	−3000.0
1	1000	0.9091	909.1
2	1000	0.8264	826.4
3	1683	0.7513	1264.5
Total = + 683		NPV =	0000.0

From this it can be seen that the DCF rate of a project is equivalent to the percentage rate by which the NCF would have to be discounted in order to give zero NPV.

Represented mathematically, this means that the DCF rate is that value of i such that

$$a_0 + \frac{a_1}{(1 + i)} + \frac{a_2}{(1 + i)^2} + \cdots \frac{a_n}{(1 + i)^n} = 0$$

The DCF rate of 10% earned by the bank in our example is often referred to as its **internal rate of return** (abbreviated to **IRR**) from that investment. This distinguishes it from the cost of capital, which is the cost of the money (also expressed as a percentage rate) to the bank itself. Clearly, if the bank is to make any kind of profit for itself from the transaction, the IRR must exceed the cost of capital.

In the following sections of this chapter we will show how the IRR or DCF rate (we use the terms synonymously) of an investment can be calculated from its net cash flow. The procedure that we describe is only valid for those investments (which in practice tend to be the majority) where the NCF has a single negative element at the very beginning, followed only by positive elements. This statement can be written as follows, for those familiar with this mathematical notation (j being the time period):

$$a_0 < 0, a_j \geqslant 0 \text{ for } j = 1, n$$

Although a full mathematical explanation for this restriction would go beyond the scope of this particular book, an intuitive explanation is possible. A negative element in the NCF means that capital has to be borrowed to meet the net cash outflow, and the cost at which it is borrowed is the cost of capital. The procedure used in making the DCF rate calculation, however, has the effect of discounting all the elements in the net cash flow at the DCF rate, whereas any negative elements should properly be discounted at the cost of capital. This does not affect the initial input made at time 0, because this does not have to be discounted, but for any later negative element it would result in an incorrect answer. (If this explanation is not sufficiently clear to you at the present stage, return to it after you have completed the chapter.)

In a later section of this chapter we will describe a method for handling this type of situation which enables the inaccuracy to be reduced to generally acceptable limits.

B — The DCF Rate of an Annuity (questions 3—7)

We begin by demonstrating how to calculate the DCF rate of an annuity, as this is the simplest application of the technique.

Remember that the DCF rate has been defined as that discount rate at which the NPV of the investment is zero. Basically, therefore, the DCF procedure in this case depends on finding the discount rate for which

$$-a_0 = da'$$

where a_0 is the initial investment (hence $-a_0$, because a_0 is negative and must be preceded by another negative sign to make it positive), d is the relevant discount factor and a' is the amount of the annual payment which is to be made under the annuity. Hence,

$$d = -a_0/a'$$

Suppose, for example, that a sum of $800 purchases an annuity of $200 for a period of n years. Then,

$$d = -(-800)/200 = 4.0000$$

Suppose that the annuity is for 5 years (i.e. $n = 5$). If we look down column 5 of the annuity tables we find the number 4.1002 opposite 7% and the number 3.9927 opposite 8%. This means that the value of i that we are seeking lies somewhere between 7% and 8%.

Let us use the symbol i_1 for the lower rate (7%) and d_1 for its discount factor (4.1002); i_2 for the higher rate (8%) and d_2 for its discount factor (3.9927). By using the following interpolation formula, which is a simplified version of the formula used in the next section, we can arrive at a reasonably close approximation of the actual value of i, the DCF rate in %:

$$\text{DCF rate} = i_1 + \frac{d_1 - d}{d_1 - d_2}$$

Applying this formula to the above data we have:

$$i = 7 + \frac{4.1002 - 4.0000}{4.1002 - 3.9927} = 7 + \frac{0.1002}{0.1075} = 7.93\%$$

Example 1

An investment of $1500 purchases an annuity of $250 for a period of 9 years. Calculate the DCF rate of return.

Solution: $a_0 = -1500$ $a' = 250$. Therefore

$$d = 1500/250 = 6.0000$$
$$n = 9$$

From column 9 of the annuity tables

$$d_1 = 6.2469, i_1 = 8$$
$$d_2 = 5.9953, i_2 = 9$$
$$\text{IRR} = i_1 + \frac{d_1 - d}{d_1 - d_2} = 8 + \frac{0.2469}{0.2516} = 8.98\%$$

C — Calculating the DCF Rate for a Non-annuity Investment — Stage I (question 8)

In the previous section we demonstrated the basic method of using present value factor tables to calculate the DCF rate of an investment.

Because the DCF rate is that value of i at which the NPV of the investment is zero, it must lie somewhere between a discount rate which gives a positive NPV and one which gives a negative NPV. By inspection, a pair of values can be found which straddle the value of i, which can then be calculated by interpolating between them.

If the investment is an annuity this procedure is, as we have seen, fairly simple and straightforward. In other cases it tends to be rather more laborious.

The first stage, in the method that we demonstrate here, is to make a guess at the approximate discount rate. This is not usually easy, without a good deal of experience. The following technique, based on the procedures described in the previous section, is a convenient way to arrive at an approximate value for i.

Consider the following project where all cash outputs arise at the end of each year.

Time (in years)	0	1	2	3	4	5
NCF in $	−10000	2000	4000	4000	2000	1000

Begin by calculating the average annual output which, in this case, is

$$\frac{2000 + 4000 + 4000 + 2000 + 1000}{5} = \frac{13000}{5} = 2600$$

Now treating the investment as an annuity of $2600 over a period of 5 years, find the discount factor by the method described in the previous section. Thus,

$$d = 10000/2600 = 3.846.$$

Then by looking down the appropriate column of the annuity tables, find the discount rate which has a factor nearest to this. In this case, looking down column 5, we find that the nearest figure to 3.846 is 3.8897, which occurs in row 9.

From this we can take 9% as a *starting* rate, on which to base the next stage in the calculation.

D — Calculating the DCF Rate — Stage II (questions 9–13)

We have defined the principles on which the DCF rate calculation is based and, in the previous section, we demonstrated a technique for estimating an approximate value of i, as a starting rate. With sufficient practice some people may find that they can dispense with this technique and proceed directly, by guesswork, to an estimate of the DCF rate which is sufficiently accurate for this first stage of the calculation. Indeed, an investor considering a new project will usually find it convenient to begin with the procedure described in chapter 2. If he then wants to find the IRR, he will already have established that it is greater or less than his discount rate, which may be close enough to it to serve as a starting rate for the DCF rate calculation.

We call this starting rate i_1 and proceed to calculate the NPV (NPV_1) at this discount rate to find out whether it is positive or negative. (If the NPV turns out to be very close to zero, the starting rate may be considered accurate enough in itself for the purpose required, and the calculation need not be taken any further.)

Repeating the data of the project in the previous section, we have:

Time (in years)	0	1	2	3	4	5
NCF in $	−10000	2000	4000	4000	2000	1000

If we take i_1 as 9% we find that

$$NPV_1 = + £357.1$$

This means that, at a discount rate of 9%, the investment would be favourable. Therefore the actual rate of return exceeds 9%.

The next stage is to try another discount rate (i_2) which will give a second NPV (NPV_2) which is, ideally, less than zero by about the same amount as NPV_1 is above, or vice versa.

Let us try 12% for i_2. At this rate, we find that

$$NPV_2 = -\$339.8$$

We can now calculate the actual value of i (to a reasonable degree of accuracy) by interpolation, using the appropriate formula of the two listed below:

formula 1, where $i_1 < i_2$:

$$IRR = i_1 + \frac{(i_2 - i_1)\, NPV_1}{NPV_1 - NPV_2}$$

formula 2, where $i_1 > i_2$:

$$IRR = i_2 + \frac{(i_1 - i_2)\, NPV_2}{NPV_2 - NPV_1}$$

(A note for those mathematically inclined: these formulae represent a method of **linear interpolation**; i.e. interpolation based on direct proportionality. Recollecting that the IRR of a project is that rate at which it has an NPV of zero, then in the case of formula 1

$$\frac{i_1 - IRR}{i_1 - i_2} = \frac{NPV_1 - 0}{NPV_1 - NPV_2}$$

and the formula is arrived at by rearrangement. Formula 2 is simply a transposition of formula 1 with i_1 and NPV_1 written in place of i_2 and NPV_2 and vice versa.)

Applying formula 1 in this example, we have

$$IRR = 9 + \frac{(12-9)\,357.1}{357.1 - (-339.8)} = 9 + \frac{3 \times 357.1}{357.1 + 339.8}$$

$$= 9 + \frac{1071.3}{696.9} = 9 + 1.54 = 10.54\%$$

Now let us try working out a complete problem.

Example 2

Use the DCF rate method to calculate the IRR of a project which has the following net cash flow: $a_0 = -\$1100, a_1 = \$500, a_2 = \$400, a_3 = \$400$.

Solution: The first rate selected by using the procedure described in the preceding section was $i_1 = 9\%$ which gives a small positive NPV of £4.3. 11% is then selected for i_2, which gives an NPV of $-\$32.4$.

(1) Year	(2) NCF	(3) $i_1 - 9\%$	(4) (2) $\times$ (3)	(5) $i_2 = 11\%$	(6) (2) $\times$ (5)
0	−1100	1.0000	−1100	1.0000	−1100
1	500	0.9174	458.7	0.9009	450.5
2	400	0.8417	336.7	0.8116	324.6
3	400	0.7722	308.9	0.7312	292.5
+ 200		$NPV_1 =$	4.3	$NPV_2 =$	−32.4

Applying interpolation formula 1 again

$$DCF\ rate = 9 + \frac{(11-9)\,4.3}{4.3 - (-32.4)} = 9 + \frac{8.6}{4.3 + 32.4}$$

$$= 9 + \frac{8.6}{36.7} = 9 + 0.234 = 9.234\%$$

i.e. if the relevant cut-off rate for the project is 7%, all other things being equal the project seems worthwhile. However if the cut-off rate is 12%, the DCF rate $< 12\%$, hence it would probably not be wise to undertake the project.

E — DCF Rate Calculation with Negative Successor Elements (questions 14—15)

In section A we pointed out that the DCF rate could not be calculated if any elements of the NCF were negative other than the initial element.

However in practice if there are only one or two negative elements in the original cash flow, and these are small, the DCF rate as calculated is usually still fairly meaningful. Nevertheless there is a way around this limitation if we know the cost of capital for the project.

In the following case, for example, the NCF for year 2 is negative. If the cost of capital for this project is 10%, how do we calculate the IRR?

Time	0	1	2	3	4	5
NCF	−2000	+500	−200	+600	+800	+800

The answer lies in eliminating the negative element in year 2 and transferring its value to the next positive year. In effect, we borrow $200 at the end of year 2 to cancel out the deficit and pay it back (with interest at the same rate as the cost of capital) at the end of the following year.

This approach is limited, of course, to those cases where the value of the cash inflow in succeeding years is greater (taking into account the time value of money) than the cash outflow in the year in question.

The procedure, broken down into steps, is described in *italics*. Its application to this particular case follows, in ordinary type.

1. *Calculate, in terms of the cost of capital, the sum of money which would have the same value at the end of the succeeding year as the negative element has in the year in which it occurs.*

Clearly the equivalent value in year 3 of −$200 in year 2, if discounted at 10%, is −$200 × 1.1 = −$220.

2. *Add this sum to the output for the succeeding year and make the negative NCF element = 0.*

Adding this amount to the NCF for year 3 we have $600 − $200 = $380. We can therefore rewrite the table as follows:

Time	0	1	2	3	4	5
NCF	−2000	+500	0	+380	+800	+800

3. *Complete the DCF rate calculation on this basis.*

From this point the calculation can proceed exactly as described in section D, and we find that IRR = 6.34%.

Let us now consider a situation in which the negative element of one year is too large to be absorbed in the following year:

Time	0	1	2	3	4	5
NCF	−3000	+1500	+1000	−300	+300	+1000

The cost of capital of the project is 8%. In this case the negative NCF of year 3 cannot be entirely absorbed in year 4. The equivalent value in year 4 of $300 in year 3, at an interest rate of 8%, is $300 × 1.08 = $324. If we borrow $300 in year 3 to cancel the deficit, in year 4 we must pay back $324, which leaves us with a figure of −$24 in year 4.

Repeating the procedure, a deficit of \$24 in year 4 has a value in year 5 of $-\$24 \times 1.08 = -\$25.9$. We can therefore rewrite the table as follows:

Time	0	1	2	3	4	5
NCF	-3000	$+1500$	$+1000$	0	0	$+974.1$

The DCF rate of this investment is then found to be 6.52%.

F — DCF Rate of Projects with Continuous Cash Flows (questions 16—18)

Thus far we have always assumed that expenditures and receipts accrue at the beginning or end of each time period. For some projects this is not a realistic practice and can give a misleading DCF rate. A rather more accurate rate is achieved in such cases by mid-pointing (i.e. assuming that all expenditures and receipts accrue at the middle of each time period) on the same principle as was demonstrated in section H of chapter 2. The procedure for calculating the DCF rate in the case of projects with continuous cash flows is illustrated in the following example.

Example 3

A certain project requires an initial expenditure of \$10,000 and will last 5 years, during which it will yield the following net cash flow in dollars:

year 1	$+2000$
year 2	$+4000$
year 3	$+4000$
year 4	$+2000$
year 5	$+1000$

This is exactly the same cash flow as that of the project discussed in sections C and D of this chapter, but in this case the receipts are considered as arising *throughout* each year whereas previously they arose at the *end* of each year.

The NCF is tabulated in the following manner:

Time (in years)	0	0.5	1.5	2.5	3.5	4.5
NCF	-10000	2000	4000	4000	2000	1000

There is no technique other than guesswork for arriving at a reasonable first estimate of the DCF rate, but in section D we found the DCF rate to be about 10½%, so let us try $i_1 = 10\%$. From this we calculate NPV_1 (in the manner of chapter 2, section H).

$$\text{NPV}_1 = -10000 + \frac{1}{(1.1)^{0.5}}\left[2000 + \frac{4000}{1.1} + \frac{4000}{(1.1)^2} + \frac{2000}{(1.1)^3} + \frac{1000}{(1.1)^4} \right]$$

$$= -10000 + \frac{11128}{(1.1)^{0.5}} \quad = -10000 + 10610 \quad = +\$610$$

NPV_1 is positive so the DCF rate exceeds 10%. Let us try $i_2 = 15\%$. We now have

$$NPV_2 = -10000 + \frac{1}{(1.15)^{0.5}} \left[2000 + \frac{4000}{1.15} + \frac{4000}{(1.15)^2} + \frac{2000}{(1.15)^3} + \frac{1000}{(1.15)^4} \right]$$

$$= -10000 + \frac{10390}{(1.15)^{0.5}} \quad = -10000 + 9689 \quad = -\$311$$

The rest of the calculation proceeds normally. Because $i_1 < i_2$ we use the interpolation formula 1 of section D. Hence

$$\text{DCF rate} = 10 + \frac{(15 - 10) \times 610}{610 + 311} \quad = 13.31$$

Notice that by this method the DCF rate works out at 13.31% as compared with our calculation of 10.54% in section D; quite a substantial difference. The reason for the higher rate is, of course, that the positive elements are being recorded half a year earlier.

G — NPV Versus DCF Rate (questions 19—20)

We have made clear that the NPV and the DCF rate calculations are both applications of the DCF method. They are not competing techniques but rather different ways of presenting basically the same information.

Nevertheless, in a practical context, there may be good reasons for using one technique in preference to the other for evaluating investments. If all you want to do is to establish whether the rate on a proposed investment is greater or less than your cut-off rate, there is little point in making a laborious DCF rate calculation when the answer can be given by simply discounting the NCF at the cut-off rate to give an NPV which is either positive or negative. Also, as we have seen, there are some limitations on the projects for which a DCF rate can be calculated at all.

On the other hand many investors, being accustomed to compare projects in terms of their rate of return, may not find the NPV very meaningful. This is particularly so when the advantages of different projects are marginal and have to be weighed against other considerations, or in situations where the cost of capital fluctuates. As has been pointed out in the previous chapter, an investor who knows that his rate of return on a project is 12%, knows at once the effect that there will be on his rate of profitability if his cost of capital rises from 9% to 10%, or drops from 9% to 8%. If, on the other hand, he has based his judgement only on an NPV calculation at 9%, he has to repeat the whole calculation at the new rate in order to find out what its effect will be.

Also of course, some method has to be found for determining a cut-off rate or checking its continued validity. One way is by calculating the actual DCF rates of existing projects, so as to establish standards which are realistic.

However, there do occur situations in which the two methods may actually seem to support contrary decisions. This condition may arise when the projects under consideration are **mutually exclusive**: i.e. of such a nature that the acceptance of one must imply rejection of the other(s). In such cases, both the NPV and the DCF calculations are required to provide the basis for a properly considered decision.

Example 4

A company has to decide whether to buy either a small computer or a sophisticated accounting machine. The computer is more expensive but it is also potentially more useful.

The estimates for the rival projects are as follows:

	Computer	Accounting machine
Initial cost	$100,000	$36,000
Annual running costs	$25,000	$10,000
Annual benefit to user (from clerical savings, more efficient operation, etc.)	$60,000	$24,000

Financing the purchase is not a problem in either case and the relevant cost of capital is 15%/annum. If both projects are assigned the same life-span of five years, what should the company do?

Solution: On this basis the IRR on the computer is found to be 22.1%, that on the accounting machine is 27.2%. It would seem, from this, that the accounting machine is the better choice.

However, taking the NPV of both projects at $i = 15\%$ the figure for the computer is greater than that for the accounting machine because of the greater amount of money involved. The relevant figures for both projects may be tabulated as follows:

Time in years	0	1	2	3	4	5	DCF rate in %	NPV $i = 15\%$
Computer NCF	−100000	35000	35000	35000	35000	35000	22.1	17300
Acc. mach. NCF	−36000	14000	14000	14000	14000	14000	27.2	10900

In the circumstances of this particular case where both projects are profitable, there is no problem in financing either purchase and we are assuming no risk, the computer is shown by the NPV calculation to be, on balance, the more financially attractive of the two alternatives, even though its DCF rate is smaller, because a larger amount of money is being invested. Contradictory results arise as the DCF rate does not take into account differences in the initial amount of capital invested.

Contradictory results may also arise when comparing projects which last differing lengths of time as the DCF rate gives no indication of the duration of the investment. Again it can be seen that both forms of calculation are required, as illustrated in a further example.

Example 5

An investor is considering two projects both costing about the same amount, $300,000. They are mutually exclusive because the investor has not the resources (e.g. factory space, staff etc.) to consider taking on both together. The estimated performances of the two projects are compared in the following table. Which project should the investor undertake if his cost of capital is 15%/annum?

Time in years	0	1	2	3	4	5	DCF rate in %	NPV $i = 15\%$
NCF Project A	−300000	100000	250000	150000			28.5	74600
NCF Project B	−300000	50000	100000	250000	150000	50000	26.4	94100

Solution: Project A has the more attractive DCF rate, project B the higher NPV. The reason for this is that project B has the longer life (5 years, as compared with 3 years for project A).

The decision in this case is not clear-cut and is likely to depend on factors (such as the nature of the investor's business, expectations and experience) which are beyond the scope of this example. If both opportunities are exceptionally attractive he may decide for project B because of its longer life and greater NPV, giving greater overall profitability. If they are not particularly exceptional (i.e. similar projects are coming up for consideration every year) he may well opt for project A on the grounds that it gives him a better rate of return and greater freedom of action (since at the end of the third year his resources will be freed and there might then be other opportunities awaiting him which would offer at least as good a rate of return as project B).

Questions

3.1 The DCF rate of an investment has been calculated and found to be 12%. Assuming the calculation has been correctly made, what would be the NPV of the project if the net cash flow were discounted at 12%?

3.2 Which of the following discount rates is the IRR for the project with $a_0 = -\$1069$, $a_1 = \$300$, $a_2 = \$600$ and $a_3 = \$400$: (i) 8%, (ii) 10% or (iii) 12%? Justify your answer.

3.3 A company can purchase a cash flow of $0.6m at the end of each of the next 5 years, for a payment of $2.0m due now. What is the present value factor (d) of the investment? Keep a note of the answer to this question for use in questions 4 and 5.

3.4 (i) Using the data of the preceding question and its answer, find i_1 and i_2. Keep a note of these values for use in question 5.
(ii) What do the terms i_1 and i_2 mean, i.e. what is their significance?

3.5 Making use of the answers to questions 3 and 4, calculate the DCF rate of the investment described in question 3.

3.6 Company A proposes to take over company B, in the same line of business. The NCF of company B is estimated at $1.0 million annually over the next 5 years. Furthermore, company A expects to achieve economies of scale, from the takeover, worth $0.2 million annually.

Calculate the DCF rate of the investment if the cost of the takeover is $4.25 million, payable at the outset. (Treat all other cash sums as accruing at the end of each year.)

3.7 Suppose, in the situation described in question 6, that the board of company A had set a cut-off rate of 11% on the investment. Anticipating an annual NCF of $1.2 million over the next 5 years, what is the maximum sum they would have been prepared to authorize as the cost of the takeover?

3.8 An investment of $1500 yields $300 at the end of the first year, $800 at the end of the second year and $600 at the end of the third and final year.

(i) Tabulate this information.
(ii) Use the method demonstrated in section C to find an approximate starting rate for the IRR of this investment. Call this i_1 and keep a note of it for use in question 9.

3.9 Calculate the IRR of the investment described in question 8.

3.10 A company which is manufacturing a product in Britain wishes to break into the US market. It expects an initial expenditure of $120,000 on advertising, establishing depots and agencies, etc., and then revenues of $40,000 and costs of $10,000 at the end of the first year increasing annually by $20,000 and $10,000 respectively.

(i) Calculate the net cash flow on the assumption that the project lasts 4 years only; and
(ii) Do a Stage I analysis on it to determine an initial starting rate for the IRR calculation. Save the answer for use in question 11.

3.11 Carry out a Stage II analysis on the data of question 10 to calculate the internal rate of return of the project.

3.12 A company proposes to purchase 3 aircraft costing with spares $1 m each, two-thirds of which is due now and one-third in a year's time. Each aircraft is expected to produce annual revenues of about $500,000 with running costs of $100,000 in the first year and $200,000 annually in subsequent years. A 4-year span of operations is visualized, at the end of which the aircraft might be worth around $100,000 each.

(i) Calculate the net cash flow for the project.
(ii) Do a Stage I analysis on it to determine an initial starting rate for the IRR calculation. Save the answer for use in question 13.

3.13 Using the data and answer of question 12, calculate the IRR for the project.

3.14 A company is considering a project, for which the board of directors requires to know the IRR before reaching a decision. The cost of capital of the project is 12% and its NCF is as follows:

Time (in years)	0	1	2	3	4
NCF (in millions)	−0.5	−0.2	−0.1	+0.4	+0.8

Rewrite the table, eliminating the negative elements in years 1 and 2, and keep a note of the answer for use in question 15.

3.15 Taking the data of question 14, calculate the DCF rate of the project.

3.16 A project that will last 3 years requires a payment of $30,000 now. The net cash inflows (revenues less expenses) are continuous and work out at $5000 during the first year, $10,000 during the second and $20,000 during the third.

(i) Prepare a net cash flow table.
(ii) Calculate the IRR for the project. (Hint: start with $i_1 = 10\%$.)

3.17 A man wishes to take over a newsagent's shop and run it himself. His initial setting-up costs will be $6000 and he expects to make a direct profit on sales of $10,000 per annum. Running costs of the premises (rent, rates, electricity etc.) are estimated at, $2000 per annum and he proposes to allow himself an annual salary of $6000. Tabulate the NCF of this project over its initial 4 years, treating all income and payments (after the initial setting-up) as accruing in the middle of each year. Keep a note of the answer for use in question 18.

3.18 From the data of question 17:

(i) If the man has to borrow the initial $6000 at 12%/annum, will the IRR exceed his cost of capital? (Hint: use annuity tables to cut down the computation required.)
(ii) Taking 12% as the starting figure of your calculation, work out the IRR of this investment.

3.19 A company whose cost of capital is 14% has to choose between two mutually exclusive projects, of which the NCFs (in mil.), IRRs and NPVs are tabulated as follows:

Time (in years)	0	1	2	3	4	DCF rate in %	NPV (in millions) $i = 14\%$
Project A	−0.4	0.1	0.2	0.3	0.2	30.2	0.163
Project B	−0.4	0.3	0.2	0.2		37.7	0.152

Explain briefly why project B has a higher IRR than project A, but a lower NPV.

3.20 A small development company has three projects currently open to it, each lasting 4 years. Its resources (of staff, etc.) are insufficient to enable it to undertake more than one of them. The NCF's (in $'000), IRR's and NPV's (with cost of capital 12%) for each of the projects are tabulated below.

Time (in years)	0	1	2	3	4	DCF rate in %	NPV (in £'000) $i = 12\%$
Build offices	−110	70	40	15	15	14.7	4.60
Build houses	− 60	10	20	20	40	14.9	4.53
Build shops	− 30	0	10	10	25	13.1	0.98

Explain why, everything else being equal, one of the projects should never be accepted and why, of the remaining two, one has a higher IRR but lower NPV than the other.

Further Reading

Essentially this is the same as for chapter 2 because of the inter-related nature of the topics covered. However, in addition to the earlier references the reader may find chapter 5 of 'Finance and Analysis' (full reference provided in chapter 2), chapter 2 of 'Capital Budgeting' (full reference provided in chapter 2) and/or chapter 5 of 'Analysis for Investment Decisions' (full reference provided in chapter 2) of interest for more detailed comparisons of the NPV and DCF rate approaches than that provided in this chapter. The first two chapter references also discuss the appropriate treatment when the DCF method is applied to a net cash flow with negative elements as we did in section E. An interesting real case study relating to a large mining project is described in chapter 6 of 'Capital Budgeting'.

4

INVESTMENT APPRAISAL TECHNIQUES: SOME ALTERNATIVE APPROACHES

This chapter concludes the description of investment appraisal techniques that has been carried on through chapters 2 and 3, by showing how these can be used to provide a common standard for evaluating alternative methods of financing. Given that you have understood the two preceding chapters, you will find the treatment of this chapter mathematically straightforward.

The chapter goes on to consider some alternatives to the DCF method, introduces the pay-back method, also known as break-even analysis, and describes various ways in which it can be applied. This part of the chapter assumes an elementary understanding of simple graphs.

A — Alternative Methods of Financing (questions 1—6)

Many projects involve the acquisition by the investor of some new **asset** (defined in the accounting sense as an item of property; e.g. a machine or building). There is often more than one way to pay for such assets. Thus far we have considered only the case of outright purchase. We list, below, three of the more common alternative ways of acquiring an asset.

1. **Lease**. This is a contract for a defined period of time between the **lessor,** who remains the owner of the property, and the **lessee** who pays for the exclusive use of it for this period of time.
2. **Rent** or **hire** (these terms are used synonymously in this book). This resembles a leasing arrangement except that its total duration is less precisely defined. Generally the period as a whole is indefinite and either side may at any time give notice of termination or of a desire to change the conditions. By contrast with a lease, a rent agreement gives more freedom of action and, by the same token, less protection to the parties.
3. **Hire purchase**. This resembles a lease in that it lasts for a defined period of time, but at the end of this time (i.e. after payment by periodic instalments has been completed) ownership is transferred to the hirer.

A person wishing to acquire a new machine may, for example, be offered 3 alternative methods of paying for it: by outright purchase from the supplier, by leasing from one financing company or by hire purchase from another financing company.

When selecting between alternatives we must stress the importance of seeking always to compare like with like as closely as possible. For example, payments made under a leasing agreement usually also cover maintenance and repair costs, for which the buyer would be responsible himself if he were to purchase the asset outright. In the latter case, therefore, the investor must estimate his maintenance costs and include these in the cash flow if he is to compare it realistically with the cost of leasing.

In the following examples we will show how to determine the least costly (i.e. most profitable) alternatives in each case. The method is basically to calculate the NPV of the NCF under each alternative method for an equal period of time, at the investor's cost of capital, in order to be able to compare them by a single common standard. In effect the NPV of a lease, when calculated in this way, represents the amount of money that would have to be invested now to yield a flow of cash sufficient to meet all the periodic payments as they fall due.

Example 1

A company requires for its transport fleet a new truck costing $6000. It may be leased from a finance company for a period of 5 years at an annual leasing charge, payable in advance, of $1800; maintenance costs to be borne by the user. Is this likely to be more advantageous than outright purchase, if the company's cost of capital is 8%/annum and the truck is expected to have a resale value of $600 in 5 years' time?

Solution: In this case we are not concerned with the profitability of the investment as such, we are merely comparing two alternative methods of financing. Therefore we can ignore all cash inflows or outflows that are identical for both. These include maintenance costs as well as running costs in this example, as these are the user's responsibility in either arrangement.

On the other hand like has to be compared with like, so if the lease is for a 5-year period and this is a reasonable lifespan in the context, the NPV must also be calculated over 5 years in the case of purchase.

Let us begin by tabulating the cash flows for the two alternative cases.

Time in years	0	1	2	3	4	5
(i) Purchase payments in $	−6000					+600
(ii) Lease payments in $	−1800	−1800	−1800	−1800	−1800	

(i) In the case of outright purchase

$$\text{NPV in } \$ = -6000 + \frac{600}{(1.08)^5} = -6000 + 408.4 = -5591.6$$

(ii) In the case of lease

$$NPV \text{ in } \$ = -\left[1800 + \frac{1800}{1.08} + \frac{1800}{(1.08)^2} + \frac{1800}{(1.08)^3} + \frac{1800}{(1.08)^4}\right]$$

This constitutes an initial payment of $600 followed by a 4 year annuity with annual payments of $600. By the use of annuity tables we have

$$NPV = -1800 - (1800 \times 3.3121) = -1800 - 5961.8 = -7761.8$$

Clearly in this particular example the leasing arrangement would prove to be considerably more expensive than outright purchase.

Example 2

A customer is offered three alternative ways to acquire a certain make of color TV set. The cost by outright purchase is $300 and he expects to be able to use it for 8 years at the end of which time it would have a second-hand value of, say, $25. A servicing contract will cost him $20/annum, payable annually in advance.

The second alternative is to rent the set for a corresponding period of 8 years, in which case the rental will cost him $80/annum for the first 4 years, decreasing in the next 4 years by $5/annum each year. This also covers the cost of full maintenance and the payments are due annually in advance.

The remaining option is hire purchase. This would involve a down-payment of $100 and five additional payments of $80, at annual intervals, to give ownership at the end of 5 years. (In practice, of course, payments in this type of rental or hire-purchase situation would be more likely to be due monthly, or even weekly. In this example, however, we have deliberately over-simplified by making the payments annual.) These payments cover full maintenance during the 5 years that the set is the property of the HP company. After ownership has been transferred, maintenance becomes the responsibility of the purchaser. These costs and the residual value are then the same as they would have been if he had purchased the set outright.

Which of these three alternatives would be cheapest for the customer if his cost of capital is 12%?

Solution: (i) For outright purchase the cash flow is

Time in years	0	1	2	3	4	5	6	7	8
Cost	−300								
Maintenance	− 20	−20	−20	−20	−20	−20	−20	−20	
Resale									+25
NCF in $	−320	−20	−20	−20	−20	−20	−20	−20	+25

$$\text{NPV in } \$ = -320 - (20 \times 4.5638) + (25 \times 0.4039)$$
$$= -320 - 91.3 + 10.1 = -401.2$$

(ii) For rental the cash flow is

Time in years	0	1	2	3	4	5	6	7
NCF in $	−80	−80	−80	−80	−75	−70	−65	−60

$$\text{NPV in } \$ = -80 - (80 \times 2.4018) - (75 \times 0.6355) - (70 \times 0.5674)$$
$$- (65 \times 0.5066) - (60 \times 0.4523)$$
$$= -80 - 192.1 - 47.7 - 39.7 - 32.9 - 27.1 = -419.5$$

(iii) For hire purchase the cash flow is

Time in years	0	1	2	3	4	5	6	7	8
NCF in $	−100	−80	−80	−80	−80	−80	−20	−20	+25

$$\text{NPV in } \$ = -100 - (80 \times 3.6048) - (20 \times [4.5638 - 3.6048])$$
$$+ (25 \times 0.4039)$$
$$= -100 - 288.4 - 19.2 + 10.1 = -397.5$$

In this example hire purchase is the cheapest method and marginally more attractive than outright purchase if the cost of capital is 12%/annum: rental is the most expensive. In no case, however, is the difference very great and, having established this point, the customer may well feel free to make his decision on other grounds.

Considering the case for outright purchase, if current interest rates are exceptionally high and the customer expects his cost of capital to decline in the near future, this could then prove to have been the cheapest method.

Considering the case for rental, there is a flexibility about this type of agreement that can work both ways. On the one hand the customer may have to accept the possibility of an increase in his rental charges some time during the next 8 years, which would have made this method even more expensive than the alternatives. On the other hand, it could prove to have been the cheapest method if for any reason the customer decides to get rid of the TV set within less than 8 years.

In the circumstances the customer could quite reasonably decide in favor of rental, despite its slightly greater cost, for the sake of the freedom of action it would give him to get rid of the set without trouble and at fairly short notice if he should wish to do so at a later date (e.g. if something more attractive should offer itself, or if he becomes dissatisfied with the maintenance service being provided).

B — The Sale and Leaseback Decision (questions 7—8)

A similar type of analysis to that described in section A is applied to evaluate the worth to a company of the **sale and leaseback** of one or more of its assets, normally to a finance or property company. In this situation a company in need of new finance will sell an asset it already owns (such as an office block or factory) for cash and lease it back from the new owners on agreed terms and for an agreed time period.

To evaluate whether this kind of transaction should be undertaken is relatively simple: the company calculates the NPV of the cash flow at its cost of capital if it enters into the transaction, then calculates the NPV of the comparable cash flow if it does not and decides on the preferable policy by comparing the results. The following example illustrates the method.

Example 3

A company owns an office block in the center of Dallas but expects to move out of Dallas in 5 years' time. It has been offered $4.5 million by a property company for the building which will be leased back to it for a 5-year period at an annual rental of $150,000 payable in arrears. At the end of the 5 years the property is expected to have a market value of $6 m. Should the company sell the building and lease it back if its cost of capital is 10%?

Solution: If the company sells the building and leases it back, the NPV of the resultant cash flow (in $m) is:

$$4.5 - \frac{0.15}{1.1} - \frac{0.15}{(1.1)^2} - \frac{0.15}{(1.1)^3} - \frac{0.15}{(1.1)^4} - \frac{0.15}{(1.1)^5}$$

$$= 4.5 - 0.57 = 3.93$$

However, if the company sells the building at the end of the 5-year period, the present value of the property is:

$$\frac{6.0}{(1.1)^5} = 3.73$$

In this particular case the company would be well advised, all other things being equal, to enter into the sale and leaseback contract which in present value terms is worth $200,000 more to it.

C — The Pay-Back Method: Break-Even Analysis (questions 9—11)

As we have seen, methods of evaluating an investment by its NPV or IRR are based on the same mathematical approach: namely, the DCF method. In this section we will consider one entirely different approach.

A business venture is said to **break-even** when the total revenues from it to date exactly equal its total expenditures to date. The point in time at which this occurs is called the **break-even point**. Until this point has been reached, the returns from the project are merely contributing towards the repayment of the money that has been put into it.

When we refer to the break-even point of an *investment,* we mean the point in time at which all payments in the form of capital expenditures and operating expenses have been recovered, which were made before the date when the break-even point was reached.

In what is called the **pay-back method** of evaluating an investment, the investor decides upon a target period of time, called the **pay-back period**, during which the project must reach its break-even point. A project is considered potentially attractive if it is expected to reach the break-even point within the pay-back period, potentially unattractive if it is not. Consider the following example.

Example 4

An investor is considering a project which is expected to yield the following net cash flow (in $'000): with all expenditures and receipts accruing at the beginning or end of a year.

Time in years	0	1	2	3	4	5	6
NCF ($'000)	−100	+10	−20	+40	+50	+60	+30

At what stage is the break-even point reached? Will he accept this project if he requires a pay-back period of 4 years?

Solution: We can begin by tabulating the data of the problem as follows:

Time in years	Total net receipts in $'000	Total net expenditures in $'000
0	0	100
1	10	100
2	10	120
3	50	120
4	100	120
5	160	120
6	190	120

By 'total net receipts' and 'total net expenditures' in this table we mean the accumulation of receipts (or expenditures) by each date, from the start of the project. Thus, by the end of year 3 the project has incurred total net outputs of $50,000 ($10,000 at the end of year 1 plus $40,000 at the end of year 3) and total net inputs of $120,000 ($100,000 at time 0 plus $20,000 at the end of year 2). By tabulating in this form it is possible to compare one directly with the other and to see at once from the table that total receipts do not overtake total expenditures until the end of year 5.

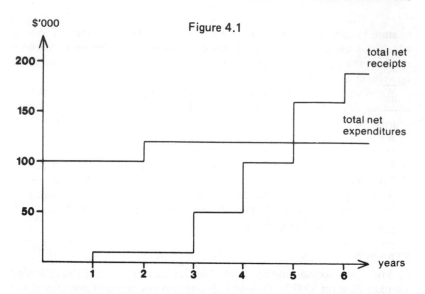

In figure 4.1 this same information is displayed graphically in the form of what is called a **break-even chart**. This graph has a stepped appearance because the expenditures and receipts all accrue at the beginning or end of each time period. The two stepped lines represent the total net expenditures and total net receipts of the project. The point at which they intersect on the chart is the break-even point. This is shown to occur at the end of the fifth year. As the investor's required pay-back period is 4 years the investment is not attractive to him.

The pay-back method is a traditional way of evaluating investments which is still quite widely used in industry. It certainly has the merit of simplicity. You will have noticed, however, that as an investment appraisal tool it is deficient in two ways.

The first defect of this approach is that it takes little or no account of the time value of money (except insofar as interest payments on borrowed funds may be made in cash and entered as such in the cash flow, and indirectly by the acknowledgement that projects which reach their break-even points quickly have an advantage over those that take longer).

Secondly, by ignoring the cash flow after the break-even point has been reached (at which stage the project has simply recovered its original costs), this method takes no account at all of the profitability of an investment.

These omissions make it generally a poor guide to the profitability of an investment, and one which is capable of leading to conclusions that are quite wrong.

Consider again our earlier example and assume that the investor's cost of capital is 10%. For this particular project, with $i = 10\%$, NPV = +$10,955 so the investment would have been profitable.

Similarly, by using the pay-back method the investor may be led to undertake a project which in fact is not profitable.

Example 5

An investor is considering a project for which the following NCF is anticipated.

Time	0	1	2	3	4	5
Costs	−20000	−2000	−3000	−5000	−10000	−12000
Revenues	0	5000	11000	15000	15000	14000
NCF	−20000	3000	8000	10000	5000	2000

If he requires a pay-back period of 4 years for the project will he accept it? If his cost of capital is 15% is the project likely to be profitable for him?

Solution: Clearly the pay-back period is 3 years, so on this criterion the investor is likely to accept the project. With $i = 15\%$, however, NPV = −\$914 so the investment would be unprofitable.

Whereas the pay-back method may not be an accurate or reliable approach to investment analysis when used on its own it can be helpful (provided its limitations are understood) when used in conjunction with NPV or IRR calculations to give a more complete understanding of a project for investment appraisal purposes. This is particularly so in the case of projects which entail risks; as obviously, other things being equal, a project that is likely to recover its costs rapidly is less risky than one which will take a longer time to do so.

D − The Pay-Back Method for Continuous Cash Flows (questions 12−14)

For those projects where income and expenditure are continuous throughout the year, graphs may be drawn which are not much more difficult than the stepped-graph used in the first example and which give a little more information.

Example 6

A company is planning to set up a new division of which the initial cost will be half a million dollars. The operating costs and revenues of this division, as estimated for the next 5 years, are shown in the following table. These costs (in the form of wages and salaries, raw materials, etc.) and revenues (in the form of payments from customers) are treated as being spread out evenly throughout the year.

Time	0	0.5	1.5	2.5	3.5	4.5
Costs (in \$m)	0.5	0.1	0.1	0.2	0.2	0.4
Revenues (in \$m)		0.3	0.35	0.4	0.4	0.4

Draw a break-even chart for the project with separate 'total net cost' and 'total net receipt' lines and use it to determine the pay-back period.

Solution: It can be seen from figure 4.2 that this graph consists of 'continuous' lines drawn by joining each point directly to its successor. The break-even point is reached at the end of the first quarter of the third year of operation, when total revenues and expenditures are each at $750,000.

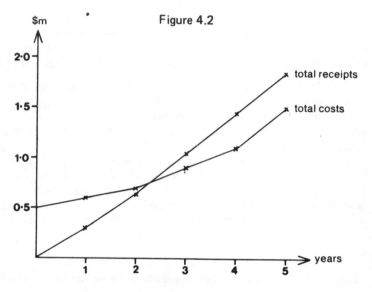

Figure 4.2

E — Break-Even Analysis in Operational Situations (questions 15—19)

The assessment of projects in terms of their break-even point is called **break-even analysis.** In the preceding section we saw how this approach was used to find the pay-back period of an investment; namely the point at which the sum of the revenues from a project has drawn level with the sum of the expenditures on that project.

Before leaving the subject of break-even analysis we should round off our treatment of it with some description of how these techniques may be used in an *operational* rather than an *investment* context. This is a far more valid use of break-even analysis as in this situation we are comparing current revenues with current expenditures; consequently, the time value of money does not enter into the problem.

Operating costs are usually of two distinct types. There are certain **fixed costs** which (in theory and within certain wide limits) are not affected by the actual volume of operations. Such costs (which may also be called indirect costs or overheads) include, for example, the rental of factory premises, the cost of rates, the cost of administrative staff, etc. Costs of this type continue to be incurred even if there is no production (e.g. if the plant is broken down, supply of raw materials has been temporarily disrupted or the work force is on strike).

As distinct from these are the variable costs or direct costs; namely costs which can be directly related to the volume of production and which vary with it. In this category are costs of raw materials, power used by machinery, wages of factory personnel, etc.

Obviously the variable costs are not always directly proportional to the volume of output, any more than the fixed costs are completely unrelated to it. For example, a temporary slow-down of production due to lack of sales will not immediately or inevitably be accompanied by a reduction in the direct labor force (although it will probably have a direct influence on the consumption of raw materials). Similarly, increases or reductions in the volume of work beyond a certain point must require changes in the amount of administrative staff or premises or equipment, all of which are treated as fixed costs. Within general limits, however, the distinction between the two types of cost is reasonable.

Even though a business may be making a direct profit on what it produces (meaning that it sells its products at more than their direct cost to it in raw materials, labor, etc.) it is not operating *profitably* until the volume of production has reached a level where the revenues from sales are also sufficient to cover its fixed costs or overheads.

Consider the case of a factory where the annual fixed costs amount to $100,000, the products are sold at $200 each and the direct cost of each items is $100. How many items does it have to manufacture and sell in the year in order to break-even?

The graphical solution to this problem is shown in figure 4.3. On this graph the sales are graduated in units along the x-axis, the costs and revenues in $ along the y-axis. Ignore for the moment the dotted line labelled profit. Total revenue increases directly with the sales, so the graph of total revenue (TR) is a straight line starting from the origin. The graph of total costs (TC) starts at $100,000 (i.e. the level of fixed costs) on the y-axis and continues from there in a straight line directly related to the volume of sales. The point of intersection of the two graphs is the break-even point. It can be seen that the factory breaks even at a rate of production of 1000 items per annum, when total costs and revenues have each reached a value of $200,000.

The profit (or loss) at any given volume of sales is represented by the distance between the TR and TC lines, as indicated by drawing the dotted line representing TR − TC in figure 4.3 labelled profit. Thus, at sales of 500 items the total revenues are $100,000 and the total costs $150,000, representing a loss of $50,000. From the diagram it can be seen how, for each additional item sold, there is an increase in the profit (or a decrease in the loss, if the break-even point has not yet been reached). At sales of

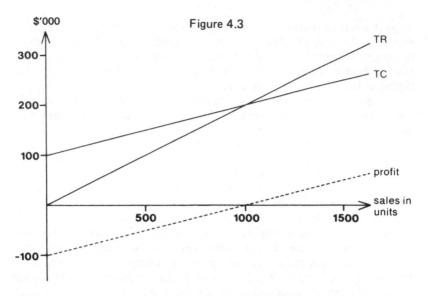

1000 units, the items are being sold at exactly what they cost to produce. The greater the margin by which sales fall short of 1000 units, the greater the loss. The greater the margin by which sales exceed 1000 units, the greater the profit.

Consider next what happens if there is an increase of 20% in direct costs (due to, say, a wage increase and/or a rise in the price of raw materials) with no corresponding increase in prices.

The new position is shown in figure 4.4, where it can be seen that the gradient of the costs graph is now steeper and an annual output of 1250 items is required to break-even.

Now let us consider a slightly more complicated problem.

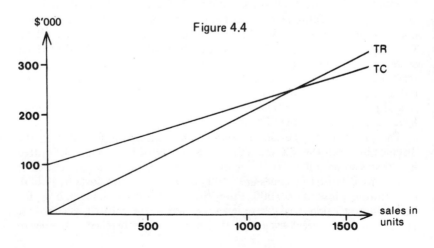

Example 7

A manufacturer is invited to make components for another company on a sub-contract basis. To undertake the job he will need to rent more factory space, involving him in total overheads of $5000/annum. He will also need to buy machines which will cost him $2000 each. He does not know whether the sub-contract arrangement will be renewed after a year or whether he will have any further use for the machines if it is not, so he needs to recover the purchase price of each machine within the sub-contract itself. Direct costs on each item produced (raw materials, labor, and power consumption) amount to $0.3 per item and the sub-contractor expects to sell each item for $0.6. Each machine has a maximum capacity of 20,000 items/annum.

Illustrate by graphs the relationship in this sub-contract between volume of production and profit.

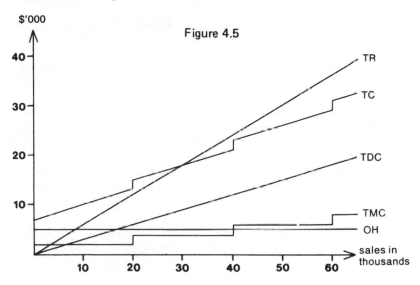

$'000

Figure 4.5

Solution: In figure 4.5, the cost of machinery is shown as a stepped line labeled TMC (total machinery costs). For each 20,000 items to be made during the year, an additional machine will have to be purchased at an additional cost of $2000.

The total fixed costs of the factory are represented by the straight line labeled OH (overheads) drawn parallel to the x-axis. The total direct costs, considered independently of the other costs, vary directly as the output and are shown by the line labelled TDC (total direct costs).

The sum of all these costs taken together is represented by the line TC (total costs). Thus, with the capacity to produce but no output at all, TC = overheads + 1 machine = $5000 + $2000 = $7000. With output of

10000 items/annum, TC = overheads + 1 machine + total direct costs = $5000 + $2000 + (10,000 × $0.3) = $10,000; and so on.

Total revenues from sales are indicated by the line TR (total revenues).

From this diagram it can be readily seen the TR intercepts TC at (30,18), indicating that the project will break-even at sales of 30000 units/annum.

At break-even point two machines are required, operating at below their full capacity. The diagram shows a relationship not only between profits and the volume of sales, but also between profits and the degree of utilization of machinery. At sales of 4000 units/annum, profits are $3000 with a capacity of two machines, fully utilized. At sales of 45000 units/annum the profits are $2500 because three machines are required at this level of output and their capacity is under-utilized.

F — Break-Even Analysis in Leasing Situations (question 20)

We have distinguished between the use of break-even analysis in capital situations (in which it is not a particularly valid approach, though sometimes useful in an auxiliary role) and in operational situations (in which its use is altogether more meaningful). In this section we touch on one case to which break-even analysis can be applied in an operational sense, although it is capital in nature.

Consider the case of a small company (or one which is newly established or undergoing rapid expansion) which is short of working capital and operating near the limit of its bank overdraft. For such a company, rental or lease may be virtually the only ways to finance new capital expenditure. In such circumstances, one possible approach is to treat the periodic rental payments simply as a fixed cost (in the same way as the other overheads in an operational situation) and establish at what level of production the cash flow of the project breaks even.

This approach introduces no new principles: it is simply an extension of the methods described in the preceding section. An example should suffice to illustrate the application.

Example 8

A small printing works with a rapidly expanding order book wishes to acquire a new multi-color printing press. It has not the capital resources to consider outright purchase but can lease the machine for 5 years at a fixed monthly rental of $360, which includes full maintenance. Other overheads which can be apportioned to this project total $150/month.

Direct operating costs (labor and power) work out at $3/hour and the output of the press will be worth $15/hour over and above the direct cost of materials (paper, inks, scrap-loss) and of setting-up time on each different job.

What is the minimum number of hours that the press must be able to operate each month for the project to break even?

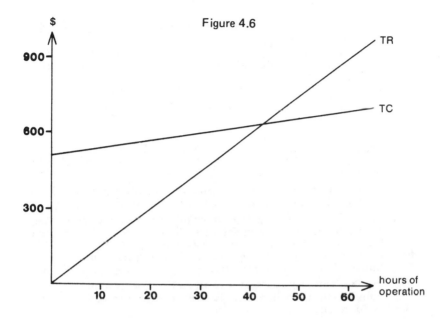

Figure 4.6

Solution: The graph of a typical month's operations is shown in figure 4.6. From the diagram it can be seen that break-even point is reached when the press operates for 42½ hours in the month.

This entire approach is of course valid only to the extent that current expenditures on a project are able to be met from its current revenues so that their present values are on the same scale. If the revenues are not to be continuous (e.g. the printing press is to be used, not for a continuous series of small orders being paid for individually, but for one or two specific large contracts with payments being made at wide intervals of time) the circumstances which could justify this type of approach cease to apply.

Questions

4.1 A company plans to refurnish its board room and directors' suite. It expects to have to repeat this operation again in 10 years' time. To buy the furniture outright will cost $10,000 and at the end of 10 years it is assumed to be out of style and hence to have no residual value. Alternatively, the furniture may be leased for 10 years at $1500/annum, due annually in arrears. If the company's cost of capital is 10%, is it more advantageous at this rate to purchase the furniture outright, or to lease it?

4.2 Taking the data of the last question; what would be the choice between purchase and leasing if the annual payment of $1500 were due in advance, not in arrears?

4.3 A construction company requires a number of dump trucks for the duration of a 4-year project. The alternative methods of acquiring these are:

     (i) outright purchase at $10,000 each, with a residual value of $2000 each at the end of the project;

    (ii) hire purchase at a down payment for each dump truck of 40% of its capital cost, followed at annual intervals by two payments of $3500; or

   (iii) lease for 4 years at $2400/annum, payable in advance.

In each case, all operating and maintenance costs are borne by the user. Tabulate the NCFs for comparison and keep a note of the answer for question 4.

4.4 Taking the data of question 3, calculate the NPV of each alternative if the company's cost of capital is 12%/annum, and establish which is the most economical in present value terms.

4.5 A company wishing to acquire a computer, which will have a life of 4 years, has the following alternative ways of paying for it:

     (i) purchase for $480,000, with maintenance contract costing $10,000/ annum payable at the beginning of each year and a potential resale value after 4 years of one quarter of its purchase price;

    (ii) lease at a monthly rental in arrears of 1/48 of its purchase price, inclusive of full maintenance service.

Treating the lease payments as a continuous cash flow of $120,000/ annum, tabulate the alternative cash flows for comparison. Keep a note of the answer for question 6.

4.6 Taking the data of question 5, calculate the NPV of each alternative if the relevant cost of capital is 9%/annum and determine which is the more economical in present value terms.

4.7 A shipping company wishing to raise some cash is offered the opportunity to sell one of its cargo vessels outright to a finance company for £0.6 million and lease it back for a period of 10 years at a yearly rental of $100,000 payable annually in arrears. The shipping company's cost of capital is 11% and at the end of 10 years the ship will be worth $50,000 for scrap. Would the proposed sale and leaseback agreement be to its advantage?

4.8 Given the data of question 7, calculate the DCF rate to the financing company of the proposed sale and leaseback agreement.

4.9 A company is considering a project which is estimated to cost $110,000 and to yield a positive net cash flow of $35,000/annum at the end of each of the succeeding 4 years. Draw a break-even chart to show the stage at which the break-even point is reached.

4.10 If the company policy is to accept projects which have a pay-back period of 4 years or less, would the project of question 9 be considered acceptable?

4.11 The cost of capital for the company in question 9 is 12%. Calculate the NPV of the project and determine whether or not it is going to be profitable, on the estimates submitted, if it has a life of 4 years.

4.12 A person who is thinking about opening a boutique forecasts an initial payment of $16,000 for fitting-up etc., fixed costs (staff, rates, etc.) of $8000 in the first year and $10,000 annually in subsequent years. He expects to make sales worth $36,000 in the first year increasing by $6000/ annum in each subsequent year, and that the cost to him of goods sold will average 2/3 of sales revenue.

Tabulate the data for 5 years' operations, assuming that all revenues and costs (except for the initial outlay) arise continuously throughout each year. Keep a note of the answer for use in questions 13 and 14.

4.13 Using the data from question 12, draw a break-even chart for the project. If the required pay-back period is 3 years, will the project be accepted?

4.14 If the person in questions 12 and 13 can borrow money at 18%, what is the NPV of the project if it lasts 5 years? Does this method of project appraisal give different results to the pay-back method used in question 13?

4.15 A garage owner has a panel-beating and paint shop on his premises. Total overhead costs allocated to this part of the business are $10,000/annum. One craftsman can handle, on average, 300 jobs/annum and costs $6000/annum in wages and insurance. Average revenue on each job is $60 with associated direct costs (excluding labor) of $20. Draw a break-even chart for up to 900 jobs/annum and keep it for question 16.

4.16 Using your break-even chart prepared for question 15, give the following information.

    (i) How many break-even points are there?
    (ii) How many craftsmen will be employed at each break-even point?
    (iii) How many jobs will be undertaken at each break-even point, and what is the significance of these figures in terms of the profitability of the operation?
    (iv) What do the costs/revenues amount to at each break-even point?

4.17 A manufacturing company makes industrial transformers which sell for $48 each. Materials consist of metal castings costing $6 each and wire costing $3 per mile. The machinery and overheads are expected to work out at $9000/annum for the project plus the wages of a skilled employee at $6000/annum for a 40-hour week, 50 weeks of the year. If each transformer requires 1 casting, 4 miles of wire and 2 hours labor, and the employee will work up to an additional 20 hours a week overtime at $6 per hour, draw a break-even chart for the project and use it to determine how many transformers will be produced at the break-even point. Save the graph for use in questions 18 and 19.

4.18 On your graph from the previous question, or on a separate graph, construct a profit curve. What will the profit be when the following numbers of transformers are produced: (i) 300; (ii) 900; (iii) 1500?

4.19 If the cost of wire doubles but the price being charged for the transformers remains unchanged, amend your TMC and TC curves on the graph drawn in question 17 and determine the new break-even point.

4.20 A manufacturing company based in Detroit wishes to set up an additional sales office in the center of Chicago, believing that in this way sales can be increased. The rental of the office is expected to be $60,000 per year and staffing the office and other overheads to cost $36,000 per year. Each item sold by the company through the office costs $60 to manufacture, about $8 for telephone calls, paperwork, packing and delivery, etc. and is sold delivered for $100. If the management has to finance the rental of the office out of additional business generated by it, what is the minimum number of additional orders that the office must generate to justify its existence?

Further Reading

1. Alternative Methods of Investment Appraisal
Chapter 10 of 'Financing and Analysis' (full reference provided in chapter 2) provides a detailed discussion of many of the ramifications in practice of leasing generally and the lease or buy decision in particular. Also, chapter 15 of Weston and Brigham's 'Managerial Finance', Holt, Rinehart and Winston, 1978; and chapter 19 of Van Horne's 'Financial Management and Policy', Prentice-Hall, 1977, analyze leasing and lease or buy decisions. compared with costs associated with the outright purchase of a computer. The approach, which we did not cover directly as the principles are the same as for the direct methods of comparison described in this chapter, is simply to compare two different projects or two alternative methods of financing the same project by subtracting the respective net cash flows from each other and determining the DCF rate for the resulting 'incremental' project. Chapter 5 of 'Analysis for Investment Decisions' (full reference provided in chapter 2) also discusses the incremental cash flow approach.

2. The Pay-Back Method
The pay-back method applied in investment appraisal and a comparison of it with the NPV and IRR approaches is provided in chapter 8 of 'Financing and Analysis'. The pay-back method is also discussed in chapters 10 and 4 in the Weston/Brigham and Van Horne books, respectively.

5

REPLACEMENT STRATEGIES

This chapter deals with techniques designed to determine the most cost-effective approach for replacing equipment, both of a capital nature and such things as light bulbs and printed circuits which once they have failed cannot be repaired. By its nature the problem of when to replace machines or plant is closely related to that of new investment, although a different approach is taken in the case of items which fail outright.

The basic mathematical knowledge required in order to be able to follow this chapter is similar to the requirements for chapter 2. It is also necessary to be familiar with the contents of chapter 2 in order to be able to understand some parts of this particular chapter.

Given that basic knowledge, and taken step by step, this chapter is not difficult to understand, though the techniques themselves can be mathematically quite laborious in their application.

A — Replacement (questions 1—3)

As a piece of equipment ages it will normally work less efficiently, require more frequent and expensive overhauls and spend more time under repair. If the solution is to replace it with new equipment of the same type, the problem is then to determine at what stage such replacement should take place in order to keep total costs to a minimum.

The costs to be taken into consideration are basically of two types. In one category we have maintenance and operating costs, which are to some extent interdependent. As the equipment ages the maintenance costs and/or the operating costs tend to increase. Among the factors which increase operating costs we can include, for example, increases in production scrap as a machine functions less efficiently and productive time lost when it breaks down or has to be overhauled.

In the other category we have **depreciation** (derived from *de* + the Latin *precium* = price) meaning literally to 'reduce in price'. If a piece of equipment which could be sold now for, say, $1000 can be expected to realize only $600 in a year's time the difference ($400) is the depreciation that occurs in that time-interval.

No doubt you have already met this term in financial accounting where its meaning is the same but its usage (due to the special conventions and purposes of financial accounting) tends to be slightly different. This difference can be confusing if it is not clarified. Thus, in financial accounting practice, if the value of an asset depreciates to zero in 5 years and the asset itself is likely to be kept for that length of time, one frequent convention (the straight line method) is to write down its book value by 20% in each of those years.

In practice, depreciation does not work in exactly that way. To a potential buyer the difference between a new machine and one a year old is much greater than the difference between, say, a 4-year old and a 5-year old machine. Hence in the first year after purchase an asset may lose, say, 30–50% of its new price in resale value, in the second year 20–30%, in the third year 10–20% and so on. The depreciation figures which concern us here are not the amounts by which the asset is written down in the annual balance sheets, but the differences in the cash price for which it can actually be sold at the end of each successive time-interval.

The operating, maintenance and depreciation costs all contribute to the **net costs flow** of the asset. Notice that we use the term 'net costs flow' rather than 'net cash flow'. This is because expenses such as depreciation, though intended to correspond with real cash values, are not necessarily being incurred in cash at the times we take account of them.

In such a flow, depreciation costs will normally diminish in successive years whereas maintenance and operating costs will increase. The effect of combining all of these costs is usually to produce a flow which (as reproduced graphically in figure 5.1) declines successively in the first years of use, reaches a minimum and then successively increases in subsequent years.

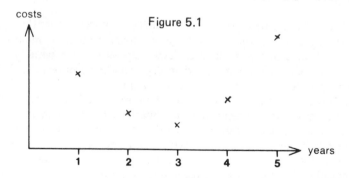

One of the assumptions made for the models used in this particular chapter is that all costs flows are of the type illustrated in figure 5.1. Another is that we generally ignore the special effects of inflation and technological innovation: in this section and the next we shall assume that each asset is replaced by another of the same type and the same costs flow. Finally, in this first section we disregard the time value of money.

In these conditions (and for the type of problems we are considering) what is called the **optimal life** or **optimum life** of an asset is the time-interval (in years) between replacements which gives the lowest average annual cost. (The terms **optimal** and **optimum** derive from the Latin word for 'best'. The word may be used in operations research terminology to include such non-quantitative factors as occupational or environmental satisfaction but we ourselves, in the limited context of this type of problem, will use it only to refer to that solution which is most profitable or, what is mathematically the same thing, least costly.) This concept is best illustrated by example.

Example 1

A factory uses a number of a certain type of machine costing $15,000 each. From experience the average operating costs for this type of machine are found to be:

Time (in years)	1	2	3	4	5	6
Costs (in $)	2000	1000	1500	3000	6000	8500

It can be seen from this table that if we exclude the first year (which carries the burden of certain exceptional costs of installation and running-in) there is a cost increase in each successive year of operation.

Resale values of the machine at the end of successive years are given in the following table, which records depreciation. As can be seen, this starts at a high rate and successively diminishes. From the fourth year the machine is assumed to have no value.

Time (in years)	1	2	3	4	5	6
Value at beginning of year ($)	15000	7000	3000	1000	0	0
Value at end of year ($)	7000	3000	1000	0	0	0
Depreciation ($)	8000	4000	2000	1000	0	0

The first step in determining the optimal life of the machine is to construct a costs flow table, as follows. The net costs flow is the sum of operating costs and depreciation.

Time (in years)	1	2	3	4	5	6
Operating costs ($)	2000	1000	1500	3000	6000	8500
Depreciation ($)	8000	4000	2000	1000	0	0
Net costs flow ($)	10000	5000	3500	4000	6000	8500

To simplify the calculations we assume in this table (and throughout all the examples and exercises of sections A–E of this chapter) that all costs accrue at the end of each year and that replacement can only take place at the end of a year. Thus, the net cost of $10,000 is assumed to occur at the end of the first year of operation. The minimum is reached at the end of the third year, with costs of $3500, after which the costs start to rise again.

We then proceed by an **iterative** process (from Latin *iterare* = to repeat); namely, by repeating calculations with successive sets of data to find out which gives the optimal result. In this case we make successive complete calculations to find out what the average annual cost would be if the machine were to be disposed of after one year, after two years and so on.

The whole process can be laid out in tabular form as follows:

(1) Year	(2) Net costs flow	(3) Total costs	(4) Average annual costs (3) ÷ (1)
1	10000	10000	10000
2	5000	15000	7500
3	3500	18500	6167
4	4000	22500	5625
5	6000	28500	5700
6	8500		

The first two columns of the above table simply list the data of the problem and column (3) shows the total costs incurred if the asset were to be sold at the end of each successive year from the beginning of the operation. Thus, in row 3 we have the costs of year 1 + costs of year 2 + costs of year 3 = 10,000 + 5000 + 3500 = $18,500.

The average annual cost is arrived at in column (4) simply by dividing this figure by the number of years of operation. Thus, if the asset is sold at the end of year 3 it will have cost $18,500 for its 3 years of use, so the average cost for 1 year is $18,500 ÷ 3 = $6167 (to nearest $).

It can be seen that the lowest average annual cost occurs if each machine is replaced after 4 years of operation. Hence the optimal life of the machine is 4 years. It is unnecessary to continue the table after the turning point has been discovered because, due to the nature of the net costs flow, there can be only one turning point after which the costs continually increase.

In this section we have demonstrated something of the approach to the problem but we have not necessarily arrived at the best answer because we have taken no account of the cost of capital and the time value of money. We take a look at these aspects of the problem in section B.

B — The Replacement Model with Discounting (questions 4 —5)

The approach to replacement is slightly different when the cost of capital is taken into account. We begin the operation in the same way by tabulating the net costs flow. We then convert these costs to their present values (exactly as we did in chapter 2, for the net cash flow — NCF — of an investment) by discounting at the relevant rate. We use these discounted costs to establish the total cost (in present value terms) that has accumulated from the start of the operation to the end of each successive time interval. The principle behind all this should require no explanation.

As in section A we then make separate calculations of what it would cost the user to replace at the end of year 1, at the end of year 2 and so on, to establish which replacement period is the most economical. What we are now trying to find, however, is not the average cost per annum, as sought by the method shown in section A, but the NPV of what we shall call the **infinite replacement chain**. This concept assumes that after a given number of years the asset is to be replaced by another of the same type and the same costs flow, which is itself to be replaced in the same way after the same number of years and so on to infinity. Thus the figures that we calculate are equivalent to those sums of cash which would have to be invested now at the relevant rate of interest (= cost of capital) so as to yield an income which would meet all the net depreciation and operating costs in the future for the particular **replacement cycle** (regular interval of time between replacements) specified.

The mathematical explanation of this process is rather complex, and references to it are given in the Further Reading section below. We have reduced the operation itself, in this book, to simple multiplication by what we call a **replacement factor** which can be found by referring to the appropriate row and column of the replacement tables given at the end of this book. They are used in exactly the same way as the present value or annuity tables. Thus, if the relevant cost of capital is 10% and the period of time is 6 years, the replacement factor (2.2961) is found at the intersection of the row headed 10% and the column headed 6.

For each successive time period, we then multiply the PV of the total cost (from the start of the operation, as calculated previously) by the appropriate replacement factor so as to arrive at a series of NPVs of infinite replacement chains. The lowest figure is the NPV of the replacement policy which minimizes total operating and depreciation costs in the long run, taking into account the time value of money.

Example 2

Taking the example used in section A, find the optimal life of each machine if the cost of capital is 20%/annum. The entire calculation is shown on the next page in tabular form.

(1)	(2)	(3)	(4)	(5)	(6)	(7)
Year	Net costs flow ($)	Discount factor $i = 20\%$	PV of net costs flow ($) (2) × (3)	PV of total costs flow ($)	Replacement factor $i = 20\%$	NPV of replacement cycle ($) (5) × (6)
1	10000	0.8333	8333.0	8333.0	6.0000	49998.0
2	5000	0.6944	3472.0	11805.0	3.2727	38634.2
3	3500	0.5787	2025.5	13830.5	2.3736	32826.9
4	4000	0.4823	1929.2	15759.7	1.9314	30438.3
5	6000	0.4019	2411.4	18171.1	1.6719	30380.3
6	8500	0.3349	2846.7	21017.8	1.5035	31600.3

The turning point occurs at the end of the fifth year, where the NPV of an infinite 5-year replacement cycle is seen to be $30,380. This is the most economical replacement policy of the various alternatives. It is not worth continuing after year 6 because we know, due to the assumption made about the nature of the costs flow, that there can be only one turning point and the NPV figure will therefore continue to increase in subsequent years.

Notice how this result contrasts with the conclusion (4 years) reached from the same data in section A.

C — Evaluation of Comparable Assets — I (question 6)

A similar approach to that demonstrated in sections A and B can be used to evaluate comparable assets. The method, when a choice has to be made between two or more pieces of equipment of similar type (e.g. as between two lathes of similar capacity offered by different manufacturers) is to estimate the net costs flow for each alternative and thence to determine the minimum NPV, as the purchaser's cost of capital, of the infinite replacement chain in each case.

Other things being equal, the asset with the lowest figure is obviously to be preferred.

Example 3

A man is buying a new motor car and has decided to make his final choice between two types, which we shall call type A and type B. They are of similar size, performance and engine capacity, but type A is an import model costing $4050 and type B an American model costing $2,850. Both types have been established for some years and their relative costs flows, taken from an article in an automobile magazine, can be tabulated as follows:

Year		1	2	3	4	5	6
Operating	A	900	750	900	1050	1200	1350
costs ($)	B	1050	900	1050	1200	1350	1500
Value at	A	2850	2400	2100	1950	1830	1740
year end ($)	B	1950	1500	1200	960	750	570

As can be seen, although the initial purchase price of type A is greater than that of type B, type A is rather cheaper to operate (due, say, to a combination of lower maintenance costs and slightly more economical fuel consumption) and holds its second-hand value rather better.

Assuming that the man would expect to replace the car of his choice in due course by another of the same type, and that his cost of capital is 8%, determine the optimum replacement cycle for each of the two types under consideration and decide which would be the more economical for him to buy.

Solution: (i) Taking the type A car first, the costs flow table can be constructed as follows:

Year	1	2	3	4	5	6
Operation ($)	900	750	900	1050	1200	1350
Depreciation ($)	1200	450	300	150	120	90
Net costs flow ($)	2100	1200	1200	1200	1320	1440

From this, using the procedure described in the preceding section, we can derive the following cost estimates for successive replacement cycles.

(1)	(2)	(3)	(4)	(5)	(6)	(7)
						NPV of
	Net		PV of	PV of	Replace-	replace-
	costs	Discount	net costs	total	ment	ment
	flow	factor	flow ($)	costs	factor	cycle ($)
Year	($)	$i = 8\%$	(2) × (3)	flow ($)	$i = 8\%$	(5) × (6)
1	2100	0.9259	1944.4	1944.4	13.5000	26249.4
2	1200	0.8573	1028.8	2973.2	7.0096	20840.9
3	1200	0.7938	952.6	3925.8	4.8504	19041.7
4	1200	0.7350	882.0	4807.8	3.7740	18144.6
5	1320	0.6806	898.4	5706.2	3.1307	17864.4
6	1440	0.6302	907.5	6613.7	2.7039	17882.8

(ii) For the type B car the costs flow is tabulated as follows:

Year	1	2	3	4	5	6
Operation ($)	1050	900	1050	1200	1350	1500
Depreciation ($)	900	450	300	240	210	180
Net costs flow ($)	950	1350	1350	1440	1560	1680

and the cost estimates for successive replacement cycles are as follows:

(1) Year	(2) Net costs flow ($)	(3) Discount factor $i = 8\%$	(4) PV of net costs flow ($) (2) X (3)	(5) PV of total costs flow ($)	(6) Replacement factor $i = 8\%$	(7) NPV of replacement cycle ($) (5) X (6)
1	1950	0.9259	1805.5	1805.5	13.5000	24374.3
2	1350	0.8573	1157.4	2962.9	7.0096	20768.7
3	1350	0.7938	1071.6	4034.5	4.8504	19568.9
4	1440	0.7350	1058.4	5092.9	3.7740	19220.6
5	1560	0.6806	1061.7	6154.6	3.1307	19268.2
6	1680					

Comparing these cost estimates it can be seen that the optimal replacement cycle for the type A car is 5 years and that for the type B car 4 years, and that the type A car is more economical as the minimum NPV of its infinite replacement chain is $1,356.2 less than the minimum for type B.

Obviously, in this particular type of problem the assumption of an infinite replacement chain may not in itself be a valid one. It is more likely to be appropriate to the needs of somebody who is operating a large fleet of vehicles of uniform type, than to a person who is buying a single car for his own use, but in neither case should the resulting figure be treated as more than an *indication* of the relative economies. Indeed, where there can be no certainty as to the alternatives that will be available in 4 or 5 years' time, no mathematical evaluation can do more than this.

D — Evaluation of Comparable Assets — II (questions 7–8)

In the previous section, where a potential buyer was evaluating between comparable pieces of equipment, we assumed that he was free to make his choice from scratch: i.e. the man in the example either had no car or had made a definite decision to dispose of the car he was currently using and replace it by one of the two types under consideration.

In this section we will take the analysis a stage further to consider the situation where the potential buyer contemplates the replacement of equipment that he already possesses by comparable equipment of a different type. In this case he not only has to decide whether the alternative would be more economical in itself but, if it is, the buyer also wants to know how much longer he should keep his existing equipment before replacing it.

Even though the comparison shows that the other type of equipment would be more economical, the replacement should not necessarily take place straight away. It has been pointed out that costs of this nature tend to follow a cycle by which they decline progressively during the first few years of operating the equipment and then start to rise again. If the existing equipment is approaching the most economical years of its particular cost cycle, it may be more profitable to continue using it for a while.

The technique to be followed in this case is therefore to combine the NPV of the infinite chain of replacements for the equipment which is to be used in the future, with the NPV of the costs of keeping the existing equipment for a number of additional years, in order to establish the minimum after which it becomes more economical to replace the existing equipment with new equipment of the other type.

What we are establishing, in effect, is the sum of money that the buyer would have to invest now, at a rate of interest equal to his cost of capital, in order to yield a sufficient annual income to meet all his costs if he were to keep his existing equipment for the given number of additional years and thereafter enter on a continuous chain of replacements using the other equipment.

We will demonstrate the approach by a modification of the example used in the previous section.

Example 4

Let us now assume that the man already possesses a type B car which he has owned for 1 year before the comparison of figures in the automobile magazine article persuades him to replace it by a type A. He has established, by the calculation of section C, that type A is the better buy and should have a replacement cycle of 5 years. However, his existing car has already incurred its heaviest initial costs and is now entering its most economical period of operation. The man's problem is to decide how much longer he should continue to use it before replacing it with the other type.

As in the earlier example of Section C, we assume, for mathematical simplicity, that all costs are payable at the end of each year.

Solution: We need to consider only the remaining years of life of the existing type B car. Consequently, the first 5 columns of the following table are basically the same as the corresponding columns of the table used in the previous section, to calculate the NPV of the infinite replacement chain for that car. The differences result from the change in our starting point, which in this case occurs a year later.

(1) Remaining years of life of B	(2) Net costs flow ($)	(3) Discount factor $i = 8\%$	(4) PV of net costs flow ($) (2) × (3)	(5) PV of total costs flow ($)
1	1350	0.9259	1250.0	1250.0
2	1350	0.8573	1157.4	2407.4
3	1440	0.7938	1143.1	3550.5

We now extend the table with three additional columns so as to complete the calculation. We will then explain what has been done.

(1) ...	(6) Minimum NPV ($) of replacement cycle of A	(7) PV ($) of (6) when A replaces B (3) × (6)	(8) Combined NPV ($) (5) + (7)
1	17864.4	16540.7	17790.7
2	17864.4	15315.2	17722.6
3	17864.4	14180.8	17731.3

In column (5) of the table we established the present value, with $i = 8\%$, of the money the man would have spent if he were to keep his existing car for one more year, for two more years, and so on.

He then replaces it with the type A car for which, as calculated in section C, an infinite replacement chain (with the optimal 5-year replacement cycle) will cost him the equivalent of $17,864.4 in lump-sum present value terms with $i = 8\%$. This is the figure inserted in column (6).

But the man is not making that investment immediately: he makes it only when the car is to be replaced in one or more years' time. Therefore the figure of column (6) has to be discounted to its present value. This is done in column (7).

Finally, in column (8), we combine the present value of what it will cost to keep the existing car for a specific number of additional years, with the present value of what it would then cost to replace it with the type A car, so as to arrive at the NPV of the complete operation.

It can be seen from the table that the turning point occurs at the end of year 2 (so it is not necessary to continue the calculations after year 3, when the turning point has been revealed). This means that, on the basis of the figures given, it would be most economical for the man to continue using his present car for a further two years before replacing it with a new type A car. By doing so, instead of replacing the existing car straight away, he would save himself the equivalent of $17,864.4 − $17,722.6 = $141.8.

In practical terms we have established that, given the data of this particular problem, the difference is not significant. If the man is being strictly businesslike about his choice, he will probably continue with his present car for another year or two and re-examine the position at that time in the light of the alternatives then available to him. If, on the other hand, he has set his heart on the type A car, he will probably decide that it is not worth waiting 2 years for the sake of such a relatively small saving and consider himself justified in making the change immediately!

E — Replacement Problems without Depreciation (questions 9—11)

Although the replacement techniques described in sections A to D are most commonly used in relation to assets such as machinery, etc., these should not be thought of as the only applications. Indeed, such techniques lend themselves to any situation which calls for recurring capital outlays followed, in each case, by a costs curve which eventually starts to rise and which can be reduced only by a further capital outlay. This capital outlay does not necessarily imply any concept of depreciation, as we shall demonstrate by example.

Example 5

A local authority is responsible for maintaining the roads in its area. The cost to it of resurfacing each mile of road is $50,000. In the first year after resurfacing, maintenance costs $15,000/mile and this cost increases by $5,000/mile in each subsequent year.

If the cost of money to this local authority is 9%/annum, determine the most economical time-cycle between resurfacings.

Solution: We assume, for computational simplicity, that all costs arise at the end of each year. This applies also to the resurfacing cost which is payable at the end of year 1 of each resurfacing cycle.

(1)	(2)	(3)	(4)	(5)	(6)	(7)
	Net costs flow	Discount factor	PV of net costs flow ($)	PV of total costs	Replace- ment factor	NPV of replace- ment cycle ($)
Year	($)	$i = 9\%$	$(2) \times (3)$	flow ($)	$i = 9\%$	$(5) \times (6)$
1	50000	0.9174	45870.0	45870.0	12.1111	555536.2
2	15000	0.8417	12625.5	58495.5	6.3163	369475.1
3	20000	0.7722	15444.0	73939.5	4.3895	324557.4
4	25000	0.7084	17710.0	91649.5	3.4297	314330.3
5	30000	0.6499	19497.0	111146.5	2.8566	317501.1

On this analysis, the most economical policy is to resurface each stretch of road at four-year intervals.

Example 6

The engineering department of the local authority proposes to build a new road. The new road will cost $150,000/mile to construct and surface and will be 20% shorter than the existing route which it will replace. Construction and initial surfacing of the new road can be completed within the year. The foundations of the new road will be more suited to modern traffic so that its resurfacing cost is expected to average $8000/mile less and its annual maintenance cost to average $3000/mile less than the corresponding costs/mile of the existing road.

Given the same resurfacing and maintenance costs per mile of the existing road as in example 5 and ignoring any savings or other advantages to the users of the new road arising from its shorter length determine whether it will be more economical to the local authority to construct the new road or to continue with the existing road.

Solution: As in the previous example, we assume that all costs are payable at the end of each year: including the initial cost of construction which arises at the end of year 1. To begin with, let us ignore the initial cost of construction and surfacing and consider only the infinite replacement (i.e. resurfacing) chain which we consider to start with the initial surfacing operation. In this example the surfacing costs for year 1 have been incorporated in the new construction costs but we shall assume that the cost/mile of initial surfacing is the same as the cost/mile of resurfacing.

Because the new road is to be 20% shorter than the existing one there will be 4/5 mile of new road for every mile of existing road.

As our purpose is to establish a comparison between the costs of the reconstructed road and those of the existing road (irrespective of its actual length) the cost of resurfacing the new road for each equivalent mile of existing road can be written as

$$\tfrac{4}{5}(50000 - 8000) = \$33,600$$

Similarly, in the first year after resurfacing (i.e. at the end of year 2 of the cycle) the maintenance cost for each equivalent mile of the existing road is

$$\tfrac{4}{5}(15000 - 3000) = \$9600$$

In the second year after resurfacing (i.e. at the end of year 3 of the cycle) the maintenance cost/equivalent mile is

$$\tfrac{4}{5}(20000 - 3000) = \$13,600$$

and so on. On this basis the complete table of iterations for the infinite resurfacing chain is:

(1)	(2)	(3)	(4)	(5)	(6)	(7)
	Net costs flow ($)	Discount factor $i = 9\%$	PV of net costs flow ($) $(2) \times (3)$	PV of total costs flow ($)	Replacement factor $i = 9\%$	NPV of replacement cycle ($) $(5) \times (6)$
Year						
1	33600	0.9174	30824.6	30824.6	12.1111	373319.8
2	9600	0.8417	8080.3	38904.9	6.3163	245735.0
3	13600	0.7722	10501.9	49406.8	4.3895	216871.2
4	17600	0.7084	12467.8	61874.6	3.4297	212211.3
5	21600	0.6499	14037.8	75912.4	2.8566	216851.4

Hence it will still be the most economical policy to resurface at 4-year intervals although the NPV of this recurring cost will be much less for each equivalent mile of the new road, as one would expect. We now turn to the initial construction and surfacing costs which, for each equivalent mile of existing road, amount to

$$\tfrac{4}{5} \times 150000 = \$120000$$

For the normal first year of a resurfacing cycle, as we have seen, the cost/equivalent mile is $33,600. Therefore, for the very first year (and for that year alone) the *extra* cost is

$$120000 - 33600 = \$86,400$$

As this arises at the end of the first year its equivalent present value (for $i = 9\%$) is $79,263.4.

We have seen, from the previous example, that if the existing road is due for resurfacing this year the minimum NPV of all future costs associated with maintaining it is $314,330.3/mile. By contrast, if the road is reconstructed this year the minimum NPV/equivalent mile will be

$$79263.4 + 212211.3 = \$291,474.7$$

Hence it will be more economical to construct the new shorter and better built road than to continue maintaining the existing road and the NPV of the resultant saving (if the existing road is due for resurfacing this year and $i = 9\%$) is $314,330.3 - 291,474.7 = \$22,855.6$.

Example 7

We now take the previous example a stage further and assume that the old road was resurfaced (i) one year previously, or (ii) two years previously.

Having established that the proposed reconstruction is desirable and should be put into effect, when would be the most economical time to do so, in each case?

Solution: Using the same type of analysis as was demonstrated in section D, the tables for cases (i) and (ii) are shown below.

(1) Remaining years	(2) Net costs flow ($) of existing road	(3) Discount factor $i = 9\%$	(4) PV of net costs flow ($) (2) × (3)	(5) PV of total costs flow ($)	(6) Minimum NPV ($) of replacement cycle (new road)	(7) PV ($) of (6) when construction occurs (3) × (6)	(8) Combined NPV ($) (5) + (7)
case (i)							
1	15000	0.9174	13761.0	13761.0	291474.7	267398.9	281159.9
2	20000	0.8417	16834.0	30595.0	291474.7	245334.3	275929.3
3	25000	0.7722	19305.0	49900.0	291474.7	225076.8	274976.8
4	30000	0.7084	21252.0	71152.0	291474.7	206480.7	277632.7
case (ii)							
1	20000	0.9174	18348.0	18348.0	291474.7	267398.9	285746.9
2	25000	0.8417	21042.5	39390.5	291474.7	245334.3	284724.8
3	30000	0.7722	23166.0	62556.5	291474.7	225076.8	287633.3

From these tables it can be concluded that:

(i) If the existing road was resurfaced one year previously it would be worthwhile to postpone construction of the new road until year 3 and the NPV of the saving achieved by doing so, instead of constructing now, would be

$$291,474.7 - 274,976.8 = \$16,479.9$$

(ii) If resurfacing of the existing road was done 2 years previously, construction of the new road should be scheduled for year 2.

F — Individual Replacement and the Steady State (questions 12—15)

We now consider another aspect of replacement — that of components (such as light bulbs) which usually have a fairly short lifespan and are not repairable in themselves: they either work or fail. (A certain loss of efficiency may in fact occur as the component ages, but for our purposes we are assuming that this is not important enough on its own to justify replacement before failure.) As the type of approach we shall deal with here is normally applied only to components that have a relatively short lifespan we shall not take into account the time value of money.

Clearly this is a different type of problem from that discussed in sections A—E. With this type of component there are no maintenance costs and depreciation is not normally considered. Also, when replacement is due the value of the component itself is often only a relatively small part of the total cost, to be considered in conjunction with others of equal or greater importance such as the cost of labor in replacing the component and certain contingency costs such as 'down time' (i.e. the loss of productive time between failure of the component and its replacement). A correct replacement strategy is one which seeks to minimize the *total* cost of replacement.

The type of case that frequently concerns us is that in which a number of components of the same kind are in use and the distribution of their life expectancy is known.

Consider a factory building which uses 10000 of a certain type of light bulb. The distribution of the life expectancy of these bulbs is given in the following table:

Life in months	1	2	3	4
Proportion of failures at that lifespan	10%	20%	40%	30%

It can be seen that all the bulbs will have failed by the end of the fourth month after their installation.

In this section we assume that the company's replacement policy is to wait until a bulb has failed before replacing it. This is called a policy of **individual replacement**. For the sake of computational simplicity, however, we assume that all such replacements are made simultaneously at the end of each time period (a month, in this particular example). This assumption, which is repeated throughout all the following sections of this chapter, is of course an artificial one but it gives results which are approximately accurate for our purpose of arriving at the 'steady state' (defined later in this section). By contrast, to assume that each component is replaced immediately on failure would greatly increase the mathematical complexity of the treatment while not making any very significant difference to the result we are seeking.

Let us represent the number of bulbs failing during (and being replaced at the end of) the first month of the factory being opened by u_1, the number failing during and being replaced at the end of the second month by u_2 and so on, and let u_0 be the initial number installed ($= 10000$).

Further, let us represent the percentage of bulbs installed which fail and are replaced within one month of their installation as p_1, those which fail and are replaced two months after installation as p_2 and so on.

Then the complete pattern of replacements of the 10000 bulbs initially installed can be tabulated as shown on the next page.

Month	Number of bulbs failing during the month (and being replaced at month end)	Number of new bulbs installed
0		10000
1	$u_0 p_1$ $= 10000 \times 0.1$	1000
2	$u_0 p_2 + u_1 p_1$ $= (10000 \times 0.2) + (1000 \times 0.1)$	2100
3	$u_0 p_3 + u_1 p_2 + u_2 p_1$ $= (10000 \times 0.4) + (1000 \times 0.2) + (2100 \times 0.1)$	4410
4	$u_0 p_4 + u_1 p_3 + u_2 p_2 + u_3 p_1$ $= (10000 \times 0.3) + (1000 \times 0.4) + (2100 \times 0.2) +$ (4410×0.1)	4261
5	$u_1 p_4 + u_2 p_3 + u_3 p_2 + u_4 p_1$ $= (1000 \times 0.3) + (2100 \times 0.4) + (4410 \times 0.2) +$ (4261×0.1)	2448
6	$u_2 p_4 + u_3 p_3 + u_4 p_2 + u_5 p_1$ $= (2100 \times 0.3) + (4410 \times 0.4) + (4261 \times 0.2) +$ (2448×0.1)	3491
7	$u_3 p_4 + u_4 p_3 + u_5 p_2 + u_6 p_1$ $= (4410 \times 0.3) + (4261 \times 0.4) + (2448 \times 0.2) +$ (3491×0.1)	3866
8	$u_4 p_4 + u_5 p_3 + u_6 p_2 + u_7 p_1$ $= (4261 \times 0.3) + (2448 \times 0.4) + (3491 \times 0.2) +$ (3866×0.1)	3342

and so on.

This table may look confusing: in fact it is very simple. Take each row individually. The top row corresponds to the number of bulbs (10000) installed at the start of the project. The row beneath it shows the number of replacement bulbs installed at the end of month 1; namely 10% of 10000 = 1000. The next row shows the position at the end of the second month, when replacements are required for 20% of the bulbs originally installed and for 10% of those installed at the end of month 1: i.e. (20% of 10000) + (10% of 1000) = 2100.

The table continues in this way, row by row. All the bulbs installed at any one time will have failed after 4 months of life. Consequently, by the end of month 4 we have replaced all the bulbs originally installed, by the end of month 5 we have replaced all of those installed in month 1 and so on; each subsequent row has to deal only with bulbs installed during the 4 immediately preceding months.

You will notice that the number of replacements required in each successive month tends to increase, then diminish, then increase again, then diminish again. These oscillations continue as the table is extended, but with decreasing amplitude, until eventually the number of replacements in each month becomes approximately constant. This is known as the steady state situation and is the one we normally consider.

Where N is the maximum number of time periods of life of a component and $p_1, p_2 \ldots p_N$ are the percentages of that component failing and being replaced in each successive time period of its maximum life, then the average life of such a component (expressed by $\bar{u}$) may be calculated by the following formula:

$$\bar{u} = (1 \times p_1) + (2 \times p_2) + \ldots (N \times p_N)$$

In our example of the light bulbs, where the values of p_1, p_2 etc. are as given and $N = 4$, then

$$\bar{u} = (1 \times 0.1) + (2 \times 0.2) + (3 \times 0.4) + (4 \times 0.3) = 2.9 \text{ months}$$

From this we can proceed to the formula for deriving the average number of failures/replacements each month in the steady state situation, which is $u_0/\bar{u}$. (This will not be proved as its proof requires advanced mathematics, however the relationship may perhaps be accepted as intuitively reasonable.)

Hence in our example, where $u_0 = 10000$ and $\bar{u} = 2.9$, the number of monthly replacements in the steady state situation is $10000/2.9 = 3448$.

Let c_1 be the total cost of replacing each item individually at failure (or, as assumed in this section, at the end of the month of failure). Then on this basis the monthly cost of replacing all the items that fail in the steady state is $c_1 u_0/\bar{u}$.

Thus in our example, assuming $c_1 = \$0.5$, the total expense of replacement in the steady state will be

$$0.5 \times 3448 = \$1724/\text{month}.$$

Applications of the principles given in this section are described in the appendix to this chapter.

G — Group Replacement (question 16)

An alternative replacement policy to that discussed in section F is that of **group replacement**; namely the collective replacement of all items of a single type at periodic intervals, whether they have failed or not.

In our example of the factory with 10000 light bulbs, the average total cost of replacement per bulb when this is done on a group basis is likely to be less than the cost of replacing each one individually after failure. Although the cost of the bulb itself is unchanged, when we consider the operations involved (i.e. getting up to the light-fitting, opening it, cleaning it, etc.) it can readily be appreciated that the labor cost of replacing a single bulb is not much less than that of replacing all the bulbs in the light-fitting together, in which case the average labor cost is correspondingly reduced for each bulb.

Let us use c_2 for the cost of replacement per item when this is done on a group basis. Then the total cost of replacing all items collectively is $c_2 u_0$.

In our example, if $c_2 = \$0.25$, then the total cost of replacing all the bulbs in the factory on a group replacement basis is

$$0.25 \times 10,000 = \$2500$$

H — Combining Group and Individual Replacements (questions 17—20)

In this section we consider a **mixed strategy** of group replacement at periodic intervals with individual replacement of any item that fails between group replacements. We continue the assumption of section F, that all individual replacements occur at the end of the time period of failure, and this of course continues to be an artificial assumption made for the sake of computational simplicity.

Let us take t as the number of time periods (months, in this case) between one group replacement and the next. Actually it is *usage* that we are normally concerned with in this type of example, not time as such, which is simply being employed here as a measure of usage; so in the general sense t can refer to any equivalent way of measuring usage. For example, when measuring the potential failures of vehicle components t could be the number of miles run: when measuring the potential failures of manufacturing tool components t could be the number of parts turned out by the machine, and so on.

If we consider a replacement cycle to consist of a group replacement followed by the series of individual replacements before the group replacement commencing the next cycle, then the total cost cycle consists of two parts:

(i) the cost of group replacement
(ii) the sum of the costs of individual replacements made between group replacements.

To determine the optimal length of replacement cycle an iterative technique similar to that of section A is used. Basically it consists in calculating the average cost of each replacement cycle for successive values of t and finding out which among them (we can call it 'optimal t') is the most economical.

Returning to our example, where the total number of bulbs is 10000, $c_1 = \$0.5$ and $c_2 = \$0.25$, the costs of alternative cycle-times are calculated and may be compared in the following table.

(1) Length of cycle in months (t)	(2) Costs incurred at end of each month of cycle ($)								(3) Total costs/ cycle ($)	(4) Average costs/month ($) (3) ÷ (1)
	1	2	3	4	5	6	7	8		
1	2500								2500	2500
2	2500	500							3000	1500
3	2500	500	1050						4050	1350
4	2500	500	1050	2205					6255	1563.75
5	2500	500	1050	2205	2130.5				8385.5	1677.1
6	2500	500	1050	2205	2130.5	1224			9609.5	1601.6
7	2500	500	1050	2205	2130.5	1224	1745.5		11355	1622.1
8	2500	500	1050	2205	2130.5	1224	1745.5	1933	13288	1661

Column (2) of this table is constructed from the group replacement cost plus the individual replacement costs for successive months as taken from the table in section F. The sum of these in column (3) gives us the total cost of the cycle t (with no discounting for cost of capital) and dividing this figure by the number of months in the cycle gives us, in column (4), the average cost/month.

It can be seen from the table that a particular cycle, say of 4-monthly duration, will consist of an initial group replacement followed by 3 individual replacements of those bulbs which fail during the first 3 months of the cycle. In this particular model we are assuming that no individual replacements occur at the end of month 4 because this would coincide with the group replacement at the beginning of the 5th month which is the start of the next cycle.

In this particular example it can be seen that with a mixed strategy the optimal solution (i.e. that which yields minimum average costs/month) is given by a 3-monthly replacement cycle. The average monthly cost of this particular strategy is $1,350, which is less than that of a policy of individual replacement.

It will be noted that there is a second turning point in the table after 6 years. Multiple turning points are common in this type of problem but in practice, in virtually all cases (including all questions to this section), the first turning point will be optimal.

Questions

5.1 In this section, what is meant by 'optimal life'?

5.2 A company uses a certain type of lathe costing $9000 to buy. Costs in use are as follows, over 7 years.

Time in years	1	2	3	4	5	6	7
Operating costs ($)	200	300	600	1000	1500	2000	3500
Resale value at year end ($)	4000	3000	2000	1000	500	0	0

Calculate depreciation and tabulate the costs flow. Keep a a note of the answer for questions 3 and 4.

5.3 On the basis of question 2, find the optimal life of this type of lathe.

5.4 Given the data of question 2, calculate the optimal life of each lathe if all costs accrue at the end of each year and the company's cost of capital is 10%. Keep a note of the answer for questions 6, 7 and 8.

5.5 Describe the nature of the result you are getting from the technique demonstrated in this section, by answering the following questions:

(i) What does the figure in the extreme right-hand column of the table represent?
(ii) How does this differ in nature from the result obtained with no discounting, in section A?

5.6 Assume that the data in question 4 relate to one type of lathe (type A) and this is now to be compared with another lathe (type B), initially more expensive but cheaper to maintain. The costs flow of the type B lathe is tabulated as follows:

Year	1	2	3	4	5	6	7
Costs flow in $	5500	1800	1200	800	1500	2500	3000

Determine the NPV of replacement costs for this lathe with $i = 10\%$ and decide from this whether the type A or type B lathe is the more profitable. Keep a note of the answer for questions 7 and 8.

5.7 The company has been operating a type A lathe for 1 year and has decided to replace it with a type B lathe. From the data of questions 4 and 6 and their answers, determine the optimal number of years that the existing lathe should be retained in use before its replacement by the other type.

5.8 If the company has been operating its type A lathe for 3 years at the time the decision is made to change over to type B, how much longer should it then decide to retain the existing lathe before making the changeover?

5.9 An oil company aims to produce a constant output for a number of years from a certain oilfield. It drills a series of similar wells (an operation that takes negligible time) and moves on to the next as it finishes with the previous one. Each well has the same costs flow as given (in $'000) in the following table; assume that all costs arise at the end of each year.

Year	1	2	3	4	5	6
Drilling costs	1400					
Operating costs	200	200	300	400	600	1000
Net costs flow	1600	200	300	400	600	1000

Determine the optimal life of each well if the relevant cost of capital is 12%, and keep a note of your results for questions 10 and 11.

5.10 The oil company has been offered a long lease on a new oilfield for $1.5m payable at the beginning of the first year of operations. Output per well and quality will be equal to that obtained from the existing oilfield but the costs flow will be less. This, and the resulting replacement cycle calculation are shown in the following table:

(1)	(2)	(3)	(4)	(5)	(6)	(7)
1	600	0.8929	535.7	535.7	9.3333	4999.9
2	100	0.7972	79.7	615.4	4.9308	3034.4
3	100	0.7118	71.2	686.6	3.4696	2382.2
4	200	0.6355	127.1	813.7	2.7436	2232.5
5	400	0.5674	227.0	1040.7	2.3117	2405.8

The cost of moving to the new oilfield is $0.5m, payable at the end of the year of moving. Moving time is negligible. The company is about to drill a new well in the existing field. Assuming that all other things are equal and that it has to choose between one field and the other, determine whether the company should move.

5.11 Assume that the company can retain an option on the new oilfield for a number of years before taking it up, and that the well being worked currently on the existing field was drilled 2 years previously. When should the company make its move to the new site?

5.12 An industrial ceramics factory has 300 diamond-tipped drills of identical type (fitted to its various drilling machines) which have to be replaced when blunted or damaged. The distribution of life expectancy is given in the following table.

Life in months	1	2	3	4	5
Proportion of failures at that lifespan	10%	15%	25%	35%	15%

Assume for mathematical simplicity that failed drills are replaced at the end of the month of failure.

If the 300 drills are initially installed together, estimate the number of replacements required at the end of each of the first 6 months. Keep a note of your results for question 17.

5.13 (i) Given the data of question 12, calculate the average life of a drill in months. Keep a note of your result for question 14.

(ii) What symbol is used in the section to signify the average life of a component?

5.14 (i) What is meant by the term 'steady state'?

(ii) Given your answer to question 13 calculate the annual number of replacements in the steady state for the data of question 12.

5.15 (i) What is meant by 'a strategy of individual replacement'?

(ii) Given the data of questions 12 to 14 and using the notation of section F, calculate the monthly cost of replacement in the steady state if $c_1 = \$7$.

5.16 (i) Given the data of questions 12 to 15 and using the notation of section G, calculate the total cost of group replacement for the 300 drills if $c_2 = \$4$.

5.17 (i) In the context of section H, what is meant by a 'mixed strategy'?

(ii) Given the data of questions 12 to 16, calculate 'optimal t' if a mixed strategy is adopted.

(iii) What is the average monthly cost of such an optimal mixed strategy and how does this compare with the cost of individual replacement strategy?

5.18 An open-cast mining operation uses a fleet of heavy scraper/dumper trucks. Each truck has 16 tires, costing $100 each to replace together in the workshop. If a tire-burst occurs on site, additional costs (down-time, etc.) of fitting a new tire amount to $100 per tire. Distribution of tire failure against mileage is given in the following table.

Mileage { from	1	10001	20001	30001
to	10000	20000	30000	40000
Failure rate	15%	25%	40%	20%

For mathematical simplicity assume tires fail at 10,000, 20,000 30,000 and 40,000 miles only. Calculate:

(i) the average life of a tire in miles,

(ii) the average cost/tire-mile of a strategy of individual replacement at failure.

(iii) the average cost/truck-mile of this strategy.

Keep a note of your results for questions 19 and 20.

5.19 Considering the data of question 18, if all 16 tires on a truck are installed together, calculate the expected number of failures per truck at the end of each 10000 miles of operation (i.e. at the end of 10000 miles, at the end of 20000 miles and so on to 50000 miles).

5.20 Considering the data of questions 18 and 19, determine 'optimal t' (in 10000 mile units) for a mixed strategy and, from this, the average cost/truck-mile. Is this cheaper than a strategy of individual replacement?

Appendix: Applications of Section F

The methods described in section F can also be used as an aid to decision-making in certain aspects of personnel management.

Each time a trained employee leaves and has to be replaced, certain costs are incurred in recruiting and training a new employee and in the time it takes that employee to build up to full working efficiency. If the total cost of replacing an average employee of a certain type is known it becomes possible to weigh such costs, for example, against the alternative costs of measures designed to reduce staff turnover. The following example illustrates the application.

Example 10

The typing pool of a large organization employs 100 copy-typists. The distribution of length of service is given in the following table.

Duration of employment in years	1	2	3	4	5 or more
Proportion of staff in that year of employment	30%	40%	20%	10%	0%

Assuming, for mathematical simplicity, that any employee leaving is replaced by another at the end of the year, determine

(i) the number of staff who leave in each of the first 8 years of the department's existence (assuming it started with 100 employees and this total number does not change),

(ii) the number leaving each year when the steady state situation is reached, and

(iii) the total annual cost of recruiting staff in the steady state if replacement of each new copy typist costs $200.

Solution: No new principles are involved in solving this problem, which is simply a special case of the general problem discussed in the section. We can therefore omit some of the more space-consuming calculations from our answers.

(i) The number of copy typists leaving at the end of each of the first 8 years of the department's existence is set out in the following table:

Year	1	2	3	4	5	6	7	8
Departures	30	49	46.7	49.6	46.4	48.0	47.6	47.7

(ii) $u_0 = 100$

$\bar{u} = (1 \times 0.3) + (2 \times 0.4) + (3 \times 0.2) + (4 \times 0.1) = 2.1$

$u_0/\bar{u} = 100/2.1 = 47.62$

(iii) in the steady state situation, the total annual cost of replacing copy copy typists in this department is

$$200 \times 47.62 = \$9524$$

Further Reading

1. The Replacement of Capital Equipment
The treatment of this technique in the conventional OR textbook tends to be quite mathematical, see for example chapter 17 of 'Introduction to Operations Research', C.W. Churchman, R. Ackoff and L.E. Arnoff, Wiley 1956, or chapter 5 of 'Operations Research: Methods and Problems' by M. Sasieni, A. Yaspan and L. Friedman, Wiley 1959. Although both texts provide mathematical derivations of the relationships for the NPV of an infinite replacement chain, neither discusses the impact on the replacement models of inflation, tax allowances and obsolescence. Chapters 19 and 20 of 'Finance and Analysis' (full reference provided in chapter 2), however, not only describe the models in more detail and at a mathematical level similar to that of this chapter but also cover the modifications to the basic models necessary to take these into account. The necessary changes are quite straightforward in principle in each case in that the net costs flow and/or discount rate is amended appropriately before the usual calculations are undertaken. Chapter 19 in addition provides a straightforward derivation of the NPV of an infinite replacement chain equation.

2. The Replacement of Items That Fail Outright
The second part of chapter 5 of 'Operations Research: Methods and Problems' (full reference provided above) gives a first class and more detailed description than that provided in this chapter of the type of model used in this situation although it makes use of elementary probability concepts and some slightly more advanced algebra. It also covers fully the associated approach discussed briefly in the appendix to this chapter for handling staff replacement.

6

INVENTORY CONTROL

In this book we use the word **stock**, or **inventory**, to refer to goods that are being held for use or disposal at a later date. These terms are used synonymously here; 'stock' being the more common term in Britain and 'inventory' in the United States. The terms may refer, for example, to raw materials for the owner's own manufacturing operations, materials for his own use (such as stationery, spare parts, etc.) or goods awaiting sale by him.

Inventory is a buffer between supply and demand. Inventory holding capacity can be used to reduce costs by exploiting the economies of large bulk orders or long production runs and failure to carry adequate stocks may result in loss of business or increased costs of various kinds caused by disruption of operations.

However, holding inventory can be expensive. The main element in inventory holding costs is normally the interest that could otherwise have been earned on the money that was used to pay for the goods in stock. Other elements include, for example, the costs of storage space and facilities, administration, handling, insurance, obsolescence or deterioration, pilferage, etc. Taking all these elements into consideration, the annual cost of inventory holding is usually of the order of 15–20% of the value of the inventory being held: i.e. an inventory with an average value of $1 million, being held throughout the year, is costing its owners $150,000–$200,000/annum simply to hold in inventory.

The problem which we will explore in this chapter is to determine how an organization can minimize its net total inventory holding and associated costs. By the application of relatively simple control techniques on the lines described here, some organizations have achieved reductions of a quarter to a third in such total costs.

A number of new formulae will be introduced in this chapter and we shall refer to these by their order of appearance in the section in which they first appear. For example, the first formula to be introduced in section A is labelled (A1), the third formula to be used in section B is labelled (B3) and so on.

This chapter follows logically from the previous one insofar as, where chapter 5 has shown how to plan an optimal replacement strategy for components which fail, chapter 6 discusses the planning of an appropriate purchasing and inventory holding strategy for the replacement items. However, the scope of chapter 6 is much wider than this, as it extends to all

82 INVENTORY CONTROL

forms of inventory. Mathematically, this chapter depends on nothing that has preceded it in this book: the concept of the time value of money is implied in the treatment of costs in this chapter so that it is only necessary, here, to have a general appreciation of that concept (such as can be grasped by reading the first half of chapter 2) in order to understand how it has been taken into account.

A – The Basic or Classical Inventory Control Model (questions 1–3)

A number of items of a particular type purchased or manufactured at any one time is called a **batch**. The simplest and most widely used method of stock control, known as the **economic batch quantity** model (abbreviated to **EBQ**), depends on the following assumptions:

(i) a uniform, continuous and known demand for the item under scrutiny (i.e. withdrawals from inventory occur at a uniform rate);
(ii) instantaneous replenishment of inventory (i.e. the inventory level is allowed to fall to zero, whereupon reordering the delivery of new items into inventory occur immediately);
(iii) stockholding cost per item is proportional to the number of items in inventory and the time for which they are held in

Let q be the order quantity in units (e.g. single items, dozens, boxes [of uniform content] etc.) and t the number of time periods (in weeks, years etc.) that it takes to exhaust this quantity. The complete cycle from replenishment of inventory to its exhaustion will be called, by us, the **reordering cycle** or **replenishment cycle**. In the basic EOQ model the inventory level over time can be expressed in graphical form as drawn in figure 6.1.

The inventory level over time during each cycle is a straight sloping line (as withdrawals from inventory are assumed to occur at a uniform rate). The rate of withdrawal in units/time-period (e.g. per month, per year etc.)

inventory level   Figure 6.1

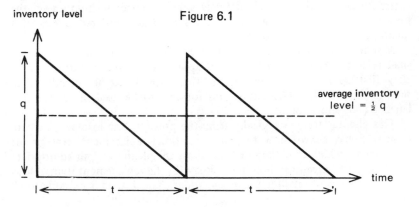

is symbolized by μ (pronounced mu, as in mew), which is the Greek alphabet equivalent of our lower case m.

There is a simple and obvious relationship between the order quantity, the rate at which it is withdrawn from inventory and the time it takes for the inventory to be exhausted, which can be expressed in a formula as follows:

$$q = \mu t \qquad\qquad (A1)$$

hence also

$$t = q/\mu \text{ and } \mu = q/t$$

Example 1

A manufacturer purchases boxes of paper towels for his factory washroom in quantities of a gross and issues them from stock at a rate of 8 boxes/week. How long will it take for his inventory to be exhausted?

Solution: $t = q/\mu = 144/8 = 18$ weeks

It will also be obvious from the graph that in this type of reordering cycle the average quantity held in inventory on a continuous basis is $\frac{1}{2}q$.

Example 2

If withdrawals of a particular item from inventory occur at the uniform rate of 75 units/month and stock is exhausted and renewed every 6 months, determine the average inventory level.

Solution: $q = \mu t = 75 \times 6 = 450$ units
average inventory level $- \frac{1}{2}q = 450/2 = 225$ units

B — Cost Basis of the Economic Order Quantity Model (questions 4–5)

In accordance with ordinary business practice we shall refer to any method of initiating a batch as an **order**.

Any purchasing or commissioning or reordering operation carries certain costs which are fixed, meaning that they do not vary with the size of the order. Such costs may be negligible or they can be very substantial, extending from the cost of administration and paperwork (e.g. placing the order, checking on delivery, etc.) to the cost of setting up for a production run. In this book we shall refer to the total initiating cost as the **set-up cost**.

The other costs of carrying inventory tend to vary with the quantity and value of the goods held in stock. These, which we shall call **inventory holding costs**, are the various costs alluded to at the beginning of this chapter, e.g. the cost of storage space, the interest rate on the value of money tied up in inventory, etc.

The combination of set-up cost with inventory holding costs we shall call **total inventory cost**. Hence total inventory cost/replenishment cycle = set-up cost + total inventory holding costs. Notice that at this stage we are not concerned directly with the purchase cost of the items: the value of this money, expressed as a rate of interest, is taken into account as part of the inventory holding costs and the time-value of the money tied up in inventory is also taken care of in this way.

Let a represent the set-up cost/reordering cycle and b the inventory holding cost/unit/time period, then total inventory holding cost/replenishment cycle = b (inventory cost/unit/time period) $\times$ ½q (average number of units in inventory) $\times t$ (number of time periods) = ½bqt. Therefore

$$\text{total inventory cost/replenishment cycle} = a + \tfrac{1}{2}bqt$$
$$= a + \tfrac{1}{2}b\mu t^2 \qquad (q = \mu t)$$

The total inventory cost/time period, which we shall call c, is generally a more useful standard for measurement and comparison than the cost/replenishment cycle. Clearly,

$$c = \frac{\text{cost/replenishment cycle}}{\text{duration of replenishment cycle}}$$
$$= \frac{a + \tfrac{1}{2} b\mu t^2}{t} = a/t + \tfrac{1}{2} b\mu t \qquad (B1)$$

We have now established a relationship between the following

q (the order size, in units)
μ (the rate of withdrawal from stock, in units/time period)
t (the duration of the replenishment cycle, in time periods)
a (the set-up cost per replenishment cycle)
b (the inventory holding cost/unit/time period)
c (the total inventory cost/time period)

Obviously if these are to be related to each other the units must all be of the same type: if the unit of quantity is to be a dozen items, then the unit values of q, μ and b must also be expressed in dozens. Similarly, the time periods must be of the same type: if the chosen time period is one week then the time values of μ, t and b must all be expressed in weeks and c is the total inventory cost per week.

Example 3

Taking the example at the end of section A, if

$$\mu = 75 \qquad \text{(in units/month)}$$
$$t = 6 \qquad \text{(in months)}$$

calculate the total inventory cost/annum if the initiating cost of each order is $7 and the stockholding cost is $4/unit/annum.

Solution: The unit of time has to be consistent and, in this case, as we are seeking a figure for annual cost, the most convenient unit is a year. Hence,

$$\mu = 75 \times 12 = 900 \quad \text{(in units/annum)}$$
$$t = 6 \div 12 = \tfrac{1}{2} \quad \text{(in years)}$$
$$a = 7 \quad \text{(in \$)}$$
$$b = 4 \quad \text{(in \$/unit/annum)}$$

By formula (B1)

$$c = a/t + \tfrac{1}{2}b\mu t = (7 \div \tfrac{1}{2}) + (\tfrac{1}{2} \times 4 \times 900 \times \tfrac{1}{2}) = 14 + 900 = \$914$$

C – Optimal Order Size (questions 6–8)

Our object is to be able to determine the reordering/replenishment cycle which gives the lowest total inventory cost per time period; in other words, the **optimal replenishment cycle**. We will use lower-case letters of the alphabet for general values of q, t and c and upper-case to mean, specifically, the optimal value of each. Thus

$$Q = \text{optimal } q$$
$$T = \text{optimal } t$$
$$C = \text{optimal } c$$

Just as there is a relationship between q, t and c; so is there a relationship between their optimal values Q, T and C, thus formula (A1) can be rewritten as

$$Q = \mu T$$

and formula (B1) as

$$C = a/T + b\mu T$$

For any given values of a, b and μ the corresponding values of T, Q and C can be found, independently of each other, by using one or other of the following three formulae (reference sources for their derivation by calculus are given in the Further Reading section):

$$T = \sqrt{\left(\frac{2a}{b\mu}\right)} \qquad \text{(C1)}$$

$$Q = \sqrt{\left(\frac{2a\mu}{b}\right)} \qquad \text{(C2)}$$

$$C = \sqrt{(2ab\mu)} \qquad \text{(C3)}$$

Example 4

A retailer buys from a wholesaler a product of which he enjoys a steady sale at the rate of 2000 items/annum. It costs him $5 to initiate each order and $2 to hold one item in stock for a year.

Determine the following:

(i) the number that he should order at a time (Q)
(ii) the optimal time between reorderings (T)
(iii) the minimum total inventory cost/time period (C)

Solution: Let a year be the time period and an item the unit of quantity. Then,

$$a = 5 \qquad \text{(in \$)}$$
$$b = 2 \qquad \text{(in \$/item/annum)}$$
$$\mu = 2000 \qquad \text{(in items/annum)}$$

(i) $\quad Q = \sqrt{\left(\dfrac{2a\mu}{b}\right)} = \sqrt{\left(\dfrac{2 \times 5 \times 2000}{2}\right)} = \sqrt{10000} = 100$

The product should therefore be reordered in batches of 100.

(ii) T can be derived from Q, thus

$$T = \frac{Q}{\mu} = \frac{100}{2000} = \frac{1}{20}$$

i.e. one-twentieth of a year, about 2½ weeks. This can also be found independently by formula (C1). This is more laborious but has the merit of providing a check on the accuracy of the first result.

$$T = \sqrt{\left(\frac{2a}{b\mu}\right)} = \sqrt{\left(\frac{2 \times 5}{2 \times 2000}\right)} = \sqrt{\left(\frac{1}{400}\right)} = \frac{1}{20}$$

(iii) The optimal cost can be found independently by formula (C3), thus

$$C = \sqrt{(2ab\mu)} = \sqrt{(2 \times 5 \times 2 \times 2000)} = \sqrt{(40000)} = \$200$$

i.e. minimum total inventory costs are $200/annum.
[Alternatively, C can be derived from T by formula (B1), thus

$$C = \frac{a}{T} + \tfrac{1}{2}b\mu T = (5 \times 20) + \frac{1 \times 2 \times 2000}{2 \times 20} = \$200]$$

Let us now extend this example a little further to see what actually happens to the total inventory cost/time period if the batch size is greater or smaller than Q. Remember that $q = \mu t$, so that formula (B1) can be written in the form

$$c = a\mu/q + \tfrac{1}{2}bq.$$

Consider first the case where $q < Q$. Taking $q_1 = 50$

$$c_1 = \frac{5 \times 2000}{50} + \frac{2 \times 50}{2} = 200 + 50 = \$250$$

Now consider the case where $q > Q$. Taking $q_2 = 200$

$$c_2 = \frac{5 \times 2000}{200} + \frac{2 \times 200}{2} = 50 + 200 = \$250$$

Notice not only that the cost is greater than C in either case but that the cost-increase is relatively much greater when $q < Q$ than when $q > Q$. Because the additional cost of ordering in batches of $\frac{1}{2}Q$ is the same as that of ordering in batches of $2Q$, this means that the extra cost/time period is as much for batches of half the optimal size as it is for batches of twice the optimal size: i.e. in this example it would be as costly to under-order by 50 units as to over-order by 100 units. The variation of cost for different values of q in this example is shown graphically in figure 6.2, such a curve being typical of this type of problem.

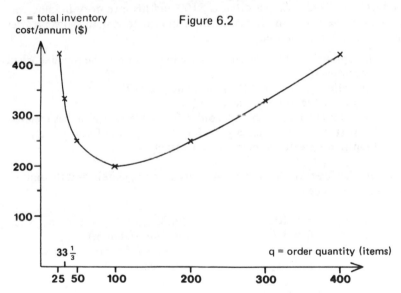

Figure 6.2

c = total inventory cost/annum ($)

q = order quantity (items)

D – Lead Time (questions 9–10)

In this section we amend the classical EBQ model and take it a stage further. You will remember that it was based on three assumptions of which the second was instantaneous replenishment of inventory. We will now assume that there has to be an interval of time between ordering the replenishment inventory and receiving it. This interval is known as lead time.

All the other assumptions and the basic formulae described in the previous section remain unchanged but it will now be necessary to reorder before the inventory level reaches zero.

Clearly if μ is the rate of withdrawal from inventory (in units per time period) and the appropriate lead time is l time periods, the number of units withdrawn from inventory between reordering and arrival of the replenishment inventory will amount to $l\mu$ units of inventory.

Obviously, if all anticipated withdrawals are to be met from inventory the next reordering cycle must be initiated while there are still $l\mu$ items in inventory or in the pipeline (i.e. due for delivery against a previous order). Let us call this quantity Q'. Then,

$$Q' = l\mu \qquad\qquad (D1)$$

Example 5

A wholesaler experiences an annual demand for 2880 units of a certain product. His fixed cost per order is $100 and his inventory holding cost per unit is $2.5/annum. It takes him a month to obtain delivery after placing his order. Determine

(i) the optimal quantity he should have in stock or in the pipeline when reordering (Q');
(ii) the optimal duration of the reordering cycle (T);
(iii) the optimal reordering quantity (Q);
(iv) the dates at which he should reorder during the year if he has received his first delivery on January 1. (For the purposes of this example, all months are treated as being of equal length.)

Solution: Let us take the unit of quantity as a single item and the unit of time as a year. Then:

$$
\begin{array}{ll}
a = 100 & \text{(in \$)} \\
b = 2.5 & \text{(in \$/unit/annum)} \\
\mu = 2880 & \text{(in units/annum)} \\
l = \tfrac{1}{12} & \text{(in years)}
\end{array}
$$

(i) $Q' = l\mu = 2880/12 = 240$ units

(ii) $T = \sqrt{\left(\dfrac{2a}{b\mu}\right)} = \sqrt{\left(\dfrac{2 \times 100}{2.5 \times 2880}\right)} = \tfrac{1}{6}$ year; i.e. 2 months

(iii) $Q = \mu T = 2880/6 = 480$ units

(iv) From (ii) and (iii) we have established that the wholesaler orders 480 units at a time and this inventory lasts two months. In fact he must reorder one month before his inventory is due to run out in order to receive delivery of the next consignment in time, so, if he received his first order on January 1 he must reorder by February 1, when he will have exactly one month's inventory in hand to carry him over. Repeat orders during that year must be placed at 2-monthly intervals from February 1, i.e. on April 1, June 1, etc.

E — The EOQ Model with Non-Instantaneous Supply (questions 11–13)

In this section we ignore the question of lead time introduced in section D and deal with the EBQ model where replenishment of stock is not instantaneous, but occurs at a rate which is greater than the rate of withdrawals.

This corresponds to the case, for example, where a company's manufacturing process turns out items at a faster rate than they are used or sold. The nature of the reordering cycle in this type of situation is illustrated in figure 6.3.

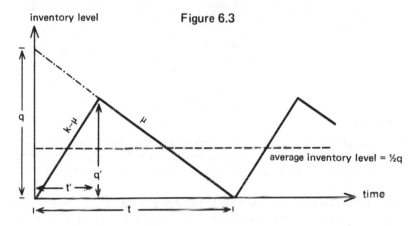

Figure 6.3

Replenishment begins when the inventory level is at zero and the order size is q units. Replenishment is not immediate but occurs at a uniform rate of k units/time period for a length of time t'. Hence

$$q = kt' \qquad\qquad (E1)$$

Thus $\qquad\qquad k = q/t' \text{ and } t' = q/k$

Withdrawals are continuous at the rate μ units/time period; $\mu < k$ and $q = \mu t$.

During the first part of the cycle replenishment and withdrawal are occuring simultaneously so that the inventory level rises at the rate $(k - \mu)$ units/time period to reach a peak at q' units which is the maximum inventory level actually achieved. Hence it can be seen that

$$q' = t'(k - \mu) = \frac{q}{k}(k - \mu) \qquad\qquad \text{(substituting for } t')$$

$$= qk/k - q\mu/k = q - q\mu/k = q(1 - \mu/k) \qquad\qquad (E2)$$

During the second part of the cycle there is no replenishment and the inventory level declines steadily, for $(t - t')$ time periods, to reach zero.

It should be clear from figure 6.3 that in this situation the average inventory level is $\frac{1}{2}q'$. Therefore, using the notation of the previous sections,

$$\text{total cost/cycle} = a + \frac{1}{2}bq't$$

If we substitute $q(1 - \mu/k)$ for q' and proceed as in section B we have

$$c = a/t + \frac{1}{2}b\mu\,(1 - \mu/k)\,t \qquad\qquad\qquad \text{(E3)}$$

From this we can derive the following formulae for T, Q and C which are simply modified versions of those in section C. (See Further Reading for reference sources for their derivation.)

$$T = \sqrt{\left(\frac{2a}{b\mu\,(1 - \mu/k)}\right)} \qquad\qquad \text{(E4)}$$

$$Q = \sqrt{\left(\frac{2a\mu}{b\,(1 - \mu/k)}\right)} \qquad\qquad \text{(E5)}$$

$$C = \sqrt{\,[2ab\mu\,(1 - \mu/k)\,]} \qquad\qquad \text{(E6)}$$

Example 6

The sales department of a manufacturing company has to meet a regular demand of 20 engines of a certain type each month. It orders these from the production department which can produce them at the rate of 2 per day.

The set-up cost for each production run is $17,000 and the cost to the company of holding one engine in inventory for one year is $850. Calculate,

  (i) the optimal order size (Q);

  (ii) the maximum number in stock at any one time (Q');

  (iii) the duration of the production run (T');

  (iv) the time interval between the start of one production run and the start of the next (T);

  (v) the minimum total inventory cost/annum (C).

Take a year as being 360 days and a month as 30 days.

Solution: Let the unit of quantity be a single engine and the time period a year. Then

$$a = 17000 \qquad b = 850 \qquad \mu = 240 \qquad k = 720$$

Hence,
$$\mu/k = 240/720 = \tfrac{1}{3}$$
$$(1 - \mu/k) = 1 - \tfrac{1}{3} = \tfrac{2}{3}$$

(i) Using formula (E5) we have

$$Q = \sqrt{\left(\frac{2a\mu}{b(1-\mu/k)}\right)} = \sqrt{\left(\frac{2 \times 17000 \times 240}{850 \times \frac{2}{3}}\right)} = 120$$

(ii) Using formula (E2) we have

$$Q' = Q(1 - \mu/k) = 120 \times \frac{2}{3} = 80$$

(iii) Using formula (E1) we have

$$T' = Q/k = 120/720 = \frac{1}{6} \text{ year, i.e. 2 months}$$

(iv) Using formula (A1) we have

$$T = Q/\mu = 120/240 = \frac{1}{2} \text{ year, i.e. 6 months}$$

Alternatively, we could find the answer independently by formula (E4): thus,

$$T = \sqrt{\left(\frac{2a}{b\mu(1-\mu/k)}\right)} = \sqrt{\left(\frac{2 \times 17000}{850 \times 240 \times \frac{2}{3}}\right)} = \sqrt{\frac{1}{4}} = \frac{1}{2} \text{ year}$$

(v) Applying formula (E6), we have

$$C = \sqrt{[2ab\mu(1-\mu/k)]} = \sqrt{(2 \times 17000 \times 850 \times 240 \times \frac{2}{3})} = \$68,000$$

Alternatively, we could derive C from T by the use of formula (E3): thus,

$$C = a/T + \frac{1}{2}b\mu(1-\mu/k)T = \frac{17000}{\frac{1}{2}} + \frac{1}{2} \times 850 \times 240 \times \frac{2}{3} \times \frac{1}{2}$$

$$= 34000 + 34000 = \$68000$$

F — Shortages and Stockouts (questions 14–17)

Many inventory control systems are based on the premise that no item shall be out of stock when required. Indeed, it is obvious that inability to meet demands from inventory will incur costs in the form of lost orders or goodwill, additional production costs (because production is disrupted by shortage of some components or raw materials) and so on.

It is often possible to assign a figure to such costs. If this is then balanced against the cost of carrying inventory, however, it may sometimes be found cheaper to permit shortages (sometimes called **stockouts**) to occur than to carry the stock needed to avoid them.

A reordering strategy based on the classical EBQ model of sections A to C but in which stockouts are deliberately permitted to occur towards the end of each cycle, is displayed graphically in figure 6.4. For simplicity we are assuming that those goods which cannot be withdrawn during the stockout are supplied from the next replenishment.

In this diagram, as in those of the preceding sections, q represents the order size and t the time it takes for this quantity to be withdrawn at the rate of μ units/time period. Because shortages are supplied immediately from the new stock as it comes in the maximum inventory level actually

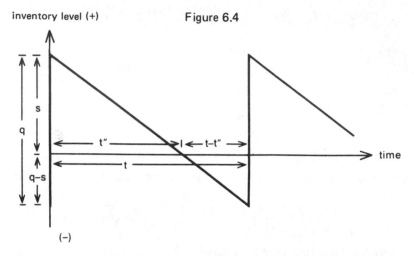

Figure 6.4

achieved is less than q and is denoted by s; it is exhausted during time t''. Thereafter the graph moves into the negative sector, as unsatisfied demand builds up during the time $(t - t'')$ and the maximum shortfall of stock is $(q - s)$.

Let us assume that the shortage carries some form of penalty cost which is proportional to the number of units out of stock and the time for which they are out of stock. Let z denote the cost/unit/time period.

It follows that we now have three elements in the total inventory cost per replenishment cycle:

(i)   the set-up cost $= a$
(ii) the inventory holding cost $= b \times \frac{1}{2}s \times t''$
(iii) the penalty cost $= z \times \frac{1}{2}(q - s) \times (t - t'')$.

[For items (ii) and (iii) the basic formula is the same, i.e. cost = cost/unit/time period $\times$ average number of units $\times$ number of time periods.] Clearly,

$$s = \mu t''$$
$$t'' = s/\mu$$
(F1)

If we substitute s/μ for t'' where it occurs in the cost equations we can arrive (by the same route as in previous sections; the algebraic processes in this case are rather lengthier but quite straightforward in themselves) at the following formula for total inventory cost/time period:

$$c = \frac{a}{t} + \frac{bs^2}{2\mu t} + \frac{z(\mu t - s)^2}{2\mu t}$$
(F2)

From this can be derived (see Further Reading for reference sources for their derivation) the following basic formulae:

$$T = \sqrt{\left(\frac{2a(b + z)}{bz\mu}\right)}$$
(F3)

$$Q = \sqrt{\left(\frac{2a\,(b+z)\mu}{bz}\right)} \qquad \text{(F4)}$$

$$C = \sqrt{\left(\frac{2abz\mu}{b+z}\right)} \qquad \text{(F5)}$$

$$S = \sqrt{\left(\frac{2az\mu}{b(b+z)}\right)} \qquad \text{(F6)}$$

where S is the value of s when we have determined the optimal (i.e. minimum cost) solution. The last two of these formulae are based on another formula for s:

$$s = \frac{z\mu t}{b+z} \qquad \text{(F7)}$$

Example 7

A sub-contractor to the motor industry produces 100000/annum of a certain type of car part. Set-up costs for a production run are $2000. Inventory holding cost per item produced is $4/annum. For late delivery there is a penalty charge of $1/item/month. Determine the following,

(i) the optimal size of production run (Q);
(ii) the number of items out of stock per cycle $(Q-S)$;
(iii) the duration of each cycle (T);
(iv) the length of time that goods are out of stock in each cycle $(T - T'')$;
(v) the minimum total inventory cost/annum (C).

Solution: Let the unit of quantity be a single item and the time period one year. Then $\mu = 100000, a = 2000, b = 4, z = 12$.

(i) By formula (F4)

$$Q = \sqrt{\left(\frac{2a\,(b+z)\mu}{bz}\right)} = \sqrt{\left(\frac{2 \times 2000 \times 16 \times 100000}{4 \times 12}\right)}$$

$$= 10000\sqrt{\left(\frac{4}{3}\right)} = 11547$$

(ii) By formula (F6)

$$S = \sqrt{\left(\frac{2az\mu}{b(b+z)}\right)} = \sqrt{\left(\frac{2 \times 2000 \times 12 \times 100000}{4 \times 16}\right)}$$

$$= 10000\sqrt{\left(\frac{3}{4}\right)} = 8660$$

$$Q - S = 11547 - 8660 = 2887$$

(iii) By formula (A1)

$$T = Q/\mu = 11547/100000$$

$$= 0.11547 \text{ year,}$$

i.e. about 42.1 days (with 1 year = 365 days). Alternatively, using formula (F3) to obtain an independent result for cross- checking, we have

$$T = \sqrt{\left(\frac{2a\,(b + z)}{bz\mu}\right)} = \sqrt{\left(\frac{2 \times 2000 \times 16}{4 \times 12 \times 100000}\right)} = \sqrt{\left(\frac{1}{75}\right)} = 0.11547.$$

(iv) By formula (F1)

$$T'' = S/\mu = 8660/100000 = 0.0866 \text{ year or about } 31.6 \text{ days}$$

Thus $$T - T'' = 10.5 \text{ days}$$

[This could also have been found directly from (ii). Clearly, duration of stockout $= (Q-S)/\mu = 2887/100000 = 0.02887$ year (365 days) = 10.5 days.]

(v) In this case it is more convenient to use formula (F5) than to derive a result from T and S using formula (F2), though both calculations may be desirable as a cross-check for errors.

$$C = \left(\frac{2abz\mu}{b + z}\right) = \sqrt{\left(\frac{2 \times 2000 \times 4 \times 12 \times 100000}{16}\right)} = \$34641$$

G – Quantity Discounts (questions 18–20)

In sections A–F of this chapter we have shown how to determine the optimal reordering quantity Q; namely that batch size which, for certain given conditions, gives the minimum total inventory cost.

So long as the other conditions remain unchanged we can assume that any smaller order quantity will be more costly than Q. On the other hand, an order for a quantity greater than Q may in some cases be rewarded by a price reduction, i.e. a **quantity discount**. The reduction in purchase price or cost/item that could be gained from ordering in larger batches may sometimes outweigh the corresponding increase in holding costs.

Consider, as an example, the case of a manufacturer of machinery who requires 25 of a certain type of small electric motor each year. His initiating cost per order is $8 and his holding cost is $4 per unit per year. The price that he has to pay for these motors varies with the order quantity, according to the following scale:

Batch quantity in units	Unit price in $
1 – 49	12
50 – 99	8
100 – 499	7
500 and above	6

In this example, using the classical EBQ model of sections A and B, if we take a year as our time period, $a = 8$, $b = 4$, $\mu = 25$, then by formula (C2),

$$Q = \sqrt{\left(\frac{2 \times 8 \times 25}{4}\right)} = \sqrt{100} = 10$$

If he reorders in batches of 10 the manufacturer will have to pay for his motors at the maximum price of $12 each. Would it be more profitable for him to order in larger batches so as to benefit from one or other of the quantity discounts?

Let us call the successive minimum ordering quantities on the discount scale q_1, q_2, q_3 and the corresponding price/unit p_1, p_2, p_3. The complete price/quantity position is displayed graphically in figure 6.5.

Obviously, the manufacturer is only interested in ordering the minimum quantity at each step in the discount scale that will enable him to benefit from the reduced price. He must therefore compare his costs for a batch of 10 with those for a batch of 50, 100 or 500. We will identify the respective costs/time period as c_1, c_2 and c_3.

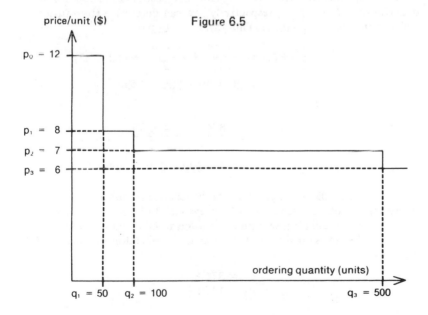

price/unit ($)   Figure 6.5

$p_0 - 12$

$p_1 = 8$

$p_2 - 7$

$p_3 = 6$

ordering quantity (units)

$q_1 = 50$ $q_2 = 100$ $q_3 = 500$

Into this comparison we must introduce the purchase price, so that we now have to consider three elements in arriving at the total cost per reordering cycle:

(i) the initiating cost $= a$
(ii) the inventory holding cost $= \frac{1}{2}bqt$
[Strictly speaking, if the purchase price is a variable then b (the holding cost/unit/time period) is also a variable, as one of the elements in b is the rate of interest on money tied up in stock. Thus if the purchase price/unit is \$12 and the cost of capital is 10%/annum, this element in the holding cost is \$1.2/annum, whereas it is only \$0.8 if the purchase price is \$8. (The other elements that contribute to b, such as the cost of storage space etc., do not vary with purchase price.) We ignore such variations here because they require a very much more complex model to deal with them. For our purposes the valuation of b must be accepted as approximate.)
(iii) the purchase cost $= pq$ (i.e. the price per unit multiplied by the batch quantity).

Hence total purchase and inventory cost/cycle $= a + \frac{1}{2}bqt + pq$

total purchase and inventory cost/time period $= \dfrac{a + \frac{1}{2}bqt + pq}{t}$

$$= \frac{a}{t} + \frac{bq}{2} + \frac{pq}{t} \ \left(\text{but } t = \frac{q}{\mu}\right) \ = \frac{a\mu}{q} + \frac{bq}{2} + p\mu \qquad \text{(G1)}$$

By using this formula to calculate the cost/time period for order quantities of $Q, q_1, q_2 \dots$ respectively, we can determine (by inspection) which is the most economical. Thus, for $Q = 10, p = 12$

$$C = \frac{a\mu}{Q} + \frac{bQ}{2} + p\mu = \frac{8 \times 25}{10} + \frac{4 \times 10}{2} + (12 \times 25)$$

$$= 20 + 20 + 300 = 340$$

for $q_1 = 50, p_1 = 8$

$$c_1 = \frac{a\mu}{q_1} + \frac{bq_1}{2} + p_1\mu = \frac{8 \times 25}{50} + \frac{4 \times 50}{2} + 8 \times 25$$

$$= 4 + 100 + 200 = 304$$

In this particular example it is hardly realistic to consider ordering in quantities of 500 (20 years' stock!) or even 100 (4 years' stock) whether or not these should prove more economical in a mathematical sense. However, the decision does not arise as the application of formula (G1) shows that

$$c_2 = 376.8$$
$$c_3 = 1150.3$$

Hence it is established that the most economical order quantity is 50 (i.e. q_1) at a purchase price of \$8/unit (i.e. p_1).

We will now recapitulate the successive stages in the calculation.

1. Use formula (C2) to calculate Q.
2. Find (by inspection) the purchase price/unit when Q is the order quantity and use formula (G1) to calculate the cost/time period of reordering in this order quantity.
3. Determine the successive minimum batch quantities $> Q$ that would give quantity discounts (i.e. q_1, q_2 ... etc. for p_1, p_2 ... etc.) and use formula (G1) to calculate c_1, c_2 .. .etc. for these batch quantities.
4. Determine (by inspection) the lowest value of c and hence the corresponding optimal order quantity. These can be labelled C' and Q' respectively to distinguish them from the optimal values C and Q where no quantity discounts apply.

Questions

6.1 (i) What do the letters EOQ stand for? (ii) List the three assumptions on which the simple or classical EOQ model is based.

6.2 A certain commodity is issued from stock at the rate of 25 units/month.

(i) What symbol is used to express this rate of issue?
(ii) What would be the minimum stock level required, without replenishment, to enable this commodity to be issued from stock at this rate for a period of exactly eight months?

6.3 With μ = 25 units/month, and regular replenishment of stock on the classical EOQ model occurring every 8 months, calculate the average inventory level throughout the time that these conditions are maintained.

6.4 (i) In section B, when we talk about the total inventory cost/replenishment cycle, what are the elements in this cost? (ii) What is done to convert the total inventory cost/replenishment cycle into cost/time period?

6.5 A certain article is ordered in quantities of 240 units and issued from stock at the rate of 40 units/month. The initiating cost for an order is \$4 and the holding cost/article/annum is \$3. Given the conditions of the classical EOQ model, show:

(i) the set-up cost/reordering cycle,
(ii) the stockholding cost/reordering cycle,
(iii) the total inventory cost/reordering cycle,
(iv) the total inventory cost/month.

6.6 A wholesaler distributes 1200 units of a certain piece of industrial equipment annually from a warehouse. The cost associated with each delivery to the warehouse is \$600 (independent of the size of the delivery) and the estimated cost of holding 1 unit in stock is \$900/annum. How often should he order a new delivery (T)? Keep a note of your answer to this question for use in questions 7 and 8.

6.7 Use the data of question 6 and its answer to calculate the optimal order size (Q): firstly by deriving this from T and then by calculating it independently, as a cross-check, by use of the appropriate formula.

6.8 Use the data of question 6 and its answer to calculate the total inventory cost/annum (C). Do this independently in the first instance, by using the appropriate formula, and then cross-check by deriving the answer from T.

6.9 A manufacturer of frozen food has to meet an annual demand for 27 million packaged TV dinners. Production set-up cost is $25,000. Lead time is 30 days and stockholding cost/package/month = $0.05. Take a year to be 360 days and a month to be 30 days. Calculate Q' and keep a note of its value for use in question 10.

6.10 Given the data of question 9, calculate Q, and T. Why is Q' greater than Q?

6.11 In a supermarket a certain product sells at the rate of 2400 items/week. There are 48 shopping hours in the week and the rate of sale of this product is fairly uniform. An employee can re-stock the shelves at a rate of 300 items/hour. This operation is done during shopping hours, so that customers are taking the product from the shelves at the same time as the employee is restocking them. If the policy is to re-stock as soon as shelves are empty, using a single employee to put in 1800 items at a time, calculate:

(i) the time required for re-stocking,
(ii) the maximum number of items on the shelves at one time,
(iii) the time-interval between the commencement of one re-stocking operation and that of the next.

Keep a note of your results for use in questions 12 and 13.

6.12 The main stock of the product of question 11 is kept in a store at the back of the shop. The operation of re-stocking the shelves in the shop from this main stock is assigned a fixed standard cost of $5.00 and the cost of holding 1 item on a shelf costs $0.005/week more than it costs to hold it in store. Given the data of question 11, calculate the total cost/week of the current re-shelving policy. Keep a note of your results for use in question 13.

6.13 Given the data of questions 11 and 12, calculate the optimal quantity to be shelved at a time and the cost of this strategy, for comparison with the existing strategy.

6.14 A motor distributor supplies an average of 150/week of a particular model of car to a number of dealers. Holding one car in stock costs $14/week, 'badwill', etc. costs about $6 for every car out of stock for a week and the paperwork and other costs associated with placing an order with the manufacturer amount to $140. Outstanding orders are met from each new delivery. Calculate the optimal size of order to be placed with the manufacturer.

6.15 Given the data of question 14, calculate the distributor's total inventory cost/annum on this model of car. Take a year to be 50 weeks.

6.16 A large hospital requires 25 bottles of special plasma daily. Reordering in the normal way involves an initiating cost of $8 per order and the storage cost is $0.05/bottle/day. In emergency, supplies can be borrowed from other hospitals and these are replaced immediately as a new delivery is received from the regular source. The cost of borrowing averages $0.2/bottle/day.

The hospital management wants to keep its costs down by pursuing an optimal reordering strategy but wants to know for safety reasons, the maximum number of bottles out of stock in each reordering cycle under the optimal reordering strategy. Calculate this and keep your results for use in question 17.

6.17 Given the data of question 16, calculate the length of time between orders and the length of time that the hospital will be out of stock of plasma in each reordering cycle.

6.18 A manufacturer of furniture has to meet a constant demand of 100/month for a certain type of chair. It costs him $1800 to set up a production run and $3 to hold a chair in stock for a year. Calculate his optimal production run according to the simple EOQ model and keep a note of your result for use in question 19.

6.19 The manufacturer of question 18 estimates that his direct costs of production per chair vary with the length of the production run, according to the following scale:

Quantity	Cost/chair in $
under 2500	13
2500–5000	12
5000–10000	9
over 10000	7

Is it likely to be worth his while to manufacture in larger batches than 1200 for the sake of the production economy?

6.20 A retailer of motor tires finds that for a certain size $\mu = 7$/week, $a = \$14$ and $b = \$1$/tire/month. Using the simple EOQ model he orders his tires at present in batches of 28 but he hopes, by offering to quadruple the size of his order, to negotiate a quantity discount. What is the minimum discount he should try to get, as a percentage of the price of $9 per tire that he is paying at present?

Further Reading

In all the different inventory models described in this chapter we assumed that the rate of demand for the item in question was known with certainty and was uniform. This of course is very rarely true in practice although in very many situations providing the actual rate does not vary too much over time and the estimated value of μ does not differ too much from the true average demand figure, models of the kind developed in this chapter prove quite satisfactory.

When unit demand per time period is not known with certainty but estimates of its distribution are available then the models of this chapter can be modified to take such information into account although knowledge of probability theory is required. These types of model are known as probabilistic demand models.

A good non-mathematical treatment of the models we have discussed in this chapter is provided, together with some more advanced material, in chapter 7 of 'Quantitative Approaches to Management' by R.I. Levin and C.A. Kirkpatrick, McGraw-Hill 1978, 4th edition. In chapter 8 of the same book various probabilistic demand models are described which allow calculation of the reorder level and reorder time with associated inventory costs for different service levels (the percentage of time on average e.g. 95%, 99% etc. that items will be in stock when required). Appendix 8 of the book provides proofs by calculus of the equations used without proof in different parts of this chapter.

A much higher level classical inventory book is provided by Eliezer Naddor, 'Inventory Systems', John Wiley & Sons, Inc., 1966. A more recent book on production-inventory systems with cases is 'Production-Inventory Systems: Planning and Control', 3rd edition by Buffa and Miller, Richard V. Irwin, 1979.

For those readers who want an exposure to modern computerized approaches to inventory control using the new MRP approach, refer to 'Production and Inventory Management in the Computer Age' by Oliver Wight, Cahners Books, 1974, and 'Materials Requirements Planning' by Joseph Orlicky, McGraw-Hill, 1975.

7

CRITICAL PATH ANALYSIS

In this chapter we deal with a method for project planning and scheduling, known as **critical path analysis**. This makes use of the theory of **network analysis**, which is the name given to the branch of mathematics dealing with networks (the terms 'critical path' and 'network' are defined and explained later in this chapter). We restrict ourselves in this book to the basic technique. There are other related approaches which deal more explicitly with the problem of uncèrtainty and are not discussed here. One of the best-known of these is called **PERT** (Program Evaluation and Review Technique), and a brief summary of this together with further reading is provided at the end of this chapter.

The contents of this chapter do not depend on anything described in the preceding parts of this book and may be studied on their own. Furthermore, although the application of critical path analysis to large and complex projects as in ship building may give rise to very complicated calculations requiring a computer for their solution, the basic method is very simple and requires no more mathematical background than the ability to add and subtract.

In the first section of this chapter we will be dealing mainly with certain graphical conventions which are necessary for a complete understanding of what follows. If the purpose of these conventions is not entirely clear to you at the first reading, they should be clear by the end of section B and it may then be a good idea to re-read section A.

A — Some Conventions of the Network Graph (question 1)

The completion of any project (from building a supersonic airliner to brewing a pot of tea) calls for a sequence of distinctive operations or jobs. For example, the action of changing the wheel of a car can be broken down into the following distinctive operations:

   (i) jack up car
  (ii) remove wheel
 (iii) put away wheel
 (iv) take out spare wheel
  (v) put on spare wheel
 (vi) release jack

In the specialized jargon of critical path analysis, each such operation is called an **activity**. Some of these activities, called **sequential activities**, are of such a type that one must precede or follow the other. For example, you cannot remove the wheel until you have jacked up the car. Other activities, described as **concurrent activities**, are of such type that there is no need for the completion of one before the commencement of any other and in fact they can be performed simultaneously. For example it makes no difference whether you take out the spare wheel before or after jacking up the car, or you can have one person taking out the spare while another operates the jack: the operations do not depend on each other.

The critical path method of scheduling this type of project (and do not be misled by its apparent simplicity for it demonstrates certain necessary basic principles) depends, in the first instance, on drawing what is called a **network graph.** In this type of graph the time taken to perform an activity is represented by an arrow. Although we do not start dealing with time until a later section of this chapter it is worth stressing here that the length of the arrow is not related to the length of time taken by the activity and is generally irrelevant. Similarly, the direction of the arrow is not relevant, though it is customarily drawn from left to right (i.e. with the head of the arrow to the right of its tail).

The start or completion of an activity corresponds to what is called an **event.** An event is simply a point in time and is represented on a network graph by a small circle or **node** (from Latin *nodus,* a knot). Figure 7.1 shows a typical representation on a network graph of an activity and its starting and finishing events which are commonly referred to, respectively, as the **tail event** and **head event** of the activity.

Figure 7.1

In the first stages of preparing a network graph it is customary to label the different activities with upper-case letters of the alphabet (e.g. A, B etc.). In figure 7.1 we have drawn the arrow that corresponds to activity X.

Activities which are sequential are drawn on a network graph in the manner of figure 7.2. This corresponds to a situation where activity Y depends on and must follow after activity X. The head event of activity X is also the tail event of activity Y: i.e. the moment in time which marks the completion of activity X is the moment from which activity Y can begin.

Figure 7.2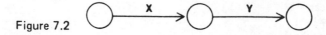

Figure 7.3 illustrates various examples of concurrent activities. In diagram (i), activities P and Q have different tail events and different head events. In diagram (ii), activities A and B have the same tail event but different head events. In diagram (iii), activities R and S have different tail events but the same head event.

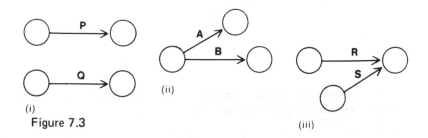

(i)

(ii)

(iii)

Figure 7.3

Finally, in figure 7.4 we show both types of activities in combination. Activity R is sequential to activities P and Q, which are concurrent: i.e. P and Q do not depend on each other but activity R depends on and must follow after both of them. Hence, activities P and Q share the same head event, which is the tail event of activity R.

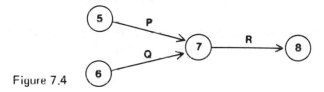

Figure 7.4

Notice that in figure 7.4 the nodes or events have been numbered. This is a normal convention after the network has been completed and, once it has been done, each activity is usually identified by the numbers given to the nodes at its tail and head. This convention is sometimes referred to as the **(i,j) system** of numbering, with i as the number of the tail event of an activity and j as that of its head event. The number of the head event of an activity should always be greater than that of its tail event. By this convention, activity P becomes activity (5,7), activity Q becomes activity (6,7) and so on.

Before we go on to an actual exercise in constructing a network, it may be convenient to conclude this section by listing some general rules of conventional or correct practice.

1. Avoid lines that are not straight. In your first attempts at drawing a network you may find it necessary to draw a crooked arrow to accommodate an afterthought, but you should then redraw the network so as to eliminate it. Figure 7.5 displays an incorrectly drawn network and, beside it, the same network with the arrow corrected.

Figure 7.5

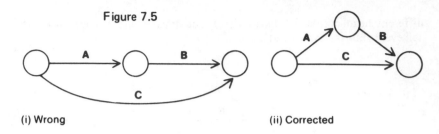

(i) Wrong   (ii) Corrected

2. Avoid lines that cross. An incorrectly drawn network and its corrected version are shown together in figure 7.6.

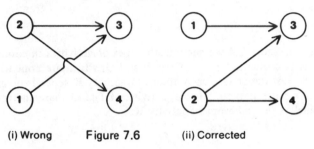

(i) Wrong   Figure 7.6   (ii) Corrected

3. Try always to draw an arrow with its head to the right of its tail. The correct and incorrect versions are illustrated in figure 7.7.

Figure 7.7

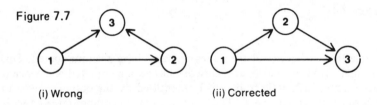

(i) Wrong   (ii) Corrected

B – Preparing the Network Graph of a Project (questions 2–4)

After breaking down a project into its separate activities, the first stage in preparing a network graph is to tabulate the relationship of these activities to each other.

In section A we described the activities into which the project of changing the wheel of a car could be broken down; we now list them in the form of what is called an **activity dependency table**. In this table we have first labelled and described the individual activities, then listed (in the right-hand column) the **immediately preceding activities** or **IPA** corresponding to each: namely, for each activity, the labels of those other activities (if any) which it must *directly* follow.

Activity	Description	IPA
A	Jack up car	—
B	Remove wheel	A
C	Put away wheel	B, D
D	Take out spare wheel	—
E	Fit spare wheel	B, D
F	Release jack	E

Obviously, if the whole project is being handled by a single person he will have to perform each activity sequentially because he cannot do more than one at a time. However, for our purpose we will assume that there is no shortage of manpower to prevent operations from being performed concurrently: this leaves us free to consider the essential relationship of the activities to each other. On this basis (and in the light of what has been said in section A) the table should be self-explanatory. For example, the operation of putting away the wheel (activity C) cannot be performed until that wheel has been removed from the axle (B) and the spare wheel taken out (D) to make room for it.

A network graph should have only one point of entry and one point of exit. Expressed graphically this means that, with two exceptions, every arrow in the network must have both its head and its tail linked at a node to the tail or head of at least one other arrow. Of the two exceptions, one arrow (the activity that starts the project) is linked only at its head and the other (the activity which concludes the project) only at its tail. Every arrow, including these two, is drawn with a node at both ends.

Two of the activities in this example (A and D) have no IPA. In order to provide a single starting point for the project we introduce an artificial initiating activity (X) which we call a **lead activity**. Similarly, if we find that there is no single activity which has to follow all the others and thus conclude the project, we introduce an artificial concluding activity (Y) which we call the **end activity**.

We are now ready to begin the network. It is customary to begin from the left and work from left to right.

The tail of an activity must start from the head of its IPA and, if two or more activities have the same IPA, this means that their tails must start from a single node. Similarly, if there is more than one immediately preceding activity, this means that the heads of those activities must meet at a single node.

We begin by drawing the initiating activity and the nodes at its head and tail. In this particular example the initiating activity is the lead activity, X. From the node at the head of X we draw the activities A and D. B follows A and the heads of the arrows representing B and D must meet at a node because both these activities immediately precede both C and E. So we draw B with its tail at the head of A and its head at the head of D. The

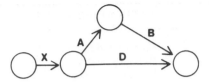

Figure 7.8

stage that we have reached so far is shown in figure 7.8. Any chain of con-
secutive activities is called a **path**. Here we have two concurrent paths,
one represented by activity D and the other by activities A and B, leading
to the single event at the heads of B and D.

We carry on in exactly the same way. Activities E and C have the same
tail event and activity F has its tail at the head of E and its head at the
head of C. From the event at the heads of F and C we lead off the end
activity, Y. Figure 7.9 displays the completed network.

Figure 7.9

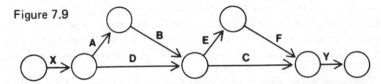

It is not as easy as it probably looks to draw a network. There are no
useful aids other than the activity dependency table and the process of
drawing up the network is itself a skill rather than a technique. Like most
skills this is developed by practice. In drawing any network, however, you
must expect to have to make a number of preliminary sketches before
achieving a satisfactory result.

There is of course no single correct version of any network by comparison with which all other versions must be incorrect, but having arrived
at a version that satisfies you and obeys the rules, you can then proceed
to number the events. Start your numbering from the extreme left of the
graph (i.e. from the tail event of the lead activity) and work towards the
right, in such a way that the head event of each activity always has a
higher number than that of its tail event. There is obviously no point in
trying to do this until a satisfactory network has been completed. Once
the events have been numbered, the activities can be identified by their
(i,j) numbers.

C – Logical Errors (question 5)

Although we have not yet begun to show how a network graph is used for
scheduling, you will probably have noticed already that the exercise of
having to think out the separate operations and their relationships towards
each other is conducive on its own to logical planning. Furthermore, the
network graph itself can be used as a tool for identifying various kinds of
planning error, some of which we will describe in this section.

The situation illustrated in figure 7.10 is called a **loop**. This is clearly logically inconsistent, as C cannot take place until A is completed nor A until C is completed. A loop situation is shown up by the (i,j) system of numbering. Because the number at the head of an arrow must always be greater than the number at its tail, the reverse situation indicates either a wrongly numbered sequence or a loop.

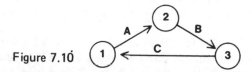

Figure 7.10

One of the assumptions of a network graph is that a project can have only one beginning and only one end. In figure 7.11 there is a lead activity X and an end activity Y, but the network also shows an activity C with nothing preceding it and an activity D with nothing following it. These are called **danglers**. The presence of danglers in a network indicates either that it has been incorrectly drawn or that the activities are not directly relevant to the project and should not have been included in the graph.

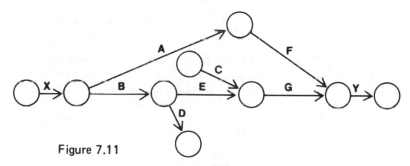

Figure 7.11

A further demonstration of incorrect planning is seen in figure 7.12, where activity C appears in two different places. It is a convention of network analysis that a label shall be used to identify a single activity, *not* a single *type* of activity: where the same type of activity has to be repeated several times in the course of a project, it should be given a different label for each time that it occurs. Clearly, no single activity may appear more than once in a network as it can be carried out only once.

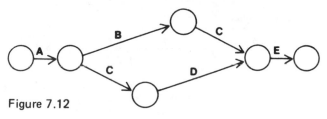

Figure 7.12

D – Dummy Activities (questions 6–7)

A useful convention of network analysis is the **dummy activity** (i.e. an imaginary activity taking zero time to complete) which is drawn as an arrowhead at the end of a dashed line.

Although it carries no label of its own, a dummy activity can be identified by the (i,j) system. Like any other activity it should be drawn with its head to the right of its tail and with the event number at its head greater than at its tail: i.e. $j > i$.

There are two principal uses for a dummy activity. One is for displaying sequential links between activities on different paths. Figure 7.13 illustrates an example of this usage, where activities A and B form one path and activities C and D another, but B cannot commence until C has been completed. Activity (3,4) is the dummy which links completion of activity C to the beginning of activity B.

Figure 7.13

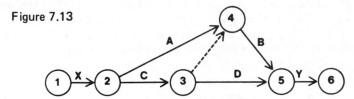

The other main usage of the dummy is to distinguish between activities that have the same head and tail events. The problem, as illustrated in figure 7.14, diagram (i), is not only one of congestion in the drawing. Our next section will show that it is difficult to perform time calculations on a network that has been drawn in this way. Alternative versions, using a dummy, are illustrated in diagrams (ii) and (iii).

Figure 7.14

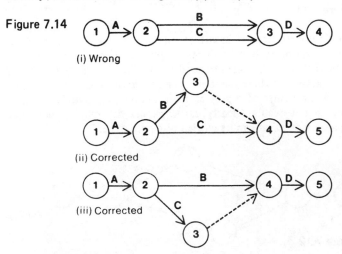

If an activity has only one IPA, then a dummy is never required. However, if there is more than one associated IPA a dummy or dummies may be necessary to show the logic. Dummies, where these are required, are drawn as an integral part of the network at the same time as their associated activities and in all respects are treated exactly like normal activities.

Avoid superfluous dummies. In diagram (i) of figure 7.15 it is clear that the dummy is redundant as activity (4,5) can only take place once activity (1,2) has been completed. The network as redrawn in diagram (ii) meets exactly the same purpose.

Figure 7.15

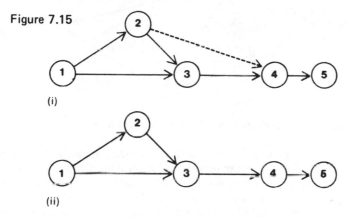

(i)

(ii)

Example 1

The following activity dependency table concerns the overhaul of a piece of equipment in a power station.

Activity	Description	IPA
A	Move tools and materials onto site	—
B	Erect scaffolding	A
C	Remove piping, valving and hoses	B
D	Fabricate piping	A
E	Check bearings	C
F	Fit cylinder wall liners	C
G	Fit hoses	C
H	Replace piping	C, D
I	Replace worn bearings	E
J	Replace valving	F, I
K	Weld and insulate	G, H, J

Construct a network graph to show the relationship between these operations.

Solution: In the network as drawn in figure 7.16,(4,7) is a dummy activity. This makes it possible to distinguish activity H, which must follow on both activities C and D, from activities E, F and G which follow from activity C alone (i.e. they do not depend on activity D).

Figure 7.16

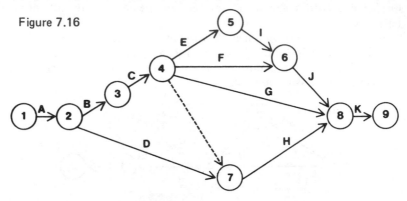

E – Duration – The Earliest Event Time (questions 8–9)

Obviously the completion of any particular activity must take a certain amount of time and this is important to the planning of the project as a whole. (An event, by contrast, is treated as instantaneous in that it merely indicates the beginning or end of an activity. If it consumes time in itself it is not an event but an activity. For example the time it takes a concrete floor to set after pouring is an activity because, though it requires no action from the builders, it requires time.)

Let us continue with example of section D and begin by rewriting its activity dependency table with a column to show the time required to complete each separate activity and the dummy activity added. We will also amend the first column of the table so as to label the activities by their (i,j) numbers.

Activity	Description	Working time required (in days)
(1,2)	Move tools and materials onto site	4
(2,3)	Erect scaffolding	1
(2,7)	Fabricate piping	5
(3,4)	Remove piping, valving and hoses	3
(4,5)	Check bearings	2
(4,6)	Fit cylinder wall liners	5
(4,7)	Dummy activity	0
(4,8)	Fit hoses	4
(5,6)	Replace worn bearings	1
(6,8)	Replace valving	2
(7,8)	Replace piping	8
(8,9)	Weld and insulate	4

We can now redraw the network graph, as shown in figure 7.17, writing the duration of each activity (in days) above the arrow. As we are now labelling the activities by the (i,j) method we no longer need the labels (A, B etc.) that we used when first preparing the network. No alterations to the graph itself are required (for example, there is no relationship between the duration of a particular activity and the length of the arrow used to show it on the graph, so there is no need to redraw the arrows).

Figure 7.17

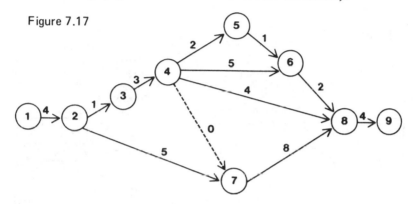

We can now start to schedule the various activities of the project, on a time basis. When considering any one particular project it is often convenient to prepare a **project calendar** so as to relate the working days required for the project (or parts of a day, or weeks etc., depending on the unit of time used) to their calendar dates. For example, in this case we shall assume that work on the project as a whole is able to commence on Monday 24 August and the following Monday (31 August) is a public holiday. Then,

Calendar	August								September						
date	24	25	26	27	28	29	30	31	1	2	3	4	5	6	7
Day of week	M	T	W	Th	F	S	Sun	M	T	W	Th	F	S	Sun	M
Project day	1	2	3	4	5	X		X	X	X	6	7	8	9	X	X	10

and so on.

If an activity is due for completion on project day 6 it is only necessary to look up the calendar to see that this is Tuesday 1 September. Only the working days are numbered as project days but it is convenient to note the holidays on the project calendar as these represent potential reservoirs of overtime capacity which may be needed to keep the project on schedule.

We can now calculate, directly from the graph, the earliest possible date by which each event can be completed and the minimum time required to complete the project as a whole. (We will work entirely in project days and ignore the calendar dates.)

The earliest date by which each activity can be completed is called its **earliest event time (EET)** and this, after it has been calculated, is conventionally written inside a rectangular frame adjoining (preferably just above) the relevant node, as in figure 7.18.

Figure 7.18

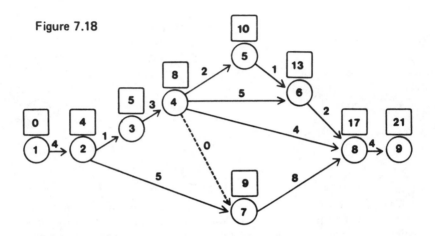

The EET of event 1 is obviously zero, as this represents the very starting point of the project. Since activity (1,2) is estimated to take four days, the earliest time at which event 2 can occur is at the end of day 4. The earliest possible starting date for activities (2,3) and (2,7) which cannot begin until activity (1,2) has been completed, is therefore the end of day 4 (i.e. the beginning of day 5). Activity (2,3) requires one day, so the EET of event 3 is the end of day 5. Similarly, activity (3,4) cannot begin until the start of day 6 and will take three days in itself, so the EET for event 4 is the end of day 8.

Now consider event 7. This cannot occur until both activity (3,4) and activity (2,7) have been completed. As we have seen, the EET of activity (3,4) is at the end of day 8 but activity (2,7) cannot be completed until the end of day 9. It is the later of these dates which represents the earliest starting time for activity (7,8).

In the same way, event 8 depends on the completion of activities (6,8), (4,8) and (7,8). The date for completing the last of these activities is the EET of event 8 which therefore falls at the end of day 17.

Event 9 corresponds to the final completion of the project. Activity (8,9) cannot commence until the beginning of day 18 and will take four days in itself, so the EET of event 9 is $17 + 4 = 21$ days. This represents the earliest date by which the project as a whole can be completed.

In summary, therefore;

> *To evaluate the EET of each node, add the duration of each activity entering the node to the EET of its tail event and set the EET for the node to be the maximum of all these.*

F — The Latest Event Time (question 10)

In the preceding section you may have noticed, while calculating the EETs, that for a number of events the completion date could have been delayed for a few days without making any difference to the duration of the project as a whole. Whenever an activity has more than one IPA it cannot begin until each of these preceding activities has been completed. If any of these takes less time than another, a corresponding delay in its completion will not affect the starting date of the sequential activity.

We now proceed to the next planning stage which is to calculate the **latest event time (LET)** for each node; namely, the latest possible time at which each particular event can be completed without holding back the completion date of the project as a whole. This also is calculated directly from the network graph. To evaluate the LET:

> *Subtract the duration of each activity leaving the node from the LET of its head event and set the LET for the node to be the minimum of all of these.*

This procedure is similar to that used for determining the EET, though in this case we work backwards through the network. Taking the same example of sections C and D, we have already established that the project will require 21 days for completion. If the latest time for event 9 is 21 days and activity (8,9) requires 4 days for its completion, then the latest possible time (which will not delay completion of the project as a whole) for event 8 is $21 - 4 = 17$ days. Conventionally, the LET of an event is written inside a triangular frame adjoining (preferably just below) the node, as in figure 7.19.

Figure 7.19

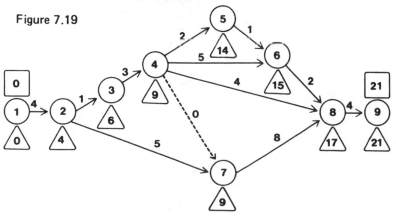

(Figure 7.19 is a further development of figure 7.18, though we have shown only the first and last EET in order to keep the diagram as free of excess detail as possible. Clearly, for the purpose of calculating every LET you need to know the EET of the final event (i.e. the duration of the project as a whole) which will also be the LET of that event. Similarly, the LET of the first event must be 0. If it is not, there must have been an error in your calculation.)

Similarly, the LET of event 6 is $17 - 2 = 15$ days and we continue in this way, working from right to left. When we come to an event such as 4 or 2, which has more than one activity leading out of it, the LET of that event is the minimum for all the activities leading out of it. Thus for event 4 the LET for the start of activity (4,5) is $14 - 2 = 12$, for activity (4,6) it is $15 - 5 = 10$; for activity (4,8) it is $17 - 4 = 13$ and for activity (4,7) it is $9 - 0 = 9$. The LET of event 4 is therefore the minimum of these, which is 9. If activity (3,4) were to be completed later than 9 project days after the start of the project, then there would be a delay in one or more of the paths leading out of that event which (unless it could be rectified, e.g. by overtime working) would be transmitted through all the subsequent stages and ultimately postpone the completion date of the project as a whole.

G — Total Float (questions 11—12)

Figure 7.20 shows the basic network of our example in section D with all the information that has been added to it in the subsequent two sections:

Figure 7.20

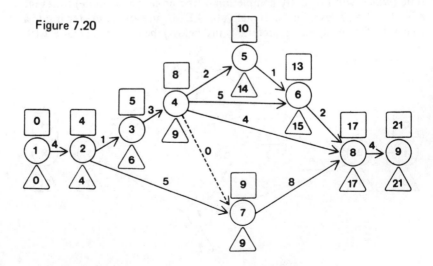

namely, the duration of each activity, and the EET and the LET of each event. You will have seen that some individual activities can be delayed without necessarily causing the project as a whole to take any longer than the time originally planned for it. This measure of permissible delay is called the **float** of the activity.

The **total float** (TF) of an activity is the maximum time that its completion can be delayed without delaying the completion of the end activity on the network, if all directly preceding activities in the network start as early as possible.

Let us consider activity (4,8). The latest time for completion of this activity (i.e. the LET of its head event) is day 17. The earliest time at which it can start (i.e. the EET of its tail event) is day 8 and it will take 4 days to complete, so that the earliest date by which it can be completed is day 12. Therefore, the total float represents the difference between the earliest and latest possible times allowed by the present schedule for completion of that particular activity; i.e. $17 - 12 = 5$ days.

The procedure for calculating total float can therefore be expressed in the following general rule:

The total float of an activity is given by the LET of its head event minus the EET of its tail event minus its duration.

Thus, for activity (2,7), the LET of its head event is 9, the EET of its tail event is 4 and its duration is 5. Therefore $TF = 9 - 4 - 5 = 0$.

The total floats of all activities can be calculated directly from the network graph, usually by simple mental arithmetic.

We can now tabulate all the activities of our example in terms of the timing of the project, as shown below. One of the reasons for this will become apparent in the next section.

Activity	Earliest starting time (at end of day ...)	Duration in days	Total float in days
(1,2)	0	4	0
(2,3)	4	1	1
(2,7)	4	5	0
(3,4)	5	3	1
(4,5)	8	2	4
(4,6)	8	5	2
(4,7)	8	0	1
(4,8)	8	4	5
(5,6)	10	1	4
(6,8)	13	2	2
(7,8)	9	8	0
(8,9)	17	4	0

H — The Critical Path (questions 13—14)

If an activity has zero total float, this means that any delay in the completion of that particular activity will lead to a corresponding delay in the final completion date of the project as a whole. Such activities are called **critical** (in the sense of 'crucial' or 'limiting', not in the sense of 'criticism').

The critical activities of a network will be found to form a path through the network from its beginning to its end. This is called the **critical path**. Usually there is only one critical path, though sometimes there can be more than one. The critical path is found, quite simply, by identifying the activities that have zero total float, and which will be found to be sequential. Continuing with our example from section D, the critical path is indicated in figure 7.21 by a heavy line. (There is in fact no standard convention for indicating the critical path, which can be represented in various ways, e.g. by a double line or by a line of extra thickness, according to your personal preference.)

Figure 7.21

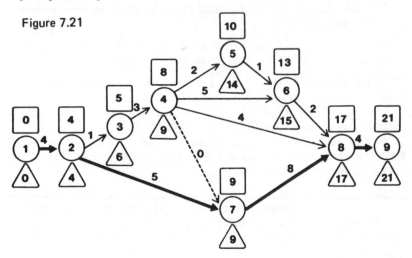

You may also have noticed that the critical path links events which have EET equal to LET. This is, indeed, a necessary condition for all activities on the critical path, but it can sometimes also be true for activities which are not on the critical path. Consider the situation illustrated in figure 7.22 (this is a detail from figure 7.25). Activity (4,8) has EET = LET for both its head event and its tail event but is not on the critical path which in fact passes through activities (4,6) and (6,8). Both these activities have zero total float, whereas the total float of activity (4,8) is $17 - 8 - 4 = 5$ days.

From a management viewpoint the activities on the critical path are those which require the closest supervision, which should be marked out for priority if there has to be any rationing of resources, and on which the

Figure 7.22

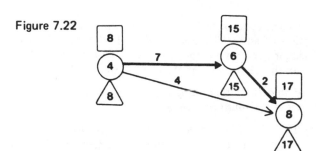

working of overtime may be justified if there is no other way to keep them on schedule.

Similarly, if the activities on the critical path can be shortened the project may be completed ahead of schedule. How far this is possible depends, of course, on the other paths. The critical path is the longest path of the network (in terms of duration) and, if the durations of the activities on that path are shortened, another path may then become the critical path.

I — Free Float (questions 15—16)

Let us consider any activities not on the critical path, such as activity (2,3) in our example. This activity has a duration of one day and a total float of one day. Suppose activity (2,3) takes two days to complete instead of one. This means that there is now no margin for delay in some of its sequential activities and we will now have a second critical path running through activities (3,4) and (4,7). The resulting position would be as shown in figure 7.23, with the criticality of the dummy activity (4,7) denoted by a heavy dashed line. You may care to confirm the correctness of figure 7.23 by undertaking the appropriate calculations yourself.

Figure 7.23

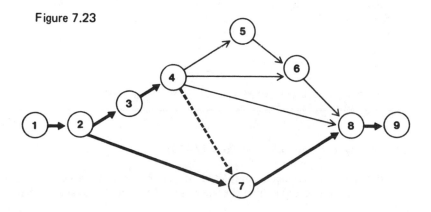

We now introduce the concept of **free float (FF)** which is the maximum time that completion of an activity can be delayed without delaying the start of any subsequent activity on the same path. Free float can be calculated directly from the network graph, by the following rule:

The free float of an activity is given by the EET of its head event minus the EET of its tail event minus its duration.

Thus, for activity (5,6) in our example, the EET of its head event is 13, the EET of its tail event is 10 and its duration is 1. Therefore FF = 13 − 10 − 1 = 2.

Hence there can be a delay of two days in the completion of activity (5,6) without postponing the start of its sequential activity (6,8).

In practice free float is found only in the last activity of a particular path. The amount of latitude that it gives to preceding activities can be seen by inspection. Activity (5,6) is preceded by (4,5). Although (4,5) has no free float it can be readily appreciated that if the completion of this activity is delayed by not more than 2 days the consequent chain reaction of delays in its sequential activities, provided none of these also take longer than planned, will stop at event 6.

We can now complete the table of section G by adding to it a final column for free float. Thus,

(1) Activity	(2) Earliest start time	(3) Duration	(4) Total float	(5) Free float
(1,2)*	0	4	0	0
(2,3)	4	1	1	0
(2,7)*	4	5	0	0
(3,4)	5	3	1	0
(4,5)	8	2	4	0
(4,6)	8	5	2	0
(4,7)	8	0	1	1
(4,8)	8	4	5	5
(5,6)	10	1	4	2
(6,8)	13	2	2	2
(7,8)*	9	8	0	0
(8,9)*	17	4	0	0

* The asterisks, in this case, mark the activities on the critical path.

J — Amending the Network (questions 17–19)

Once the network has been completed, it can be used if necessary as a basis for revising and replanning the operation. Suppose, for example, that

the total completion time of 21 days required for our power-station overhaul is unacceptably long, and has to be reduced.

The activities which need to be reduced in duration are those on the
critical path. Shortening the time required for any other activities will not
have any direct influence on the duration of the project as a whole. Taking
those activities that are on the critical path it is necessary either to rethink
the activities themselves so as to find ways of executing them more quickly,
or to allocate greater resources of manpower and equipment to them,
possibly at the expense of others which are less urgent.

Example 2

By replanning the method of fabricating the piping, activity (2,7) can be
reduced in duration by two days. What effect does this have on the total
duration of the project (originally 21 days)?

Solution: The new position is shown in figure 7.24. Activity (2,7) was on
the critical path but reducing its duration by two days has made it non-
critical and has shifted the critical path through activities (2,3), (3,4) and
(4,7). The total duration of the project is therefore reduced by only one
day. To reduce it any further, attention must now be concentrated on
activities which are on the new critical path.

Obviously, the tighter the planning of a project, the greater will be the
number of its critical paths or potentially critical paths. This increases the
number of potential emergency situations and the amount of replanning
required if any of these activities should be at all behind schedule. At the
same time it reduces the resources that are capable of being diverted (from
other activities in the same project) for the purpose of keeping a critical
activity on schedule.

Figure 7.24

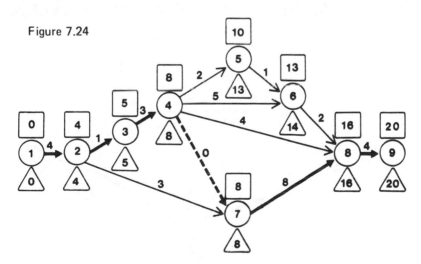

In practice it is rare for any operation to proceed exactly as planned, or without any need for amendments to the programme while it is actually under way. Components promised for delivery by outside suppliers at a certain date may be late in arriving, some part of the operation may be delayed by sickness of key personnel, resources that have been reserved for the project may have to be withdrawn to meet an emergency elsewhere, and so on. Obviously, if the network is to continue to be a useful document it must be kept up to date and changed to reflect the current project situation. This is known as **updating** the network.

At each updating, event times and floats are recalculated to determine the new minimum project duration and new critical path. (Any necessary measures for keeping employees or colleagues informed of those changes of plan that affect them must obviously be taken at the same time.)

The procedure is simply to go back to the stage where the alterations begin and then to recalculate the subsequent stages. It is quite straight-forward but there are no short cuts.

The following examples, all relating to the original network for the same power station project, illustrate the approach to different contingencies.

Example 3

What happens to the network if activity (4,6) is increased in duration: (i) by one day? (ii) by two days?

Solution: (i) Increasing the duration by one day takes up only one of the two days' total float available. It forces activity (6,8) to start one day later but will not put either activity on the critical path or increase the duration of the project as a whole.

(ii) If activity (4,6) is completed two days later then activity (6,8) must also start two days later. The revised position, as drawn in figure 7.25,

Figure 7.25

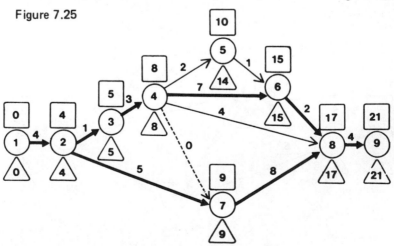

shows no change in the time required for completion of the project as a whole, but there are now two critical paths.

Example 4

By 1 September the following things have been discovered:

 (i) Removal of the piping, valving and hoses will in fact be completed by the end of the following day;
 (ii) due to the poor state of existing valving, the fitting of new cyclinder wall liners will take two days longer than expected;
 (iii) it seems likely, after partially taking down the existing plant, that the hoses will have to be fitted before the pipes are replaced and not concurrently as previously believed.

Solution: In this example we have to consider not only some changes of timing but also a change of logic which may require amendments to the network. We should consider this first, and begin by referring back to the activity dependency table of section D.

Activity G (fit hoses) is now an IPA of activity H (replace piping). Activity C can no longer be an IPA of activity II as activity G, which also depends on the completion of activity C, must come between them.

After amending the activity dependency table, we turn to the network of figure 7.16 to see what amendments are required to that. In fact the alteration proves to be quite simple and is achieved in this case by substituting activity G for the dummy activity (4,7) and eliminating (4,8) from the network.

We next consider the changes in timing. The duration of activity (3,4) is now two days instead of three and that of activity (4,6) is now seven days instead of five. [1 September is day 6 of the project calendar.

Figure 7.26

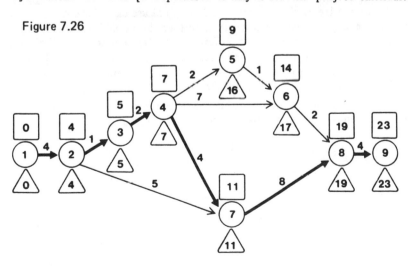

Assuming that the activities taking place before the end of day 6 have proceeded according to schedule, activity (3,4) would have begun at the beginning of day 6 and will be completed at the end of day 7 — i.e. a duration of 2 days — and a similar argument applies for activity (4,6).] The rest of the calculation is as shown in figure 7.26 and is self-explanatory. It requires merely a repetition, on the basis of the new information, of the processes followed through in sections E–H.

It can be seen that the route of the critical path is changed and that the total duration of the project has been increased by 2 days. The table of total float and free float of section I should also be appropriately amended.

K — Use of Bar Charts (question 20)

The network graph is, as we have seen, a very powerful tool for project planning and scheduling but it is not the ideal type of diagram for progressing or for demonstrating, to those people (such as foremen, etc.) responsible for executing the project, the roles that they are to play. For this purpose it is sometimes useful to transfer the relevant parts of the information on to another type of diagram such as a bar chart, which is easier to read and follow.

The **bar chart** is one of the simplest forms of statistical graph and we can reasonably assume that you are already familiar with its use. Its application to this type of situation is best illustrated by example, as in figure 7.27.

This is the bar chart that relates to our basic example, as developed in the preceding sections. It incorporates all the important information about schedules from the table of section I; i.e. the starting date, duration, total float and free float of each activity.

An alternative version of this bar chart would use calendar dates in place of project days so as to reduce even further the possibility of misunderstanding or errors in reading. This method can also be used to highlight the non-working days which are available, if necessary, for overtime. Lack of space prevents us from showing the complete chart, but figure 7.28 shows enough of it to indicate what is meant.

Any alterations required to the working programme while it is in operation must also, of course, be recorded on the bar chart.

Figure 7.27

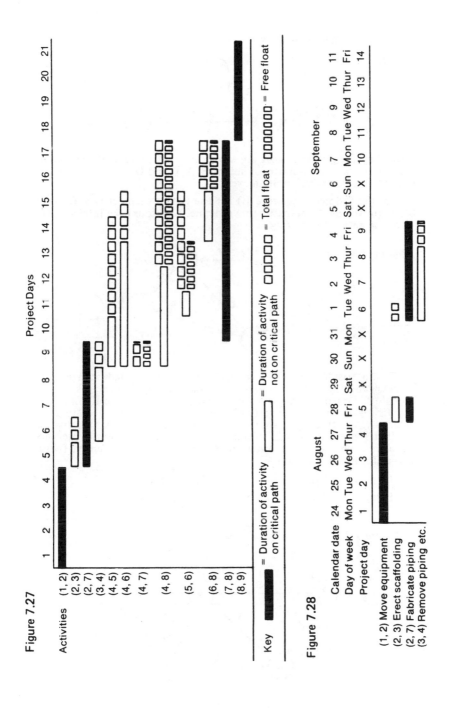

Project Days

Key   ■■■■■ = Duration of activity on critical path   ▭▭▭ = Duration of activity not on critical path   ▯▯▯▯▯ = Total float   ❑❑❑❑❑❑ = Free float

Figure 7.28

Calendar date	24	25	26	27	28	29	30	31	1	2	3	4	5	6	7	8	9	10	11	12	13	14
Day of week	Mon	Tue	Wed	Thur	Fri	Sat	Sun	Mon	Tue	Wed	Thur	Fri	Sat	Sun	Mon	Tue	Wed	Thur	Fri	Sat	Sun	Mon	Tue	Wed	Thur	Fri
Project day	1	2	3	4	5	X	X	X	6	7	8	9	X	X	10	11	12	13	14

August   September

(1, 2) Move equipment
(2, 3) Erect scaffolding
(2, 7) Fabricate piping
(3, 4) Remove piping etc.

Questions

7.1 (i) In the following network:

Figure 7.29

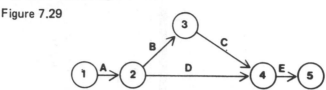

(a) List the activities that are sequential and those that are concurrent.
(b) Give the (i,j) numbers of activities A, C and D.
(ii) What is the duration of an event?

7.2 In the following network (i) list the IPA of each activity; (ii) describe the sequence of the activities in words; i.e. give your own interpretation of what the network is stating.

Figure 7.30

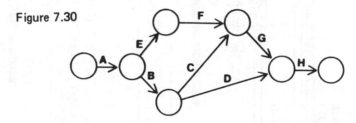

7.3 A motorist drives into a garage, has his tank filled with gas, his oil checked and filled, his tire pressures adjusted, pays for the gas and oil and drives off. Prepare an activity dependency table, listing only the activities specifically described (i.e. do not insert additional intermediate activities such as 'take off gas cap' or add others such as 'refill radiator') and assuming that there are enough attendants to permit operations which do not actually depend on each other to be performed concurrently. (Note the answer for use in question 4.)

7.4 Prepare a network graph from the data of question 3.

7.5 Identify the logical errors in the following network.

Figure 7.31

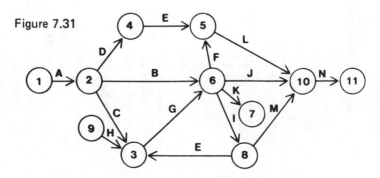

7.6 A person makes himself a cup of tea in the following sequence of operations:

A   Fill kettle and bring to boil
B   Place tea in teapot
C   Pour boiling water on tea in teapot and stir
D   Pour milk in cup
E   Pour tea ón milk in cup
F   Put sugar in tea and stir

Prepare an activity dependency table and list those activities which *may* need a dummy to precede them. Keep a note of your answer for use in question 7.

7.7 Given the data of question 6, draw a network graph for this project.

7.8 Given the following project calendar,

Calendar date	5	6	7	8	9	May 10	11	12	13	14	15
Day of week	F	S	Sun	M	T	W	Th	F	S	Sun	M
Project day	1	X	X	2	3	4	5	6	X	X	7

(i) On what day of the week is the project scheduled to start?
(ii) Give the calendar date corresponding to day 4 of the project.
(iii) Give the project day which corresponds to 13 May.

7.9 Given the following network graph, calculate each EET and state the minimum time required to complete the project as a whole. Keep a note of your answer for use in later questions.

Figure 7.32

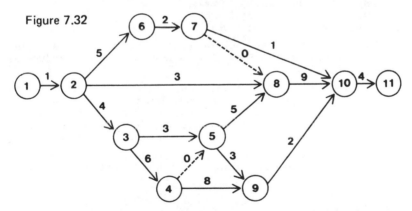

7.10 Given the data of question 9, calculate each LET. Keep a note of the EET and LET of all events in this network, for use in questions 11, 12, 13 and 16.

7.11 From your answers to questions 9 and 10, calculate the total float of the following activities: (6,7) (3,4) (3,5) (8,10).

7.12 From the answers to questions 9 to 11 tabulate, in the manner of the section, the total floats of all the activities of the network in terms of the timing of the project which it represents. Note the answer for questions 13 and 16.

7.13 From the answer to question 12, list the chain of activities which forms the critical path and mark the path of your network.

7.14 What does the critical path actually signify in a project; i.e. in what ways does it differ from any other path and in what ways are its activities particularly important?

7.15 (i) What is meant by 'free float'? (ii) If an activity has zero free float, does this mean that a delay in completing that activity is likely to delay the completion date of the project as a whole?

7.16 Given the answer to question 9, calculate the free float of all activities in the network.

7.17 Given the following network, describe the effect on the timing of the project as a whole of each of the following changes in duration (shown in weeks) considered separately:

Figure 7.33

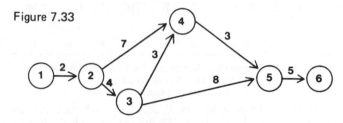

(i)   activity (2, 4) reduced by 3 weeks,
(ii) activity (4,5) increased by 2 weeks,
(iii) activity (3,4) increased by 1 week,
(iv) activity (3,5) reduced by 1 week.

7.18 Given the original network of question 17, what would be the effect on the project if activity (3,5) is replanned so as to reduce its duration by 3 weeks?

7.19 Suppose the project, as shown in its revised form in the answer to question 18 above, has not yet been started. Due to technical changes, the activity shown as (3,4) is now to follow directly from (1,2) and will run concurrently with (2,3) instead of consecutively. What effect will this have on the project? Keep a note of your answer for use in question 20.

7.20 The project, as replanned in the answer to question 19 above, is now ready to go ahead. Prepare a bar chart in the manner described in section K.

Further Reading

This chapter has concerned itself with the basic principles of critical path analysis (CPA). At the beginning of the chapter we referred to an associated technique known as PERT (Program Evaluation and Review Technique), which is explicitly designed to deal with the problem of uncertainty in activity time estimates, and the need to use the computer in the analysis of virtually any real project because of the number of activities involved — often of the order of several thousand.

The PERT technique is widely used in the US although not so extensively in the UK. It recognizes that whereas a single estimate of the duration of an activity may usually be about right, the job may be completed earlier or later for various reasons and requires three estimates of its duration: the usual time (U), an optimistic time (O) and a pessimistic time (P). O and P are so chosen that the actual duration will fall outside the optimistic — pessimistic range only about one in a hundred times. The critical path is then calculated as in this chapter using activity duration estimates given by $(O + 4U + P)/6$ and the likelihood of the overall project finishing at different times determined using probability techniques.

Good basic introductions to CPA are provided by Levin and Kirkpatrick, 'Planning and Control with PERT/CPM', McGraw-Hill, 1966; and 'A Management Guide to PERT/CPM', second edition, 1977, by Wiest and Levy. Additionally, OR textbooks such as Cook and Russell's and Anderson, Sweeney, and Williams's 'An Introduction to Management Science', second edition, West, 1979, provide basic material and further examples.

8

LINEAR PROGRAMMING

Many decision problems revolve around the allocation of finite resources or capacities. If resources of various kinds (e.g. labour, capital, certain types of raw material, the capacities of particular machines) are available only in limited quantities and a number of different and competing demands are being made on these resources, then it is necessary to determine the most effective (i.e. usually the most profitable or least costly) way of allocating the resources to meet the demands being made on them.

A technique which is commonly used nowadays for this type of problem is known as **linear programming** which is defined, technically, as the 'optimization of a linear objective function subject to certain constraints'. In the following sections we will see what these words mean.

The principles of linear programming are not mathematically very difficult but, if you are approaching the subject for the first time, you will find many of its concepts unfamiliar. In the first three sections of this chapter we will describe the basic approach, broken down into successive stages. The rest of the chapter will be used to extend this basis.

It is worth making the point, now, that in this book we are not trying to do more than introduce the concept of linear programming, explain the principles on which it is based and show you how to use it in certain limited applications. The nature of these limitations and the reasons for them will become apparent later in the chapter but it should be pointed out here that the full use of linear programming techniques in practical situations normally requires a computer. In addition the commonly used computational technique, known as the **Simplex method**, goes beyond the scope of this particular book, and is based on a rather different mathematical approach from that described here. The appendix to this chapter, however, illustrates the use of the computer in the solution to linear programming problems.

Mathematically this chapter depends on nothing that has preceded it in this book and may be studied on its own.

A — Constraints and Inequalities (questions 1—3)

We will begin by defining the idea of a **constraint**. This is simply a limitation, expressed mathematically for our purposes, on what can be done. A simple example should explain the principle.

A man insists on two lumps of sugar with his cup of white coffee. If he has ample coffee and cream in front of him but only six lumps of sugar, this means that he cannot drink more than three cups. The number of lumps of sugar represents a constraint which can be identified as 'the sugar constraint' in this particular situation. Alternatively, if he has plenty of sugar and cream but there is only enough coffee in the pot for five cups, this may be identified as 'the coffee constraint' which obviously prevents him from being able to drink more than a corresponding number of cups of coffee.

Let us now go a stage further. The man and his wife are taking coffee at a restaurant. Having paid for what is on the table they want to try to drink as many cups of coffee between them as they can. The man likes his coffee in the proportion of three parts of coffee to one part of cream, with two lumps of sugar per cup. His wife, who is slimming, takes five parts of coffee to one part of cream and no sugar, though she takes one saccharin tablet per cup.

The coffee-pot contains the equivalent of 6 full cups, the cream jug holds 1½ full cups and the sugar bowl has eight lumps of sugar. The woman has five saccharin tablets in her handbag.

Had either person been alone the problem would have been a simple one: he or she merely continues to drink until coffee or cream or sweetener is all consumed, the limitation being set by whichever runs out first. With several demands of different types the situation becomes more complicated, not least because of the variety of the data. This aspect of the problem is often best dealt with by tabulating the data in the first instance, as in the manner shown below:

| Ingredients | Amounts per cup | | Total available |
	His (x)	Hers (y)	in units
Coffee	¾	⅚	6 (cups)
Cream	¼	⅙	1½ (cups)
Sugar	2	0	8 (lumps)
Saccharin	0	1	5 (tablets)

We will now identify the constraints. This, and the sorting out of the relevant data, tends to be the most difficult part of any linear programming problem. Once it has been completed, the rest is usually straightforward.

Let us use x for the number of cups to be consumed by the man and y for the number to be consumed by his wife. We will deal with the constraints individually, starting (for simplicity, in this particular example) from the bottom of the table and numbering each constraint. There are five saccharin tablets and the wife wants one per cup, so she cannot have more than five cups. This is 'the saccharin constraint', which can be expressed algebraically as follows:

$$y \leqslant 5 \qquad (1)$$

The sign $\leqslant$ means 'equal to or less than' and this type of statement is termed an **inequality** expression. In this particular context it means, in effect, that she can have five cups of coffee or she can have fewer than five cups, but she cannot have more than five cups.

The sign $\leqslant$ itself is a combination of two commonly used mathematical signs of different meaning that you are already familiar with; one of these is the sign used to express an equation. Thus, $y = 5$ means 'y is equal to 5'. This type of equation is called an **equality**. The other sign, as in $y < 5$, means 'y is less than 5' and this expression is called a **strict inequality** which is a statement that two quantities are *not* equal, i.e., depending on the sign used, that one is either greater or less than the other. (It should be noted that such an expression is still a relationship (in the sense that one quantity is being balanced against the other) and can be treated, in many respects, like an equation.)

In the same way, taking the second line from the bottom of the table we have

$$2x \leqslant 8$$
$$x \leqslant 4 \qquad\qquad (2)$$

meaning that the man can have four cups of coffee or fewer than four cups, but he cannot have more (because there are only eight lumps of sugar and he requires two for each cup). This is the sugar constraint.

Now for 'the cream constraint'. The man requires a quarter of a cupful of cream for every cup of coffee he takes. Therefore, if he drinks x cups of coffee his total requirements of cream will be $\frac{1}{4}x$ cupfuls. Similarly, his wife requires one sixth of a cupful of cream for every cup of coffee, so if she drinks y cups of coffee her total requirement of cream will be $\frac{1}{6}y$ cupfuls. Therefore the total consumption of cream by both together will be given by

$$\tfrac{1}{4}x + \tfrac{1}{6}y \text{ cupfuls.}$$

The maximum amount of cream available to them is $1\frac{1}{2}$ cupfuls, so the cream constraint as a whole can be expressed algebraically as

$$\tfrac{1}{4}x + \tfrac{1}{6}y \leqslant \tfrac{3}{2} \qquad\qquad (3)$$

In the same way the coffee constraint can be expressed as

$$\tfrac{3}{4}x + \tfrac{5}{6}y \leqslant 6 \qquad\qquad (4)$$

To these four constraints we can add two more; the so-called **non-negativity constraints**. Obviously neither the man nor his wife can drink a negative number of cups of coffee (less than no cups of coffee). Therefore we can complete the list by adding:

$$x \geqslant 0 \qquad\qquad (5)$$
$$y \geqslant 0 \qquad\qquad (6)$$

(The sign $\geqslant$ means 'equal to or greater than'.)

These six contraints then represent all the restrictions on the couple that prevent them from drinking as much coffee as they want. Within these constraints an infinite number of arrangements or solutions are possible, i.e. they may have 1 cup each, the man may have four cups and his wife none, and so on.

By defining the constraints and expressing them as inequalities we have completed the first stage of the formulation of the problem. (In fact the complete formulation of the problem consists in the definition and expression in mathematical form of both the constraints and the objective function. At this stage the problem has been only partly formulated; the objective function is discussed in section C.)

You may by now have noticed the logic in the way that the data of this problem were tabulated. The quantities of coffee, cream, sugar and saccharin available, and the proportions in which these are mixed, are represented by the **constants** in these equations; i.e. they are fixed and known amounts. The number of cups of coffee drunk by the man and his wife are represented by the **variables** (i.e. values which are not fixed), x and y. By having the constraint names as row headings and the variable names as column headings, each row of the table gives the terms of an inequality: hence the inequalities can be read directly from the table.

We conclude this section with some examples of a more conventional type which we will take to the same stage of completion and continue in the following sections.

Example 1

A chemical company manufactures two types of fertilizer; Super-Nitrate and Phosphate—R. Both fertilizers make use of the same three chemicals, in different proportions. These chemicals, the proportions (as a percentage by weight) of each that are used in the two fertilizers and the total quantity of each chemical available for the year are listed in the following table.

Chemical	Super-Nitrate %	Phosphate—R %	Maximum quantity available (tons)
Nitrate	20	10	2500
Phosphate	10	15	2000
Sulphate	20	20	3000

The company is under contract to supply 3000 tons of Phosphate—R to one of its customers but is otherwise free to apportion its production between the two types of fertilizer in the most profitable manner. Define the constraints and express them as inequalities.

Solution: Let us use x for the number of tons of Super-Nitrate to be produced in the year and y for the number of tons of Phosphate—R. Then the inequalities are as follows:

1. For the 'nitrate constraint' $\frac{1}{5}x + \frac{1}{10}y \leqslant 2500$, i.e. for every ton of Super-Nitrate produced there will be a requirement of 20% (i.e. $\frac{1}{5}$) of a ton of nitrate, for every ton of Phosphate—R there will be a requirement of $\frac{1}{10}$ ton of nitrate, and the total consumption of nitrate cannot exceed 2500 tons.
2. For the 'phosphate constraint' $\frac{1}{10}x + \frac{3}{20}y \leqslant 2000$.
3. For the 'sulphate constraint' $\frac{1}{5}x + \frac{1}{5}y \leqslant 3000$.
4. For the 'contract constraint' $y \geqslant 3000$.
5. For the 'non-negativity constraints' $x \geqslant 0$ and $y \geqslant 0$.

But we have already established that $y \geqslant 3000$ and, as $3000 > 0$, $y \geqslant 0$ becomes a **redundant constraint**: i.e. a constraint that should be ignored as it serves no useful purpose. Thus the constraints are written as

$$\frac{1}{5}x + \frac{1}{10}y \leqslant 2500 \qquad (1)$$
$$\frac{1}{10}x + \frac{3}{20}y \leqslant 2000 \qquad (2)$$
$$\frac{1}{5}x + \frac{1}{5}y \leqslant 3000 \qquad (3)$$
$$x \geqslant 0 \qquad (4)$$
$$y \geqslant 3000 \qquad (5)$$

Example 2

The manager of a metal foundry must add to each ton of molten iron in his furnaces at least 24 oz of element A and 12 oz each of elements B and C. One lb of compound P contains 8, 2 and 1 oz of these elements respectively, and one lb of compound Q contains 3, 2 and 3 oz. Define the constraints and express them as inequalities.

Solution: We can tabulate the relevant data as follows:

Element	Contents of compound P in oz	Contents of compound Q in oz	Minimum requirements of each element in oz
A	8	3	24
B	2	2	12
C	1	3	12

Let us use x for the number of lbs of compound P added to each ton of molten iron, and y for the number of lbs of compound Q.

In this example we are specifying minimum limits for each chemical (by contrast with the preceding examples where maximum limits were being specified) so in this case the inequalities are written as follows:

$$8x + 3y \geqslant 24 \qquad (1)$$
$$2x + 2y \geqslant 12 \qquad (2)$$
$$x + 3y \geqslant 12 \qquad (3)$$
$$x \geqslant 0 \qquad (4)$$
$$y \geqslant 0 \qquad (5)$$

(i.e. taking the first inequality, the addition of x lb of compound P to each ton of molten iron will give it $8x$ oz of element A, the addition of y lb of compound Q will give it $3y$ oz of element A, and the total amount of element A in each ton of molten iron must not be less than 24 oz. The other inequalities are interpreted in the same way.)

B — The Feasible Region (questions 4—7)

In this section we will express the statements made in section A in graphical form.

Figure 8.1

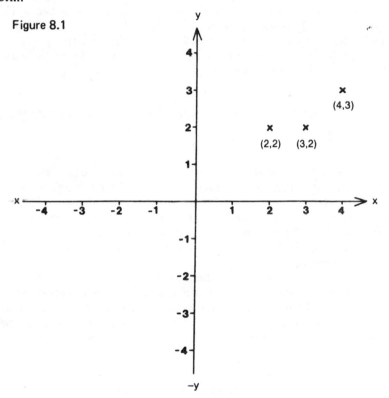

Continuing with our example of the coffee-drinking couple, let us begin (figure 8.1) by laying out the two axes of a graph and let the x-axis represent the number of cups drunk by the man and the y-axis the number of cups drunk by his wife. Then, if he drinks 4 cups and she drinks 3, this is shown as the point (4,3) on the graph; if he drinks 3 cups and she drinks 2, this is shown as the point (3,2); if they drink two cups each, this is shown as the point (2,2) and so on. Any such combination can therefore be expressed as a point somewhere on the face of this graph which can be identified by a pair of coordinates.

However, because of the constraints we know that certain combinations are possible, or **feasible**, and others are **infeasible** (impossible in these circumstances; e.g. the man cannot have 5 cups, even if his wife does not have any, because there is not sufficient sugar on the table for his own needs). The next stage of the process is to block in those parts of the graph which are infeasible, so as to enclose that area of the graph, called the **feasible region**, in which all feasible combinations or points must lie.

Beginning with the non-negativity constraints, you will have noticed that the points marked in figure 8.1 are all in one corner of the graph. This is the corner which is to the right of the y-axis and above the x-axis. This is in fact the only possible quarter of the graph for our purposes, as both x and y must be positive. We can ignore the other three quarters.

Let us now see how the other constraints can be shown on the graph. We shall begin with the coffee constraint which is

$$\tfrac{3}{4}x + \tfrac{5}{6}y \leqslant 6$$

For the moment we shall ignore all values less than 6 and deal with this as an equation. If all the coffee in the pot is consumed, then

$$\tfrac{3}{4}x + \tfrac{5}{6}y = 6.$$

There is an infinite range of values of x and y which could satisfy the conditions of this equation. For example, if $x = 4$ then $y = 3\tfrac{3}{5}$, if $x = 5\tfrac{1}{3}$ then $y = 2\tfrac{2}{5}$ and so on. Each of these possible pairs of values of x and y can be represented as a point on the graph but it will be found that all these points will be on a straight line (see figure 8.2 below). This is true for all equations of this type of form and for this reason such equations are called **linear equations**.

In order to draw the graph of this equation, all we need to do is to find any two pairs of values of x and y which satisfy the conditions of the equation, plot them on the graph and join them with a straight line which can be extended as far as we like in either direction. In practice, the two easiest points to find are usually those for which one or other of the unknowns is zero.

For example, with $y = 0$

$$\tfrac{3}{4}x = 6 \text{ and } x = 6 \times \tfrac{4}{3} = 8$$

This gives us one pair of coordinates (8,0). Next, with $x = 0$

$$\tfrac{5}{6}y = 6 \text{ and } y = 6 \times \tfrac{6}{5} = 7\tfrac{1}{5}$$

so our second pair of coordinates is (0, 7⅕). We plot these two points on the graph and join them with a straight line, as in figure 8.2. It is unnecessary to try to extend this line beyond either axis of the graph as this would mean that either x or y would be negative, which is impossible for this type of problem.

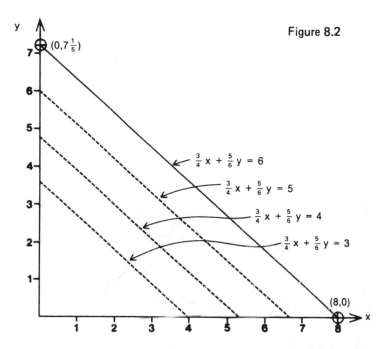

Figure 8.2

On the same diagram we have drawn the graphs as broken lines of some of the values of

$$\tfrac{3}{4}x + \tfrac{5}{6}y < 6$$

specifically, those of equalities with values of the RHS of 5, 4 and 3, with the initials **RHS** standing for the 'right-hand side' of the equation, i.e. everything to the right of the equality/inequality sign. (Similarly, the left-hand side of the equation may be referred to as **LHS**.)

Notice that the lines are parallel: i.e. whatever the value of the right hand side of the equation, the slope or **gradient** of the graph is the same. Furthermore, the graph of this equation moves further to the left as the value of its RHS decreases, and moves to the right as it increases. Therefore it can be said that *all* points for which LHS $\leqslant 6$ lie either on or to the left of the graph of $\tfrac{3}{4}x + \tfrac{5}{6}y = 6$. We indicate this, as in figure 8.3, by shading that side of the line for which the conditions of the inequality are *not* satisfied. By doing the same thing along the x and y axes, to exclude all values for which x or y would have to be negative, we have now defined the feasible region for these three constraints.

By drawing the graphs of the other inequalities for cream, sugar and saccharin, we can delimit the feasible region even further as shown in figure 8.4. The sugar and saccharin constraints are drawn simply as lines perpendicular to the appropriate axis, at the appropriate point. Thus, for the sugar constraint, $x \leqslant 4$ irrespective of the value of y. This is the same as saying that $x \leqslant 4$ for all possible values of y.

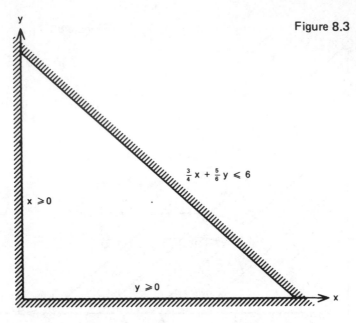

Figure 8.3

$\frac{3}{4}x + \frac{5}{6}y \leqslant 6$

$x \geqslant 0$

$y \geqslant 0$

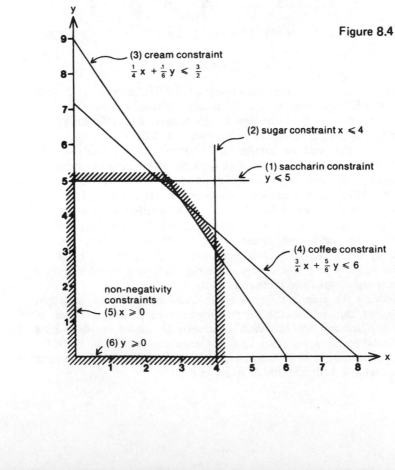

Figure 8.4

(3) cream constraint
$\frac{1}{4}x + \frac{1}{6}y \leqslant \frac{3}{2}$

(2) sugar constraint $x \leqslant 4$

(1) saccharin constraint
$y \leqslant 5$

(4) coffee constraint
$\frac{3}{4}x + \frac{5}{6}y \leqslant 6$

non-negativity
constraints
(5) $x \geqslant 0$

(6) $y \geqslant 0$

All the points within the feasible region, as now drawn, satisfy the conditions of *all* the inequalities. The solution of the problem, which we will deal with in the next section, consists in finding the particular point within the feasible region which corresponds to the greatest number of cups of coffee.

We can now draw the feasible regions for Examples 1 and 2 of section A:

Example 3

It is convenient to begin by calculating the reference points of the more complex inequality constraints. Thus,

	Inequalities set to equalities	For $y = 0$ $x =$	For $x = 0$ $y =$
(1)	$\frac{1}{5}x + \frac{1}{10}y = 2500$	12500	25000
(2)	$\frac{1}{10}x + \frac{3}{20}y = 2000$	20000	13333
(3)	$\frac{1}{5}x + \frac{1}{5}y = 3000$	15000	15000

Making these calculations in advance provides a guide to the sizes and scales required for the axes. The corresponding graph, shaded around the boundaries of the feasible region, is shown in figure 8.5.

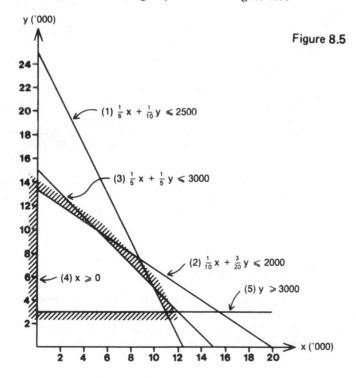

Figure 8.5

Example 4

For this example the reference points can be tabulated as follows:

Inequalities set to equalities	For $y = 0$ $x =$	For $x = 0$ $y =$
(1) $8x + 3y = 24$	3	8
(2) $2x + 2y = 12$	6	6
(3) $x + 3y = 12$	12	4

and the corresponding graph is drawn in figure 8.6.

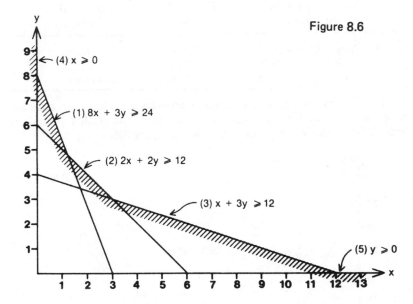

Figure 8.6

Notice that in this case we are dealing with constraints on the *minimum* values so the feasible region contains all those points that correspond to values of (x,y) equal to or greater than those on the shaded lines; i.e. those on the far side (of the shaded lines) from the origin.

C — The Objective Function (questions 8—12)

We are now ready to solve our coffee problem: namely, to determine the maximum number of cups of coffee the couple can drink together. If the man drinks x cups and his wife y cups, then obviously the total number of cups of coffee that they drink between them is $x + y$. Let us use z for the total number of cups of coffee drunk. Then

$$x + y = z$$

This equation is called the **objective function** (abbreviated to **OF**); namely, the function that corresponds to our objective, which in this case is the total number of cups of coffee. (When the value of one variable varies according to the value of another variable, it is known as a **function** of that variable. For example, if $x + y = z$ but $z = 4$, then $y = 4 - x$ and y is a function of x.)

Our purpose is generally to **optimize** the objective function, namely, to establish the best possible value that is permitted by the constraints of the problem. If we wish this value to be as large as possible, we seek to **maximize** the OF. If we wish it to be as small as possible, we seek to **minimize** the OF. In our coffee problem we are seeking to maximize the objective function, which means, in the context of the particular example, to drink as many cups of coffee as possible.

The method, as illustrated in figure 8.7, is to take our graph showing the feasible region and draw on it the graph of the objective function for any value of z, say $z = 4$. With respect to this graph you will recall, from section B, that

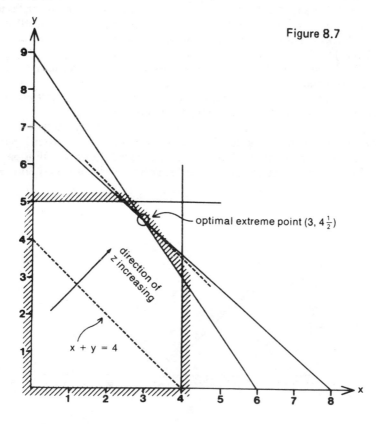

Figure 8.7

optimal extreme point $(3, 4\frac{1}{2})$

direction of z increasing

$x + y = 4$

(i) all points on the graph of an equation satisfy the conditions of the equation;

(ii) if we draw the graphs of $x + y = 5, x + y = 6$ and so on, these will be parallel to it and progressively further away from the origin as the value of z increases, or closer to it as the value of z decreases for x and $y \geqslant 0$. In figure 8.7 we have shown, by an arrow, the direction of z increasing.

Our purpose, in the first instance, is to establish the gradient of the graph and its location for a particular value of the objective function. We next draw a parallel line as far as possible (if the objective function is to be maximized) from the origin of the graph which still touches the feasible region at one point. (It may happen that, if one of the constraints has the same gradient as the OF, the OF will lie along its boundary. This case is discussed two paragraphs further down.) The coordinates of this point represent what is called the **optimal solution** or **optimum solution** of the problem; namely that feasible value of the objective function that is best for our purpose (i.e. greatest if it is to be maximized, least if it is to be minimized). In figure 8.7 the appropriate OF graph is drawn as a broken (dotted) line and it will be seen that it touches one corner of the feasible region (3,4½). Thus, the maximum total consumption is achieved if the man drinks 3 cups and his wife 4½ cups (total consumption is therefore 7½ cups).

This is the point where the boundaries of the coffee constraint and the cream constraint meet each other, meaning that all the coffee and all the cream will be used up and a little of the sugar and saccharin left over (two lumps and half a tablet respectively, by simple calculation).

In most examples of this type of problem the optimal solution lies at one of the corners of the feasible region, which are called **extreme points**. It may sometimes happen, however, that the gradient of the OF is parallel to the gradient of one of the constraints. This type of situation is illustrated

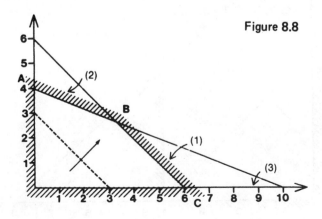

Figure 8.8

generally in figure 8.8, in which the graph of the optimal OF lies along the side BC of the feasible region.

This is a case of what are called **multiple optima**, meaning that all values of (x,y) along the line BC are potential optimal solutions. For all of them you will be at the limit of constraint (1). If you choose the combination represented by the coordinates of point B you will also be at the limit of constraint (2) whereas if you choose that represented by the coordinates of point C you will be at the limit of constraint (3).

In practice, once the gradient of the OF has been established it is often unnecessary to draw a line parallel to it as the extreme point of the feasible region can be judged by eye.

We now establish the optimal solutions for the examples of sections A and B.

Example 5

This example is intended to be a little more realistic, and is therefore a little more complicated, than the coffee example. The objective of the management of the fertilizer factory is not to use up as much raw material as possible but rather to obtain the most profitable combination possible of the two fertilizers that it makes. If the net profit from every ton of Super-Nitrate sold is $5 and that for every ton of Phosphate—R is $3, solve the problem.

Solution: The total profit on the annual production is $\$(5x + 3y)$, i.e. $5 multiplied by the number of tons of Super-Nitrate produced plus $3 multiplied by the number of tons of Phosphate—R. If we use P for the profit in $'s, then $P = 5x + 3y$ is the objective function and the object is to maximize P. The data of such a problem can be tabulated in such a way as to give the OF as well as the constraints. In this case the table looks as follows:

Chemical	Super-Nitrate %	Phosphate—R %	Maximum quantity available (tons)
Nitrate	20	10	2500
Phosphate	10	15	2000
Sulphate	20	20	3000
Profit ($ per ton)	5	3	

From this layout, which is self-explanatory, all the constraints (except the non-negativity constraints) can be read off the successive rows of the table and the OF can be read off the bottom row. All that is necessary additionally is to insert the inequality signs for each of the constraints.

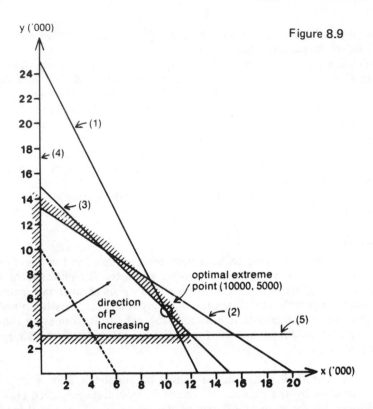

Figure 8.9

To solve the problem we proceed in exactly the same way as for our coffee example by imposing the graph of $P = 5x + 3y$, for any value of P, on the graph of the feasible region and establishing, by a line drawn parallel to it, the maximum value of P at which it is possible to satisfy the constraints. This is illustrated in figure 8.9 where we have chosen the convenient value of $P = 30$ and have therefore drawn the graph of $5x + 3y = 30$. From the figure 8.9 the maximum possible value of P is seen to be at the point (10000,5000) corresponding to the production of 10000 tons of Super-Nitrate and 5000 tons of Phosphate—R. At this optimal solution the maximum profit is achieved, namely

$$P = 5x + 3y = (5 \times 10000) + (3 \times 5000) = \$65,000$$

Example 6

In the case of the metal foundry the OF is to be *minimized*; our purpose is not to increase a profit but to reduce a cost. Essentially there is no difference between these objectives; they represent the same objective achieved in an opposite way. This corresponds, equally, to the difference in their mathematical treatment. If 1 lb of compound P costs $7 and 1 lb of compound Q costs $4, solve the problem.

Solution: The data of this problem can be reconstructed in tabular form, as follows:

Element	Compound P	Compound Q	Minimum requirement (oz)
A	8	3	24
B	2	2	12
C	1	3	12
Cost ($ per lb)	7	4	

If C is the total cost in $ of the amount of these compounds used per ton of iron, then $C = 7x + 4y$. This is the objective function and it is to be minimized.

As with the other examples, the graph for any convenient value of the OF is drawn on the graph of the feasible region, as shown in figure 8.10 for the value of $C = 56$. In this case, as the OF is to be minimized the direction in which it must move is *towards* the origin, as indicated by the arrow. It can be clearly seen that the extreme point is at the intersection of the limits of the element A constraint and the element B constraint, which is the point ($1\frac{1}{5}$, $4\frac{4}{5}$). Hence we require $1\frac{1}{5}$ lb of compound P and $4\frac{4}{5}$ lb of compound Q for each ton of molten iron, of which the cost is as follows:

$$C = (7 \times 1\frac{1}{5}) + (4 \times 4\frac{4}{5}) = \$27.60$$

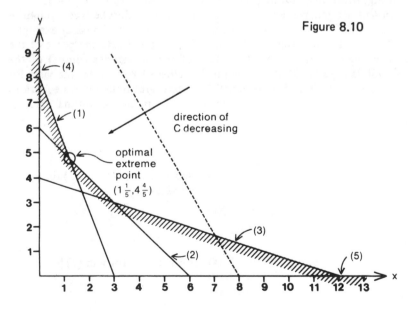

Figure 8.10

   This combination will give us the minimum amount of elements A and B required for the melt, but slightly more than the minimum required of element C.

   We conclude this section with an important point. In all the examples that we have chosen the products have been infinitely divisible. This is not true of all types of product. One of the exercises to this section deals with the problem of a tailor making two types of dress. The optimal solution to this particular problem is expressed in each case as a **mixed number** (i.e. a whole number or **integer** and a fraction) but clearly such an answer cannot be optimal in the full sense as there is no profit in making, say, two-thirds of a dress.

   For our purpose we either have to ignore this practical aspect of the problem or meet it by rounding down the answer in each case to the nearest whole number. However, it is worth mentioning that there exists a special branch of mathematical programming known as **integer programming** which is designed for this type of situation although the actual treatment of the technique goes beyond the scope of this particular book.

D — Solution by Algebra (questions 13–14)

There is often more than one mathematical way to solve a problem. In sections B and C we demonstrated the solution of linear programming problems by graphical methods. These methods have certain limitations, one of which is that their accuracy is limited by the accuracy of the drawing, which may not be precise enough for the purpose required.

   In this section we set out to show the relationship between graphical and algebraic methods of solving this type of problem. Consider examples 1, 3, and 5 from sections A, B and C. The optimal extreme point of the feasible region was at the intersection of the boundaries (limits) of the constraints (1) and (3). At this point the values of x and y are the same for both the constraints. Set to equalities, these are simultaneous equations and can be solved, as such, algebraically, to determine the optimal extreme point as follows:

$$\tfrac{1}{5}x + \tfrac{1}{10}y = 2500 \qquad\qquad (1)$$
$$\tfrac{1}{5}x + \tfrac{1}{5}y = 3000 \qquad\qquad (3)$$

$$\tfrac{1}{10}y = 500 \quad \text{[subtracting (1) from (3) to eliminate } x\text{]}$$

i.e.
$$y = 5000$$

and

$$\tfrac{1}{5}x + 500 = 2500 \quad \text{[substituting for } y \text{ in (1)]}$$
$$\tfrac{1}{5}x = 2000$$
$$x = 10000$$

Similarly, for examples 2, 4 and 6 the optimal extreme point occurred at the point of intersection of the graphs of

$$8x + 3y = 24 \qquad (1)$$
$$2x + 2y = 12 \qquad (2)$$

Multiplying both sides of equation (2) by 4 and subtracting equation (1) from the result to eliminate x we have,

$$5y = 24$$
$$y = 4\tfrac{4}{5}$$

and

$$2x + 9\tfrac{3}{5} = 12 \quad [\text{substituting for } y \text{ in (2)}]$$
$$2x = 2\tfrac{2}{5}$$
$$x = 1\tfrac{1}{5}$$

Even though the simultaneous equation method is to be used it is still necessary to graph the feasible region so as to establish which two equations intersect at the optimal extreme point, but for this purpose alone a rough sketch is often sufficient.

Example 7

Maximize the OF $= 7x + 6y$ given the following constraints:

$$5x + 6y \leqslant 100 \qquad (1)$$
$$x + 3y \leqslant 36 \qquad (2)$$
$$5x + 2y \leqslant 80 \qquad (3)$$
$$x \geqslant 0 \qquad (4)$$
$$y \geqslant 0 \qquad (5)$$

Solution: Sketching the constraints and the OF, in figure 8.11, shows that the optimal extreme point is at the intersection of the limits of constraints (1) and (3) at C. It must therefore satisfy the conditions of

$$5x + 6y = 100 \qquad (1)$$
$$\text{and } 5x + 2y = 80 \qquad (3)$$
$$4y = 20 \quad [\text{subtracting (3) from (1)}]$$
$$y = 5$$
$$\text{and } 5x + 10 = 80 \quad [\text{substituting for } y \text{ in (3)}]$$
$$5x = 70$$
$$x = 14.$$

Thus $\quad$ OF $= \quad 6x + 7y = 84 + 35 = 119.$

If the sketch is not precise enough to identify the optimal extreme point with certainty, the answer can be checked by comparing the value of the OF at the most likely extreme point with its value at the two extreme points on either side. If it is greater than both in a maximization problem or less than both in a minimization one, then it is the optimal solution. (It should be noted that in those cases where the OF lies parallel to a constraint, one of the adjacent extreme points will yield a lower value for the OF and the other will yield the same value, for a maximization problem, and a greater value and equal value respectively in a minimization type.) For example, it will be found by calculation that at point B in figure 8.11

$$x = 28/3, y = 80/9, \text{ and the OF} = 118\tfrac{2}{3}.$$

And at point D

$$x = 16, y = 0, \text{ and the OF} = 112.$$

i.e. in both cases the value of the OF is less than it is at point C.

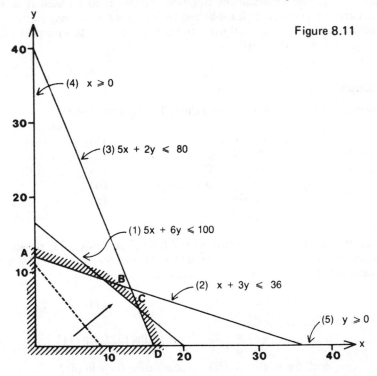

Figure 8.11

E — Dual Values (questions 15—17)

In the fertilizer factory example (examples 1, 3 and 5) you will recall that the optimal extreme point was located at the intersection of the boundaries of the nitrate and sulphate constraints. This is the point at which the nitrate and sulphate are completely used up, though there is still some phosphate left over.

Now let us consider what happens if the amount of nitrate available is increased by one ton. The nitrate constraint can now be rewritten as follows:

$$\tfrac{1}{5}x + \tfrac{1}{10}y \leqslant 2501$$

and the graph of this inequality expressed as an equality can be redrawn parallel to the previous one but a little further away from the origin; as sketched in figure 8.12. (In this example the changes of position are too small to be shown properly on a graph drawn to scale. The new position of the optimal extreme point has been determined by the simultaneous equation method.)

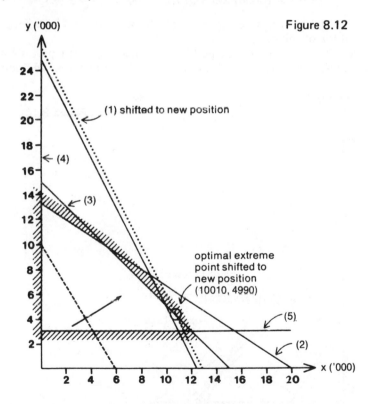

Figure 8.12

The extreme point now occurs at (10010,4990) and the value of the objective function is now

$$OF = (5 \times 10010) + (3 \times 4990) = \$65,020$$

as compared with $65,000 previously, an increase of $20. It is usually more convenient to calculate the difference (which is what really interests us) directly by the following method, which is self-explanatory:

$$(10010 - 10000) \times 5 + (4990 - 5000) \times 3 = 20$$

This indicates that it would be worth paying up to $20 extra for one additional ton of nitrate (i.e. $20 more than the normal price, which has been taken into account in arriving at the net profit figures for the two types of fertilizer).

In the same way, if the available quantities of nitrate and phosphate were to remain unchanged but the quantity of sulphate available were to be increased by one additional ton, the graph of the new constraint would be as sketched in figure 8.13 with the extreme point now at (9995,5010) for which the difference in the value of the objective function is

$$(9995 - 10000) \times 5 + (5010 - 5000) \times 3 = 5.$$

Hence it would be worth paying up to $5 above the normal price for one additional ton of sulphate.

In the circumstances of this problem it would be worth paying four times as much extra for an additional ton of nitrate as for an additional

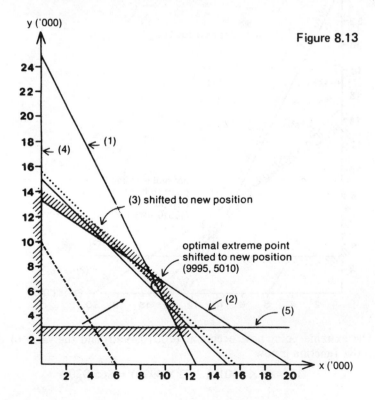

Figure 8.13

ton of sulphate. Indeed, from looking at the graph, it is obvious that shifting the nitrate constraint to the right moves the extreme point further away from the origin, in the direction of travel of the objective function, than shifting the sulphate constraint a similar distance.

Now consider the phosphate. Obviously, since there is already a surplus of this chemical, the purchase of additional phosphate will not bring any increase in profitability. The effect on the graph of an increase of one ton in the amount of phosphate available is sketched in figure 8.14. There is no change in the position of the extreme point.

The potential increase in profit that can derive from easing one of the constraints by the amount of a single unit is called the **dual value** or the **shadow price** of the constraint (in this book the terms dual value and shadow price are treated as synonymous).

If we apply the same approach to the conditions of the metal foundry example (examples 2, 4 and 6), where the objective function has to be minimized, the principle remains the same. In that example the extreme point occurs at the intersection of the boundaries of the element A and element B constraints. If either of these constraints can be relaxed the cost can be reduced, whereas a relaxation in the constraint for element C will have no effect if the other conditions have remained unchanged.

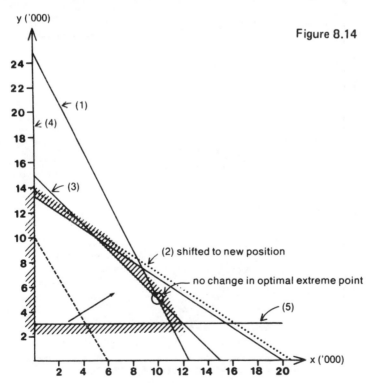

Figure 8.14

In practice, of course, the constraints in this case are of a type that cannot be relaxed because, if they were, the resulting alloy would not be to its correct specification. This does not affect the general principle and is not true of all problems for which the objective function is to be minimized.

Clearly, there is a limit on the amount by which it is worth trying to ease any one constraint, as the effect after a certain stage is simply to transfer the extreme point to the intersection of the boundaries of a different pair of constraints. It is therefore important to be able to find out the maximum amount by which it is worth trying to ease any particular constraint and beyond which the effect will be non-existent or even perhaps counter-productive: as in our fertilizer example, where it would lead to the accumulation of stocks of a particular chemical which have to be paid for but cannot be used during the year.

Take another look at figure 8.12. We could have continued to shift the graph of the nitrate constraint to the right until its boundary intersected with the boundaries of constraints (3) and (5). This point (12000, 3000) would then have become the optimal extreme point, as can be clearly seen

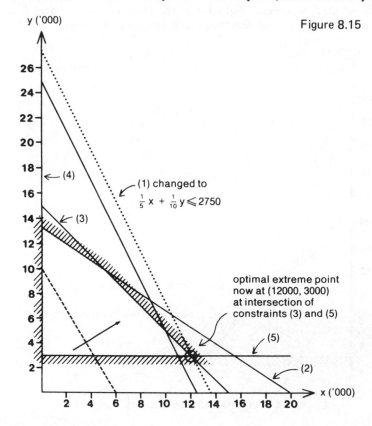

y ('000)

Figure 8.15

(4)

(1) changed to
$\frac{1}{5} x + \frac{1}{10} y \leqslant 2750$

(3)

optimal extreme point
now at (12000, 3000)
at intersection of
constraints (3) and (5)

(5)

(2)

x ('000)

from the sketch. To discover how many tons of nitrate are required to manufacture a total of 12000 tons of Super-Nitrate and 3000 tons of Phosphate—R, we simply have to multiply these figures by the amount of nitrate required per ton of each fertilizer: thus $\frac{1}{5}$ (12000) + $\frac{1}{10}$ (3000) = 2700 tons as compared with the 2500 tons originally formulated in constraint (1). If all other conditions are unchanged (and if the extra output can be sold!) it is therefore worth buying up to 200 additional tons of nitrate for which, as we have shown earlier in this section, it is worth paying up to $20 per ton above the price paid for the original consignment.

On the other hand, it is clearly not desirable to buy more than 200 tons of nitrate as the surplus cannot be used (at least, not in the year considered, or without relaxing some of the other constraints). The effect of buying, say, 250 extra tons is shown graphically in figure 8.15, where it can be seen that the graph of the boundary of $\frac{1}{5}x + \frac{1}{10}y \leqslant 2750$ is now outside the feasible region altogether and passes to the right of the optimal extreme point, (12000, 3000), at the intersection of the boundaries of constraints (3) and (5).

On the other hand, it would be worth buying more than 200 additional tons of nitrate if more sulphate were also to be purchased.

F — The Dual Problem (questions 18—20)

You may have noticed that none of the examples that we have used hitherto contained more than two variables. This is an obvious limitation of the graphical method that we have been using. Because such graphs are drawn in two dimensions they cannot have more than two axes and, as each axis corresponds to a variable, there cannot be more than two variables.

There is such a thing as a **three-dimensional graph** which uses the technique of solid-figure drawing, having three axes which makes it possible to deal with three variables at a time. We will not, however, go into this further in this book, as it goes beyond the basic mathematical knowledge assumed. The graphical method can go no further than three dimensions, as we are unable to visualize a graph in four or more dimensions.

There are various ways of getting round the limitation that this imposes on linear programming. One such method, which we shall describe in this section, is based on the use of shadow prices, although it is restricted to the case of two constraints excluding the non-negativity constraints.

Example 8

Let us consider the example of a footwear manufacturing company which can produce men's shoes, women's boots, women's shoes or children's shoes. The factory has 20 machines and employs 50 skilled men working a

40-hour week. The machine-hours and skilled-man-hours required to manufacture one pair of each type of footwear are listed in the following table, together with the net profit on each product.

Time required	Men's shoes	Women's boots	Women's shoes	Children's shoes	Total hours available
Machine-hours	$\frac{3}{2}$	1	1	$\frac{8}{3}$	800
Man-hours	$\frac{5}{2}$	9	5	1	2000
Profit in pence	60	90	70	40	

The problem is to decide how many of each type of footwear to produce each week, in order to maximize the profit.

Solution: Let us use a for the number of pairs of men's shoes produced each week, b for the number of pairs of women's boots, c for the number of pairs of women's shoes and d for the number of pairs of children's shoes.

The machine-hours constraint is therefore

$$\tfrac{3}{2}a + b + c + \tfrac{8}{3}d \leqslant 800$$

the skilled-man-hours constraint is

$$\tfrac{5}{2}a + 9b + 5c + d \leqslant 2000$$

and the non-negativity constraints are

$$a, b, c, d \geqslant 0.$$

Finally we have

$$\text{OF} = 60a + 90b + 70c + 40d$$

which is to be maximized.

This straightforward formulation of the constraints and objective function is known as the **primal problem**. We cannot solve it directly by the methods described hitherto as it contains four variables. However, there are only two *constraints* (other than the non-negativity constraints) and we know that each of these has a shadow price associated with it in the optimal solution.

If we use x for the shadow price on the machine-hours constraint and y as the shadow price on the skilled-man-hours constraint (both expressed in cents), we can make these the variables and the profits on the individual products become the constraints.

Perhaps the clearest way to demonstrate what is being done is to rewrite the table (in effect, turn it on to its side) to fit the conventions we have been using hitherto, using the product names as row headings, and the original constraint names as column headings. Thus,

Product	Machine hours	Man hours	Profit in cents
Men's shoes	¾	⁵⁄₂	60
Women's boots	1	9	90
Women's shoes	1	5	70
Children's shoes	⅔	1	40
Total hours available	800	2000	

In each case we want the profit per item to be not less than (i.e. equal to or greater than) the figure in the right hand column, so the new constraints can be written:

$$\tfrac{3}{2} x + \tfrac{5}{2} y \geqslant 60 \qquad (1)$$
$$x + 9y \geqslant 90 \qquad (2)$$
$$x + 5y \geqslant 70 \qquad (3)$$
$$\tfrac{8}{3}x + y \geqslant 40 \qquad (4)$$
$$x, y \geqslant 0$$

We want to keep costs as low as possible, so if x is the shadow price per hour of machine-time and y the shadow price per hour of man-time, then the OF $= 800x + 2000y$ and is to be minimized.

This reformulation of the primal problem is called the **dual problem**. The two types of problem are equivalent and their relationship can be stated as a general rule in the following manner:

To every primal problem there is always associated an equivalent dual problem and the dual of this dual problem is the original primal problem.

At the optimal solution of both problems the value of the objective function is the same: i.e. the optimal value of the OF in primal problem = the optimal value of the OF in dual problem.

The graph of the dual problem is sketched in figure 8.16 and this problem can now be solved in the normal manner. The optimal solution is at the intersection of the limits of constraints (1) and (3) which occurs at (25,9). Therefore,

$$OF = (800 \times 25) + (2000 \times 9) = \$380.$$

As the optimal value of the objective function of the primal problem is the same as the dual, we have now also calculated the optimal value of the

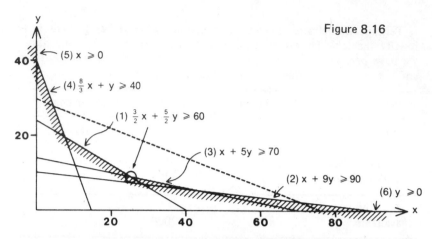

Figure 8.16

OF of the primal problem. We now need to find what combination of products gives this optimal value. In the dual problem, the dual values or shadow prices of the principal constraints in the optimal solution will be the optimal values of a, b, c and d respectively in the primal. But we have used only the constraints for a and c (men's shoes and women's shoes) to determine our optimal point, so only these two constraints have dual values not equal to 0. The dual values associated with the constraints for b and d (women's boots and children's shoes) will be 0.

To find the actual values of a and c we simply apply the technique described in the preceding section. Thus, if all other constraints remain unchanged but the RHS of inequality (1) is increased by one unit, then we have the following simultaneous equations:

$$\tfrac{3}{2}x + \tfrac{5}{2}y = 61$$
$$x + 5y = 70$$

Solving these we have $x = 26$ and $y = 8\tfrac{4}{5}$.
Therefore the objective function of the dual problem increases by

$$(26 - 25) \times 800 + (8\tfrac{4}{5} - 9) \times 2000 = 800 - 400 = 400$$

Performing the same operation for inequality (3), the resultant increase in the objective function is 200.

Therefore, in the primal problem $a = 400$, $c = 200$, and b and $d = 0$. Thus by solving the dual problem we have obtained answers to the primal problem and have discovered that the factory should produce 400 pairs of men's shoes, 200 pairs of women's shoes and no women's boots or children's shoes. The resultant profit for the week will be $380.

We have also found that the shadow price is 25¢ on the machine-hours constraint and 9¢ on the skilled-man-hours constraint. It is therefore worth paying, for additional hours of machine time or skilled labor time, that much per hour above the normal cost.

We can check this, if required, by solving the primal problem. With $b = 0$ and $d = 0$, this can be rewritten as:

$$\begin{aligned}
\text{maximize } & 60a + 70c \\
\text{subject to } & \tfrac{3}{2}a + c \leqslant 800 \\
& \tfrac{5}{2}a + 5c \leqslant 2000 \\
\text{with } & a, c \geqslant 0
\end{aligned}$$

From this calculation the extreme point will be found to be at (400,200) yielding a maximum profit of \$380/week, with dual values of 25¢ on the first constraint and 9¢ on the second.

This method can be applied to problems containing any number of variables (within reason) as long as there are only two constraints (apart from the non-negativity constraints) in the primal problem. However, the answer will be given in terms of a maximum of only two variables in all situations. That is to say, not more than two of the variables will have non-zero values: all the others will have zero values. The reasons for this are beyond the scope of the book.

Questions

8.1 A tailor has 32 meters of silk, 60 meters of cotton and 60 meters of wool in stock. He makes dresses of 2 designs, the first requiring 2 meters, 3 meters and 1½ meters of these materials respectively and the second 1, 4 and 5 meters. Tabulate the data in the form demonstrated to you in section A, and keep a note of your answer for question 2.

8.2 Given the answer to question 1, name the constraints that prevent the tailor from making as many dresses of both types as he wants and express each constraint as an algebraic inequality, using x for the number of dresses of design 1 and y for the number of dresses of design 2 produced. Write down the non-negativity constraints. Keep a note of the answer for later questions.

8.3 A health-drink manufacturer specifies on the label of his product that each cc contains not less than 5 mg of vitamin A, 7 mg of vitamin B and 10 mg of vitamin C (1 cc $\simeq$ 1000 mg: the rest of the volume is made up with water, flavourings etc.). To supply these ingredients he buys concentrates from two sources. Analysis shows that, in each cc, concentrate X contains 15, 14 and 50 mg and concentrate Y contains 15, 28 and 20 mg respectively of vitamins A, B and C. If x is the number of cc of concentrate X and y the number of cc of concentrate Y the manufacturer uses in each cc of health drink, list the constraints, including the non-negativity constraints, and express them as algebraic inequalities. Keep a note of the answer for questions 7 and 11.

8.4 (i) What is meant by 'the feasible region' and what is its significance? (ii) On the sketch graph below, show the values of x, y which correspond to the coordinates (0,2½), (2,3) and (5,2).

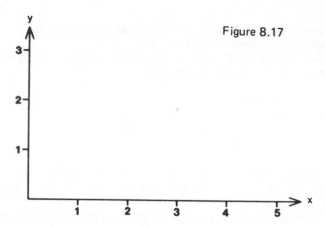

Figure 8.17

8.5 Take the tailoring problem of questions 1 and 2 and consider the silk constraint.

(i) Express the inequality as an equation in the manner of the text.
(ii) For this equation, if $x = 0$ what is the value of y?
(iii) And if $y = 0$, what is the value of x?
(iv) Draw a sketch graph to show this equation and the non-negativity constraints, and shade around the outside of the feasible region that they enclose.

8.6 Now draw the complete graph of the tailor problem (i.e. the graph of the constraints given in the answer to question 2) and shade around the boundaries of the feasible region. Keep the graph for use in question 10.

8.7 Taking the data of question 3 and its answer, graph the constraints of this problem and shade those sides of the constraints that are *outside* the feasible region. Keep the graph for use in question 12.

8.8 (i) Formulate the objective function for the tailoring problem of previous questions on the assumption that he makes an equal profit on each design of dress. (ii) Now reformulate it on the assumption that his profit is $5 on each dress of design 1 and $3 on each dress of design 2. (iii) In each case, is the OF to be maximized or minimized? (iv) Try to give a brief description, in words, of the difference in the nature of the tailor's objective in each case.

8.9 Now take an arbitrary figure for the tailor's total profit from making both types of dress, say $60, and sketch the equation $5x + 3y = 60$ as a graph. Then,

(i) say what this graph means in this particular context, and
(ii) draw an arrow to show in which direction graphs of $5x + 3y > 60$ would lie.

8.10 Now draw the graph of the OF on your graph of the feasible region for the tailor problem, determine the optimal solution and state the profit that the tailor would receive from it. (Note: the optimal quantity of dresses of both designs will be fractional, so round down in each case to the nearest whole number.) Keep your full answer for use in question 15.

8.11 Suppose that the costs to the health-drink manufacturer of question 3 of concentrates X and Y are 0.5 cents/cc and 0.4 cents/cc respectively.

(i) Combine this information with the data you were given in question 3 and lay it all out in a single table, as you would do if you were formulating the problem as a whole.

(ii) What is the objective function, and is it to be maximized or minimized?

8.12 Given the answers to questions 3, 7 and 11:

(i) state the constraints which intersect at the optimal extreme point, and explain what this means in relation to the specification of the product;

(ii) determine the optimal cc of concentrates X and Y in each cc of the tonic;

(iii) calculate the cost to the manufacturer, for each cc of tonic, of the optimal combination of concentrates X and Y. Keep your graph for use in question 17.

8.13 Given that the following constraints apply for a given problem

$$
\begin{aligned}
x + 2y &\geqslant 10 &(1)\\
\tfrac{1}{3}x + \tfrac{1}{5}y &\geqslant 2 &(2)\\
x + y &\geqslant 8 &(3)\\
x, y &\geqslant 0
\end{aligned}
$$

and that OF $= 5x + 4y$ and is to be minimized; use a sketch graph and the simultaneous equation method to calculate the optimal values of x and y. Save your graph for use in question 14.

8.14 From the answer to question 13, calculate the values of the OF at the extreme points on each side of the optimal extreme point so as to confirm that it is in fact optimal.

8.15 (i) Assume that the tailor of earlier questions can earn a proportional profit on fractions of a dress. On this basis, calculate the shadow prices on (a) silk, and (b) cotton.

(ii) Say why the shadow price on wool is zero. Keep a note of your observations for question 16.

8.16 If the tailor could buy no more silk or wool of the same pattern as his existing material, but could buy more cotton at the normal price, calculate:

(i) the number of dresses of each type that this would enable him to produce,

(ii) the total profit,

(iii) (approximately) the optimal number of additional metres of cotton that he should buy.

8.17 Given the information contained in the answer to question 12, state the effect on the health-drink manufacturer's optimal purchasing policy for concentrates X and Y if he were to relax his minimum specification either:

(i) for vitamin A, from 5 to 4 mg/cc; or

(ii) for vitamin B, from 7 to 6 mg/cc.

What reduction (if any) in his costs could be achieved through each of these changes?

8.18 Consider the following linear programming problem.

$$\text{Minimize } 80a + 80b + 60c$$
$$\text{Subject to } 10a + 3b + 6c \geqslant 80$$
$$3a + 10b + 5c \geqslant 50$$
$$a, b, c \geqslant 0$$

Formulate the dual to this problem and keep a note of your solution for questions 19 and 20. (Hint: you may find it helpful to begin by constructing the table from which these constraints and OF would have been derived. Then treating the rows as variables and the columns as constraints rewrite the table to reformulate the primal problem as its dual problem, turning it on its side to fit the previous conventions if this makes it easier.)

8.19 By sketching a graph for the dual problem of question 18, solve it. Keep a note of the answer for question 20.

8.20 By calculating the shadow prices of the dual problem, solve the primal problem.

Appendix: The Use of Computers

To illustrate the use of the computer in the solution of linear programming problems, output from a typical interactive linear programming computer package that runs on a computer time-sharing system is shown overpage. This employs the Simplex method of solution (in fact a variant entitled **Revised Simplex**) and is used to solve the fertilizer example of the chapter. Needless to say the package would normally be used to solve much larger problems indeed. Nevertheless common principles apply.

The package is entitled LPCU (Linear Programming at City University) and was written for the use of students at the City University Business School on the University's ICL computer time-sharing system through a terminal. Although it was specially developed for the use of students with a limited mathematical background it is typical of the many available on commercial time-sharing computer systems.

The package minimizes an objective function subject to constraints of the form we are already familiar with. Thus if the problem is a maximization one the coefficients of the objective function are set negative and this is then minimized since minimizing a negative objective function is equivalent in linear programming to maximizing a positive function i.e. max (OF) = − min (−OF). This is illustrated in the fertilizer example in which the chemical company manufactures two types of fertilizer, Super-Nitrate and Phosphate−R, both of which make use of the same three chemicals in different proportions. The data of the problem is reproduced below from section C in a slightly amended form so that it can be processed directly by the package in that

(i) the percentages are expressed in decimal form
(ii) the profit figures are now negative 'losses'
(iii) the constraint relationships are laid out explicitly in the table and
(iv) the constraint that at least 3000 tons of Phosphate−R must be produced is now incorporated directly in the table.

The problem is then to minimize the negative loss/ton objective function subject to the constraint set.

In the package output at the terminal, which follows, the tons of Super-Nitrate produced are termed X1 and the tons of Phosphate—R produced X2 instead of the x and y used in the chapter. The commands to the computer and the data input for the problem are underlined; all the other printing originates from the computer. The results can be readily compared with those arrived at by hand computation in the chapter.

Constraint	Super-Nitrate	Phosphate—R	Inequality	Maximum quantity available (tons)
Nitrate	0.2	0.1	$\leqslant$	2500
Phosphate	0.1	0.15	$\leqslant$	2000
Sulphate	0.2	0.2	$\leqslant$	3000
Contract	0	1	$\geqslant$	3000
loss ($/ton)	−5	−3		

Further Reading

In this chapter we dealt only with the basic principles of linear programming and considered problems which could be solved using simple algebra or two-dimensional graphs. In a practical situation such as the blending of different hydrocarbons in an oil refinery to satisfy certain technical requirements and capacity constraints while maximizing profits there may well be several thousand variables and constraints in the model. A very large computer program taking several hours to run on a computer would be required to solve such a problem using the Simplex method which can handle essentially any number of variables and constraints.

There is an enormous literature on linear programming although most of it is highly mathematical. The reader of this book with a relatively modest mathematical background who wishes to explore the area further might best be advised to concentrate on learning the fundamentals of the Simplex method from a relatively non-mathematical operational research text. Texts that can be recommended for this purpose, among others, are 'Quantitative Approaches to Management' by R.I. Levin and C.A. Kirkpatrick, McGraw-Hill 1978, in which in chapter 9 they discuss linear programming in a related way to the approaches taken in this chapter and in chapter 10 using the Simplex method, and 'Introduction to Linear Programming' by R.S. Stockton, Irwin, 1971.

Slightly more advanced treatment, more applications and examples can be found in Cook and Russell's 'Introduction to Management Science', second edition, Prentice-Hall, 1981; and 'Linear Programming for Decision Making' by Anderson, Sweeney, and Williams, West, 1974.

```
TYPE JOB NUMBER← MGA182
TYPE PASSWORD
%BBBBD
DATE: 14/03/78 CHANNEL: 3
19-39-53← LPCU
•••INTERACTIVE SOLUTION OF LINEAR PROGRAMMING PROBLEMS
VERSION OF 04/02/78
AVAILABLE OPTIONS (FIRST 4 CHARACTERS SIGNIFICANT)
INPUTDATA   LISTDATA    CHANGEDATA   STOREDATA   HELP   SOLVEPROBLEM
INVBASIS    CSENSITIVITY RSENSITIVITY  PICTURE    FINISH  ALL RESULTS


OPTION?←INPUTDATA

IS DATA FROM A SUBFILE?←NO
TYPE NUMBER OF VARIABLES
←2
TYPE NUMBER OF CONSTRAINTS
←4

ENTER MATRIX ROW BY ROW TYPING EVERY ELEMENT SEPARATED BY SPACES
TYPE ROW 1
←.2 .1
TYPE ROW 2
←.1 .15
TYPE ROW 3
←.2 .2
TYPE ROW 4
←0 1
TYPE THE R.H.S.(S) OF CONSTRAINT EQUATIONS
←2500 2000 3000 3000
TYPE CONSTRAINT TYPES, L FOR < =, E FOR =, G FOR > = FOR EACH ROW.
←L L L G
TYPE THE COEFFICIENTS OF THE OBJECTIVE FUNCTION.
← −5 −3

OPTION?←SOLVEPROBLEM
SOLUTION IS
  X1 =    10000.000
  X4 =      250.000
  X6 =     2000.000
  X2 =     5000.000


OPTIMUM VALUE = −65000.000
DUAL VALUES (SHADOW PRICES) ARE
−20.000       <
  0.000       <
− 5.000       <
  0.000       >


OPTION? ←FINISH

19-46-17← LOGOUT
CONNECTED FOR    7 MINS
MILL TIME USED   6 SECS
SESSION COST     1.23
```

This identifies the user for accounting purposes.

This password for security purposes is only known to the user and is obscured by the computer automatically.

The name of the package required. The preceding numbers indicate the time of day in hours, minutes and seconds.

Options available in the package (we will use only a limited number)

This command indicates we wish to put the data for the problem into the package. The package asks if the problem data is already held in the computer. As it is not we input via the terminal as follows.

Note the negative coefficients for the objective function (see the text).

This command instructs the package to solve the problem. The solution follows with 10000 tons of Super-Nitrate (X1) and 5000 tons of Phosphate–R (X2) produced. X4 and X6 are termed slack variables and are required for mathematical reasons by the Revised Simplex method. They should be ignored.

Because the problem is a maximization one the optimum result requires a sign change to 65000 for correct interpretation (see the text).

The dual values are provided automatically. Again for correct interpretation they require a sign change. The zero dual values for the slack variables X4 and X6 should be ignored.

This command indicates we have finished the analysis.

This signs off from the computer.

These indicate the length of time we were connected to the computer and how much time was spent by the computer in actual computation of our problem. The session cost is expressed in $ and gives an approximate indication of what such an analysis might cost using a commercial time-sharing computer center.

9

THE TRANSPORTATION PROBLEM

In this final chapter we deal with the application of linear programming techniques to certain types of distribution problem such as, for example, the minimization of transportation and associated costs when certain goods are distributed from a number of different sources to a number of different destinations. The technique is widely used in practice, for example, to determine the optimal way to distribute coal from collieries to power stations or cement from cement works to depots and on to individual retailers and building sites, to route tankers and even to allocate primary school pupils to secondary schools. Because of its applicability to this particular situation, this special case of linear programming is commonly known as the **transportation problem**; but the approach is also used in problems which, as in the case of certain production scheduling problems, can be formulated in a similar manner.

The specialized nature of this problem enables it to be handled rather differently from the general linear programming problem discussed in chapter 8. The particular advantage of this treatment is that it makes it possible to handle quite complex problems without the use of a computer. The appendix to this chapter, however, illustrates the use of the computer in the solution of transportation-type problems.

This chapter does not depend on anything in chapters 2–7. Although it is a special case of the general linear programming problem described in chapter 8, it depends on that chapter only for one or two concepts. In all other respects it can be studied independently.

Mathematically, this chapter is not difficult. It requires no more preliminary knowledge than the ability to add, subtract and multiply in simple arithmetic. However, the full process is rather long drawn-out and introduces a number of concepts which, though simple enough in themselves, may be unfamiliar to you. For this reason we have used section A to introduce the concept of the 'tableau', which is necessary background knowledge, and we have spread the description of the basic process over the next four sections, B–E. You should find the arrangement of the rest of the chapter to be self-explanatory.

A – The Tableau (question 1)

A **tableau** (plural **tableaux**; derived from the French word signifying a

162

scoreboard, roster, mathematical table, etc.) is a table: i.e. a rectangular arrangement of data in rows and columns, such that each datum corresponds to a row heading and a column heading. The distinction between a tableau and a table is a distinction of usage, not of arrangement. A tableau is a representation of data in tabular form, expressed in a convenient manner so that arithmetic operations can be performed on it in fairly straightforward fashion. By contrast, the word 'table' tends to be applied to arrangements of data that are made purely for the purpose of organizing or displaying the subject matter.

To illustrate the construction of a tableau, we will perform here a preliminary operation for the example which is to be developed in the next four sections. This deals with the case of a company which has factories located at New York, Baltimore and Newark supplying warehouses at Philadelphia, Pittsburgh, Buffalo and Washington. The factories manufacture an identical product, which is transported by road to the warehouses at a uniform rate of $0.04/ton/mile (i.e. it costs 4 cents to transport each ton of the product a distance of one mile).

One of the things we need to know before we can decide on the optimal method of allocation is the cost/ton of transporting the product from each of the three factories to each of the four warehouses. To do this, we begin by laying out a hypothetical table of distances in the following manner, which is self-explanatory. By convention, we have the factories (i.e. the suppliers) as row headings. In this particular table all distances are given in miles.

	Phila.	Pitts.	Buffalo	Wash.
New York	90	200	210	240
Baltimore	90	120	370	80
Newark	80	160	220	240

To convert this table of distances into a table of transport costs (in $/ton) all we need to do is multiply each mileage figure by 0.04 to achieve the following result, laid out in the same tabular form.

3.6	8.0	8.4	9.6
3.6	4.8	14.8	3.2
3.2	6.4	8.8	9.6

If we conceive of these as successive stages in an operation then, provided we maintain a consistent arrangement of row and column headings we do not need to rewrite the headings themselves. In a tableau each box or frame at the intersection of a row with a column is referred to as a **cell** or **element** which is conventionally identified by its row and column numbers, listed in that order within brackets. Thus, the cell at the intersection of row 2 with column 4 is identified as cell (2,4) and is the cell which corresponds in this particular tableau to the company's cost ($3.20 per ton) of transporting its products from the factory at Baltimore to the warehouse at Washington.

B — Formulating the Transportation Problem (question 2)

Let us take the case of the company described in section A a stage further and assume that, in a given week, the production from the 3 factories and the demand from 4 warehouses is as laid down in the following tables (all figures in tons):

	Factory	Production		Warehouse	Demand
I	New York	500	I	Philadelphia	300
II	Baltimore	250	II	Pittsburgh	400
III	Newark	400	III	Buffalo	250
			IV	Washington, D.C.	200
	Total	1150		Total	1150

In the general treatment of this type of problem we describe each factory as a **source** or **origin** and each warehouse as a **destination**. The problem is to decide in what proportions to allocate the goods from all the sources to all the destinations, so as to incur the minimum possible total transportation cost.

From now on, as we develop this problem, we shall refer where necessary to the factories at New York, Baltimore and Newark as sources of origins I, II and III respectively. Similarly we shall refer to the warehouses at Philadelphia, Pittsburgh, Buffalo and Washington respectively as destinations I, II, III and IV.

Let us assume that all transportation is by road, that the cost/ton of delivery from each source to each destination is as calculated by us in section A and that the production costs at each factory are equal.

This assumption has been made so as to keep the problem in its simplest form. If production costs are not equal the method of approach is to modify the costs tableau by adding any differences in costs at source on to the transportation costs from that source. All subsequent stages in the formulation and solution of the problem are continued on the basis of the amended costs tableau. (The costs tableau is defined below.)

For example suppose that the product costs \$3.7/ton to manufacture at the New York source, \$3.9/ton at Baltimore and \$3.4/ton at Newark. Then the amended costs tableau is derived by taking the cheapest cost (\$3.4/ton) as basic and adding the differences in production cost on to the transportation costs from each of the other sources:

	I	II	III	IV
New York I	3.6 + 0.3 = 3.9	8.0 + 0.3 = 8.3	8.4 + 0.3 = 8.7	9.6 + 0.3 = 9.9
Baltimore II	3.6 + 0.5 = 4.1	4.8 + 0.5 = 5.3	14.8 + 0.5 = 15.3	3.2 + 0.5 = 3.7
Newark III	3.2	6.4	8.8	9.6

The first stage in the solution of any such problem is to formulate it, which is done in this case by laying out two tableaux. One of these, the **costs tableau**, contains all the transportation costs from each source to each destination and has already been prepared, in Section A, for this particular problem, based on the assumption of transportation by a uniform method at a uniform rate/ton mile.

This assumption is, however, not necessary. A costs tableau is simply a tabulation of the best cost per unit for transportation from each source to each destination by whatever method is appropriate to the circumstances: e.g. the figure in cell (2,3) could equally have been the cost in \$/ton of transportation by air from Baltimore to Buffalo, that in cell (3,2) the cost in \$/ton of transportation by rail from Newark to Pittsburgh, and so on. Clearly, however, the units of quantity and value have to be uniform throughout the tableau: i.e. if the transportation cost in one cell is expressed in cents/carton, then the transportation costs in all the other cells must similarly be expressed in cents/carton from source to destination in each case.

The other tableau, commonly referred to as the **O/D tableau** (origins/ destinations tableau) is laid out in the same way as the costs tableau with origins or sources as row headings and destinations as column headings. However, the cells are left empty at this stage. Against each source (i.e. at each row heading) we show the capacity at that source; against each destination (i.e. at each column heading) we show the requirement at that destination.

The costs tableau (repeated from the end of section A) and O/D tableau for our example are laid out side by side on the next page.

(i) Costs tableau (all costs in \$/ton):	(ii) O/D tableau (all figures tons)

3.6	8.0	8.4	9.6
3.6	4.8	14.8	3.2
3.2	6.4	8.8	9.6

	300	400	250	200
500				
250				
400				

Having formulated the problem in this way, our objective is now to fill the cells of the O/D tableau with the tonnages to be assigned from each source to each destination so as to satisfy the constraints of the problem (i.e. to meet the requirements of each destination and not exceed the capacity of each source) at minimum transportation cost. The method of doing this is described in the following sections C–E.

C – The Basic Feasible Solution – Vogel's Rule (I) (question 3)

Having formulated the problem in the manner described in section B, the first stage in solving it is to find a **basic feasible solution** in linear programming parlance; namely, any solution which:

(i) satisfies the constraints of the problem (meaning that, of the total amount delivered from all sources to all destinations, the amount supplied by each source equals what that source is producing and the total amount delivered to each destination equals that destination's requirement) and

(ii) utilizes $m + n - 1$ routes; where m is the number of origins and n the number of destinations. In this example, where there are 3 origins and 4 destinations, this means that the feasible solution must use $3 + 4 - 1 = 6$ routes. ($m + n - 1$ routes must be used, as the use of more or fewer routes can produce a solution which is feasible, but not basic. The mathematical explanation is beyond the scope of this book, but it is not necessary to understand it in order to be able to apply the technique.)

There are usually a number of basic feasible solutions to a problem of this type. Some will be more costly than others and the problem is solved when we have found a basic feasible solution which is also optimal; i.e. least costly. The procedure we adopt is iterative; having found a feasible solution we establish whether it is optimal (there may be more than one optimal solution) and if it is not we repeat the process with successively modified basic feasible solutions, each one less costly than its predecessor, until an optimal solution is achieved.

It is often possible to get fairly close to the optimal solution at the first attempt by using **Vogel's Rule** (after W.R. Vogel, who published the technique in 1958). In the following description, each stage of the general rule is printed in italics and then illustrated in ordinary type and with a diagram in terms of our example carried over from the previous section.

1. For each row and each column in the costs tableau, determine the least and second least cost elements and write the difference against each row and column respectively.

3.6	8.0	8.4	9.6	4.4
3.6	4.8	14.8	3.2	0.4
3.2	6.4	8.8	9.6	3.2
0.4	1.6	0.4	6.4	

The effect is as shown (all costs being given in $). Beginning with row 1, the cheapest cost is 3.6 and the next cheapest is 8.0. The difference between these ($8.0 - 3.6 = 4.4$) is written against the row on the right hand side. Similarly, the figure 0.4 which is written beneath the first column is the difference between the cheapest cost, 3.2 and the second cheapest cost, 3.6. The other rows and columns are treated in the same way.

2. Now determine the least cost cell in the row or column with associated greatest cost difference and write the largest feasible delivery figure in the corresponding cell of the O/D tableau.

(i) Costs tableau: (ii) O/D tableau:

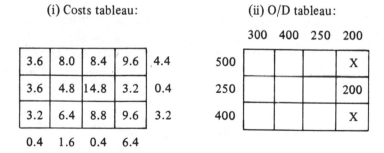

In this example the greatest difference, 6.4, is found at the foot of column 4 and the least cost cell in that column is cell (2,4). The total demand from destination IV is 200 tons, which is less than the total output from source II. We therefore write 200 tons in the appropriate cell. In the other two cells of that column we can insert an X as the full requirement of that particular destination has been satisfied and it will not require any supplies from either of the other two sources.

3. Amend the costs tableau by eliminating any parts of it that are now no longer relevant because requirements have been satisfied; then repeat stages 1 and 2.

(i) Costs tableau:

3.6	8.0	8.4	~~9.6~~	4.4
3.6	4.8	14.8	~~3.2~~	1.2
3.2	6.4	8.8	~~9.6~~	3.2

0.4   1.6   0.4

(ii) O/D tableau:

	300	400	250	200
500	300			X
250	X			200
400	X			X

The costs tableau is shown as amended. The whole of column 4 has been deleted as no longer relevant (because the full requirement of that destination has been satisfied) and the cost differences have been amended accordingly. The greatest cost difference is now 4.4, against row 1, and the lowest cost figure in that row occurs in cell (1,1). Again, the entire requirement (300 tons) of that particular destination can be met from the single source so the figure 300 is written in the appropriate cell of the O/D tableau and X in the other two cells of that column, as nothing is required from either of the other two sources.

4. Repeat the process of stage 3 successively, until the capacities of each origin and the requirements of each destination have been satisfied.

In this particular example the total capacity of all the sources was initially equal to the total requirement of all the destinations. (In later sections we deal with the case where these are not identical. Our object at present is to take the simplest possible case, in order to demonstrate the principle of the operation.) The completed O/D tableau for this problem is now shown as follows:

	300	400	250	200
500	300	X	200	X
250	X	50	X	200
400	X	350	50	X

The procedure by which the remainder of this tableau was filled in should be self-explanatory and you should try to complete the intervening stages yourself.

By applying Vogel's rule we have now arrived at a basic feasible solution to this particular problem which, in this case, is in fact fairly close to the optimal solution. We can now calculate the total transportation cost for the week if this particular solution is adopted, so as to be able to compare it with the total cost of the optimal solution which is established in section E. The total cost calculation is achieved simply by multiplying the figure in each cell of the O/D tableau by the figure in the corresponding cell of the costs tableau. Thus we have:

(1) Cell no.	(2) No. of tons conveyed by this route	(3) Transport cost per ton ($)	(4) cost/cell ($) (2) × (3)
(1,1)	300	3.6	1080
(1,3)	200	8.4	1680
(2,2)	50	4.8	240
(2,4)	200	3.2	640
(3,2)	350	6.4	2240
(3,3)	50	8.8	440
Total tonnage:	1150	Total cost:	6320

D — Determining Whether a Basic Feasible Solution is Optimal (questions 4—6)

Having established a basic feasible solution, the next problem is to determine whether this particular solution is in fact optimal. This is done by making use of the concept of dual values: namely, if any of the product were to be despatched by any of the routes other than the chosen ones, would there be a saving in total transportation costs?

In this section we will describe the procedure to be followed and give a simplified explanation of what it means using the basic feasible solution produced by application of Vogel's Rule in section C. A full mathematical exposition would exceed the scope of this book and is not necessary to enable you to work the process itself. The procedure probably sounds laborious and complicated as we describe it, but in application it is quite simple and straightforward.

Begin with the original costs tableau and ring each cell that corresponds to a route which it is proposed to use. Then write an arbitrary number (say, 0) against any row (say, the row with the greatest individual ringed cost) as demonstrated on the following page.

(3.6)	8.0	(8.4)	9.6
3.6	(4.8)	14.8	(3.2)
3.2	(6.4)	(8.8)	9.6

0

The figure 0 that has been written against the bottom row in this demonstration is an example of what is called a **fictitious cost**: signifying that it is supposed to represent a cost, though not one that is meaningful in any accounting sense. Written against a row, such a figure can be interpreted as the relative price of one ton delivered (on used routes) from that source: written above a column, it represents the relative cost of one ton delivered (on used routes) to that destination. The figure so written against a row or column can be positive, zero or negative: its absolute value is not important to us; what we are concerned with is its value relative to the dual values of the other sources or destinations.

These values, relative to the first value that we have assigned, are calculated by applying the following rules:

1. Add the cost of a used (ringed) route to a source (row) dual value to obtain a destination (column) dual value.
2. Subtract the cost of a used (ringed) route from a destination (column) dual value to obtain a source (row) dual value.

We will now show how these rules are applied to arrive at the dual values for all the sources and destinations of the costs tableau in our example. At the moment we have assigned a dual value only to source III but, by applying rule 1, we can calculate the dual values for destination II (6.4 + 0 = 6.4) and destination III (8.8 + 0 = 8.8). The position is as shown:

	6.4	8.8	
(3.6)	8.0	(8.4)	9.6
3.6	(4.8)	14.8	(3.2)
3.2	(6.4)	(8.8)	9.6

0

We can now use these destination dual values to calculate the dual values of source II (6.4 − 4.8 = 1.6) and source I (8.8 − 8.4 = 0.4). The position is now as shown:

	6.4	8.8	
0.4	(3.6)	8.0	(8.4)	9.6
1.6	3.6	(4.8)	14.8	(3.2)
0	3.2	(6.4)	(8.8)	9.6

Then by applying rule 1 again, we are able to calculate the dual values of destination I (3.6 + 0.4 = 4.0) and destination IV (3.2 + 1.6 = 4.8). The completed set of dual values is as shown:

	4.0	6.4	8.8	4.8
0.4	(3.6)	8.0	(8.4)	9.6
1.6	3.6	(4.8)	14.8	(3.2)
0	3.2	(6.4)	(8.8)	9.6

From this we can see that the price of one ton delivered from source I is $0.4 greater than that from source III, but $1.2 less than from source II. Similarly, if we examine the column dual values we can see that the cost of one ton delivered to destination IV is $0.8 greater than that of one ton delivered to destination I, but $4.0 less than the cost of one ton delivered to destination III. Clearly, it does not matter which row or column we decided to start with, or what arbitrary dual value we chose to assign to it. Whatever the figures themselves might be, their *relative* values (i.e. the differences between them) would have been the same. (This can be verified if you wish by starting afresh, assigning a zero to one of the other sources or destinations and repeating the process described.)

We can now use these fictitious costs in order to arrive at a profit for each individual cell which, although equally fictitious in any accounting sense, provides a guide to the relative profitability of using that route. For this purpose the profit per unit of using any particular route is defined as:

cost at destination − transportation cost − price at source.

This formula is used to calculate the profit (in $ per ton, in this example) on each individual route and the answer is conventionally written inside a box within the individual cell. To start with, the relative profits on the routes corresponding to the ringed cells must obviously be 0, though it is a good plan to work them out in order to check the arithmetic. Thus, for route (2,2) the profit is $6.4 - 4.8 - 1.6 = 0$. Similarly, for route (1,3) the profit is $8.8 - 8.4 - 0.4 = 0$. The position at this stage is shown as follows:

	4.0	6.4	8.8	4.8
0.4	0 (3.6)	8.0	0 (8.4)	9.6
1.6	3.6	0 (4.8)	14.8	0 (3.2)
0	3.2	0 (6.4)	0 (8.8)	9.6

By applying the same rule we can now go on to calculate the profit on each of the remaining routes. If the result is a negative figure, this indicates a loss by the use of this particular route: i.e. if this route were used total transport costs would be increased. Similarly, if the result for any particular route is positive this indicates a profit, meaning that if this route were used total transport costs would be reduced.

On this basis, we now proceed to calculate the profits for the remaining cells. Thus, for route (1,2) the profit is $6.4 - 8.0 - 0.4 = -2.0$; that for route (2,3) is $8.8 - 14.8 - 1.6 = -7.6$, and so on. The completed calculation is shown below:

	4.0	6.4	8.8	4.8
0.4	0 (3.6)	-2.0 8.0	0 (8.4)	-5.2 9.6
1.6	-1.2 3.6	0 (4.8)	-7.6 14.8	0 (3.2)
0	+0.8 3.2	0 (6.4)	0 (8.8)	-4.8 9.6

It can be seen that, for the cells which are not ringed, the results are all negative with the exception of cell (3,1) which is positive.

You will note that in this example and also in some of the questions and answers we have shown the full figures in the corners of the cells. This is so that you can follow exactly what is happening and compare our results with your own. In practice, all we really want to know is whether the profit on a route is negative, zero, or positive. If it is negative we do not need to know the exact figure, though we sometimes want this information if the profit is positive (for reasons which will become clear in section G). Thus, in the cells (1,2) or (1,4) of this particular example it is obvious that:

transportation cost + price at source > cost at destination.

So the profit on the route will be negative. As we do not need to know by exactly how much it is negative, we do not need to waste time making the full calculation. We could therefore have completed the tableau in the following manner, which would have been quite informative enough for our purpose:

	4.0	6.4	8.8	4.8
0.4	[0] (3.6)	[–] 8.0	[0] (8.4)	[–] 9.6
1.6	[–] 3.6	[0] (4.8)	[–] 14.8	[0] (3.2)
0	[+0.8] 3.2	[0] (6.4)	[0] (8.8)	[–] 9.6

In this way then we have established that in this example the initial feasible solution arrived at by applying Vogel's Rule is not an optimal solution as each ton carried on route (3,1), up to a certain limit, would reduce total transport costs by $0.8.

This latter information can be used, as shown in the next section, to amend the initial feasible solution into one with lower total transport costs, and the process is repeated as necessary until an optimal solution is achieved.

E — The Optimal Solution (I) (questions 7 and 8)

In section D we established that, in our example, a saving of $0.8 can be achieved on every ton conveyed by route (3,1) instead of by the routes specified in the initial feasible solution, which was shown not to be optimal. To take full advantage of this potential saving we obviously want to transport as many tons by this particular route as we are permitted to within the constraints of the problem.

To do this we return to the O/D tableau prepared at the end of section C. We want to add something to the figure in cell (3,1) so as to bring this up to the maximum number of tons that can be carried on that particular route. As we do not yet know how much we can add, we express this amount by the symbol θ (the lower case letter *theta*, which is the Greek alphabet equivalent of our *th*) so we insert $+\theta$ in cell (3,1). However by adding θ tons to the figure in cell (3,1) we are throwing the other cells of row 3 and column 1 out of balance; meaning that the constraints of the problem are no longer satisfied. To rectify this we have to subtract θ tons from one or more of the other routes in that row or column to compensate for what we have added to route (3,1).

Let us begin with column 1. Obviously we cannot take anything away from route (2,1) because it is not used, so we must insert $-\theta$ in cell (1,1) to restore the balance of that column. The position is shown as follows:

	300	400	250	200
500	300$-\theta$		200	
250		50		200
400	$+\theta$	350	50	

Clearly, if destination I can only take 300 tons, the contents of column 1 cannot total more than 300. The contents of the three cells of column 1 now add up to $300 - \theta + \theta = 300$ tons which is equal to the demand, so this column is now in balance.

However, row 1 is now out of balance so we have to rectify this by adding $+\theta$ somewhere else in the row. The only other used route in this row is (1,3) so we add $+\theta$ to this route which brings row 1 into balance but throws column 3 out of balance.

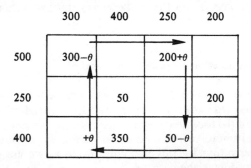

	300	400	250	200
500	300$-\theta$		200$+\theta$	
250		50		200
400	$+\theta$	350	50$-\theta$	

To correct the balance of column 3 we have to subtract θ from route (3,3) which also has the effect of correcting the imbalance which existed in row 3. The whole tableau is now in balance again.

You will notice that we have drawn arrows on the tableau to show the sequence of operations required to bring each row or column into balance. If these operations have been completed correctly the arrows will be found to have formed what is called a **closed loop**: namely, the arrows are all linked in such a way that the head of each arrow meets the tail of one other arrow. The loop can, of course, run equally well in either direction, so every arrow could equally well be drawn facing the opposite way.

We are now able to determine the *maximum* possible value of θ which, clearly, cannot be more than 50 tons as it is not possible to take more than 50 tons away from route (3,3) to add to route (3,1). The revised tableau is now shown as follows:

	300	400	250	200
500	250		250	
250		50		200
400	50	350		

We now have a new feasible solution and have to determine whether or not is it optimal. We do this by the identical procedure that was used for testing the feasible solution in section D and the result is as follows:

	3.6	6.8	8.4	5.2
0	(3.6) [0]	8.0 [−]	(8.4) [0]	9.6 [−]
2.0	3.6 [−]	(4.8) [0]	14.8 [−]	(3.2) [0]
0.4	(3.2) [0]	(6.4) [0]	8.8 [−]	9.6 [−]

In the new costs tableau all the unused cells show a negative profit, meaning that the solution which we now have is optimal.

It should, however, be noted before we continue that although in this example we were able to arrive at an optimal solution after only one iteration, this is frequently not possible. If the amended O/D tableau is found not to be optimal, the whole cycle has to be repeated for as many times as necessary. With each iteration it will be found that total transport costs are reduced until finally an optimal solution is achieved. This subject will be treated further in section G, using a more complex example.

Since we have rerouted 50 tons on route (3,1) and expect to achieve a saving, by doing so, of $0.8 per ton, we should expect a total saving of $50 \times 0.8 = \$40$. We can verify this by recalculating the complete transportation cost for the week, which we can compare with that of the feasible solution arrived at in section C. Thus, multiplying the figures in the filled cells of the O/D tableau in the optimal solution, by the figures in the corresponding cells of the costs tableau, we have

(1) Cell no.	(2) No. of tons conveyed by this route	(3) Transport cost per ton ($)	(4) cost/cell ($) (2) × (3)
(1,1)	250	3.6	900
(1,3)	250	8.4	2100
(2,2)	50	4.8	240
(2,4)	200	3.2	640
(3,1)	50	3.2	160
(3,2)	350	6.4	2240
Total tonnage:	1150	Total cost:	6280

The total cost for the week of $6280 compares with the cost of $6320 arrived at in section C for the initial feasible solution: a saving of $40, as expected.

F — Vogel's Rule (II) (questions 9—10)

This section and the next deal with points of detail that are necessary for full treatment of the earlier part of this chapter. If you would prefer to begin by getting an overall picture of the transportation problem as a whole (insofar as this book is able to deal with it), you can by-pass these two sections and their questions at present and return to them after completing the remainder of the chapter.

In section C we gave a description of Vogel's Rule in its simplest form, illustrated by an example which had been selected for this purpose because it offered no complications of treatment. In this section we display, by means of a worked example, certain complications which may be encountered in practice and the methods of overcoming them.

Consider the following pair of tableaux which have been prepared in the usual manner with origins as row headings and destinations as column headings.

(i) Costs tableau:

13	5	8	6	11
3	7	5	22	10
9	14	6	8	5
10	31	17	18	9
11	9	8	15	11

(ii) O/D tableau:

	18	12	20	11	15
12					
13					
22					
20					
9					

We will not demonstrate every step in applying Vogel's Rule to arrive at an initial feasible solution, but only those at which complications arise. It would be a useful exercise on your own part to follow this operation on a separate piece of paper, completing the straightforward intermediate steps for yourself.

After filling the cells in row 2 of the O/D tableau we come to our first complication as shown below:

13	5	8	6	11	1
X	X	X	X	X	
9	14	6	8	5	1
10	31	17	18	9	1
11	9	8	15	11	1
1	4	2	2	4	

	18	12	20	11	15
12					
13	13	X	X	X	X
22					
20					
9					

Here there are now two columns, column 2 and column 5, with equal associated greatest cost difference of 4. When a tie of this kind occurs, you should fill that cell in the O/D tableau with corresponding route that can carry the greatest load; if the loads are equal, fill any of the cells in question (it does not matter which). Route (1,2) can carry a maximum load of 12 units. The alternative choice, route (3,5), can carry a maximum load of 15 units. We therefore select the latter and the result is as follows:

13	5	8	6	X	1
X	X	X	X	X	
9	14	6	8	X	2
10	31	17	18	X	7
11	9	8	15	X	1

      1   4   2   2

	18	12	20	11	15
12					X
13	13	X	X	X	X
22					15
20					X
9					X

The next step is straightforward but in the following one we arrive at a further complication, as shown:

X	5	8	6	X	1
X	X	X	X	X	
X	14	6	8	X	2
X	31	17	18	X	1
X	9	8	15	X	1

        4   2   2

	18	12	20	11	15
12	X				X
13	13	X	X	X	X
22	X				15
20	5				X
9	X				X

If we insert 12 in cell (1,2), we satisfy the full output of source 1 and the full requirement of destination 2 simultaneously. However, if we were to eliminate the remaining unfilled cells of both row 1 and column 2, we would end up with fewer than $m + n - 1$ routes in use. It was pointed out in a previous section that a basic feasible solution must have $m + n - 1$ used routes (i.e., in this particular example, $5 + 5 - 1 = 9$ routes), so we meet this particular problem by deciding to eliminate either the remaining cells in row 1 or the remaining cells in column 2; but not both. (The effect will be that, in the completed feasible solution, one of the routes will carry zero load.) The choice is arbitrary: it does not matter which is selected. In this case we will eliminate the remaining cells in the column. We now have the following situation:

X	X	8	6	X	2
X	X	X	X	X	
X	X	6	8	X	2
X	X	17	18	X	1
X	X	8	15	X	7
		2	2		

	18	12	20	11	15
12	X	12			X
13	13	X	X	X	X
22	X	X			15
20	5	X			X
9	X	X			X

The next two steps include one example of a tie of the type we have met already, and which is solved in the same way by filling the cell (3,3), which carries the greatest load. This brings us to the following situation:

X	X	8	6	X	2
X	X	X	X	X	
X	X	X	X	X	
X	X	17	18	X	1
X	X	X	X	X	
		9	12		

	18	12	20	11	15
12	X	12			X
13	13	X	X	X	X
22	X	X	7	X	15
20	5	X			X
9	X	X	9	X	X

Here the rule indicates that cell (1,4) should be filled. However, the entire output of source 1 has already been allocated to route (1,2) so the maximum possible figure that we can insert in cell (1,4) is 0. (A similar situation is that in which nothing can be put into a cell as the full requirement of the destination has been satisfied. In this case, again insert 0 in the cell.) The position is now as follows:

X	X	X	X	X
X	X	X	X	X
X	X	X	X	X
X	X	17	18	X
X	X	X	X	X

	18	12	20	11	15
12	X	12	X	0	X
13	13	X	X	X	X
22	X	X	7	X	15
20	5	X			X
9	X	X	9	X	X

We complete the initial basic feasible solution, with 9 cells filled, by filling in the remaining two cells (4,3) and (4,4) with a 4 and 11, so that the requirements on row 4 and columns 3 and 4 are satisfied.

	18	12	20	11	15
12	X	12	X	0	X
13	13	X	X	X	X
22	X	X	7	X	15
20	5	X	4	11	X
9	X	X	9	X	X

G — The Optimal Solution (II) (questions 11—13)

In section F we used a worked example to illustrate those situations in which the application of Vogel's Rule to arrive at an initial basic feasible solution occasionally requires a choice to be made between different courses of action, and to demonstrate how such situations should be handled.

Similar situations can arise at the later stages of solving the problem. We demonstrate them, in this section, by taking the same worked example through to a solution.

As in section F, we will not describe every stage in detail but will concentrate only on those that require a choice to be made between alternative decisions. It will help you to follow this explanation if you perform the straightforward intermediate stages for yourself on a separate piece of paper.

At the end of section F we arrived by Vogel's Rule at the following initial basic feasible solution:

(i) Costs tableau:

13	5	8	6	11
3	7	5	22	10
9	14	6	8	5
10	31	17	18	9
11	9	8	15	11

(ii) O/D tableau:

	18	12	20	11	15
12		12			
13	13				
22			7		15
20	5		4	11	
9			9		

We now have to determine whether it is optimal and, by applying the procedure described in section D, we find that in fact it is not. The following tableau shows three routes with positive profits.

	10	17	17	18	16
12	13 [−, 0]	(5)	8 [−, 0]	(6)	11 [−]
7	(3) [0]	7 [+3]	5 [+5]	22 [−]	10 [−]
11	9 [−]	14 [−]	(6) [0]	8 [−]	(5) [0]
0	(10) [0]	31 [−]	(17) [0]	(18) [0]	9 [+7]
9	11 [−]	9 [−]	(8) [0]	15 [−]	11 [−]

Of these three routes we select that which has the greatest profit per unit transported: namely, route (4,5). The next operation, which is a straight-forward repetition of the procedure described in section F, results in the transfer of 4 units from cell (4,3) to cell (4,5), an increase of 4 units on route (3,3) and a decrease of 4 units on route (3,5). Route (4,3) is now unused. Checking the revised feasible solution to find out whether it is optimal results in the following situation, where four routes are found to show a positive profit.

	10	17	10	18	9
12	13 [−, 0]	(5)	8 [−, 0]	(6)	11 [−]
7	(3) [0]	7 [+3]	5 [−]	22 [−]	10 [−]
4	9 [−]	14 [−]	(6) [0]	8 [+6]	(5) [0]
0	(10) [0]	31 [−]	17 [−]	(18) [0]	(9) [0]
2	11 [−]	9 [+6]	(8) [0]	15 [+1]	11 [−]

	18	12	20	11	15
12		12		0	
13	13				
22			11		11
20	5			11	4
9			9		

The revised O/D tableau is therefore still not optimal and the cycle must be repeated, though we now have to choose between two routes which show an equal greatest profit of +6. In this case we make an arbitrary choice, say route (5,2). We show, here, the complex nature of the loop which is required to satisfy the constraints.

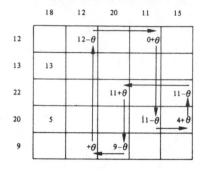

	18	12	20	11	15
12		12−θ		0+θ	
13	13				
22			11+θ		11−θ
20	5			11−θ	4+θ
9		+θ	9−θ		

The maximum possible value of θ is 9, so the next stage of revising the O/D tableau and testing whether it is optimal is laid out as follows [with route (5,3) now unused] :

	10	17	10	18	9
12	13	(5)	8	(6)	11
7	(3)	7	5	22	10
4	9	14	(6)	8	(5)
0	(10)	31	17	(18)	(9)
8	11	(9)	8	15	11

	18	12	20	11	15
12		3		9	
13	13				
22			20		2
20	5			2	13
9		9			

The revised O/D tableau is found to be still not optimal. Of the two routes showing a positive profit we select route (3,4) on which the profit is greater, and the resulting loop is shown below:

	18	12	20	11	15
12		3		9	
13	13				
22			20	θ	2 − θ
20	5			2 − θ	13 + θ
9		9			

In writing out the revised O/D tableau we now once again have to make a choice between different courses of action. The maximum possible value of θ is 2, which is the content both of cell (3,5) and also of cell (4,4). We cannot eliminate both routes from the solution because, if we did, we would have fewer than $m + n - 1$ routes used. We therefore make an arbitrary decision to eliminate one of the routes and leave the other one in at zero level. (Whichever route is eliminated, in fact, the optimal solution ultimately arrived at will be the same. One choice is likely to require more subsequent iterations than the other, but there is no simple way of determining in advance which this would be.) We decide to eliminate route (4,4) and the resulting revised O/D tableau, with the test of whether it is optimal, is as follows:

	10	11	10	12	9
6	13	⑤	8	⑥	11
7	③	7	5	22	10
4	9	14	⑥	⑧	⑤
0	⑩	31	17	18	⑨
2	11	⑨	8	15	11

	18	12	20	11	15
12		3	9		
13	13				
22			20	2	0
20	5				15
9		9			

It can be seen that we have now finally arrived at an optimal solution, as no positive profit is shown on any of the routes. There are two features of this particular solution, however, that are worth noting.

The first is that route (3,5) in this optimal solution is used at zero level. It differs from the routes represented by empty cells in the final O/D tableau in that it is not an unused route. It forms part of the optimal solution but no load is actually carried on it. This type of situation, where one or more routes in the optimal solution is used at zero level, is known as **degeneracy**.

The second feature worth noting is that (5,3) shows zero profit even though it is an unused route. This indicates the existence of **multiple optima**; meaning that there are one or more other optimal solutions which have the same total costs but use a different combination of routes.

In fact, if we introduce route (5,3) into the solution we obtain either of the following optimal solutions (each with total costs of 510 units as in the original optimal solution), depending on whether route (1,4) or route (5,3) is eliminated (with the other being used at zero level).

	18	12	20	11	15
12		12			
13	13				
22			11	11	0
20	5				15
9		0	9		

	18	12	20	11	15
12		12		0	
13	13				
22			11	11	0
20	5				15
9			9		

H — Excess Capacity (questions 14 and 15)

Previously we have assumed that the total quantity available at the origins exactly balances the total quantity required at the destinations. In this section and the next we will consider the situations where this is not so.

In this section we will describe how to modify the costs and O/D tableaux so that the transportation algorithm (an **algorithm** is a method of computation by pre-arranged steps designed to solve a specific type of problem) can handle problems of excess capacity: i.e. situations where the total quantity available from all the sources is greater than the total quantity required at all the destinations. We will do this by modifying the example used in sections B—E of this chapter.

Let us increase the capacity of source II (the factory at Baltimore) from 250 tons to 550 tons, while leaving all the other figures unchanged. The total capacity of all the sources now exceeds the total requirement of all the destinations by 300 tons. We continue to assume that costs at source are equal for all three factories, so that we are concerned only with transportation cost in deciding how the output should be allocated from each source to each destination and the production level at each source.

We handle this by introducing into the problem an additional destination which is a 'dummy', with transport costs of $0/ton from all three sources and a requirement exactly equal to the excess capacity. Total capacity is now exactly equal to total requirements, so let us see what happens if we proceed on this basis. The costs tableau and O/D tableau are written out as follows:

    (i) Costs tableau: (ii) O/D tableau:

3.6	8.0	8.4	9.6	0
3.6	4.8	14.8	3.2	0
3.2	6.4	8.8	9.6	0

	300	400	250	200	300
500					
550					
400					

By the procedure described in earlier sections (using Vogel's Rule to arrive at an initial basic feasible solution, checking whether it is optimal and, if not, iterating until an optimal solution is achieved) we arrive at the following minimum transportation cost solution:

	300	400	250	200	300
500			250		250
550		350		200	
400	300	50			50

It can be seen from this tableau that 250 tons are allocated to the dummy destination from source I, and 50 tons from source III. These represent the quantities that are not transported: which means, in practical terms, either that they are stockpiled at source or production at the sources is cut back by corresponding amounts.

Ignoring the final column of the O/D tableau, the total cost of the tonnage actually transported during the week (i.e. the tonnages listed in the first four columns of the tableau) amounts to $5700, which compares with the optimal transportation cost of $6280 arrived at from our earlier model in section E.

I — Excess Requirements (question 16)

In this section we consider the converse situation (to that of section H) where the total quantity required at all the destinations is greater than the total quantity available from all the sources.

To demonstrate how to handle this situation we again modify the original example of sections B—E by supposing that the requirement for the week is increased by 50 tons at each of the 4 destinations. If the original capacity of the 3 sources remains unchanged, the total requirement now exceeds the total capacity by 200 tons. In practice this means, of course, that distribution must in some way be rationed: i.e. one or more of the destinations must be allocated less than its requirement. The problem we are seeking to solve, here, is to determine the optimal allocation policy in terms of transportation costs alone.

We proceed in basically the same way as for the previous section by creating in this case a dummy source with a capacity exactly equal to the total excess requirement (200 tons in this case) and a transportation cost to each destination of $0/ton. With total capacity now nominally equal to total requirements, the costs tableau and O/D tableau can be laid out as follows:

(i) Costs tableau: (ii) O/D tableau:

3.6	8.0	8.4	9.6
3.6	4.8	14.8	3.2
3.2	6.4	8.8	9.6
0	0	0	0

	350	450	300	250
500				
250				
400				
200				

Proceeding in the normal fashion the optimal O/D tableau given below is arrived at:

	350	450	300	250
500	350	50	100	
250		0		250
400		400		
200			200	

The optimal allocation of the product to minimize total transportation costs is as shown in the tableau, with destination III (the warehouse at Buffalo) receiving only 100 tons of its total requirement of 300 tons.

This solution gives a total transportation cost for the week of $5,860.

J — Routes Which Must or Must Not Be Used (questions 17—18)

It may sometimes happen in practice that a certain route must or must not be used. Continuing with our original example of sections B—E, let us assume that the products of the three factories are similar but not exactly homogeneous, and that the specification produced by the factory at Baltimore is not acceptable to the principal customer at Washington. In other words, route (2,4) must not be used.

We assume further that the company management insists that all 250 tons required at Buffalo be transported on route (3,3) due to the availability of a return load on that route. We continue to assume that production costs are equal at all three sources.

To deal with these requirements it is necessary to reformulate the problem in a particular manner. The way to ensure that a particular route is not used is by assigning it an artificial transport cost per unit which is so high as to ensure that the route never enters the optimal solution.

To ensure that route (2,4) is not used we will therefore assign it a transportation cost of $100/ton. (This is an arbitrary figure that is intended purely to prevent that route from entering the calculation. It bears no relationship to the real transportation cost.)

Similarly, the way to ensure that a particular route *is* used is by assigning it an artificial transportation cost so low that it *must* enter the optimal solution and have the greatest possible load allocated to it. We therefore assign route (3,3) an artificial transportation cost of −$100/ton. The costs tableau and O/D tableau can now be written out as follows:

(i) Costs tableau:

3.6	8.0	8.4	9.6
3.6	4.8	14.8	100
3.2	6.4	−100	9.6

500
250
400

(ii) O/D tableau:

	300	400	250	200
500				
250				
400				

By proceeding in the normal fashion we can arrive at the optimal O/D tableau given below:

	300	400	250	200
500	300	0		200
250		250		
400		150	250	

It can be seen from this tableau that, as required, route (2,4) is now unused and route (3,3) is now used to carry its maximum possible load of 250 tons.

In arriving at the actual total transportation cost, the load transported on route (3,3) must obviously be costed at its true rate which is $8.8/ton and not at its artificial cost of −$100/ton which was applied simply to ensure the full use of the particular route. The total transportation cost for the week in this new situation is found to be $7360.

K — The Dual Transportation Problem (questions 19–20)

We conclude this chapter with some description of how the transportation algorithm can be used to maximize a profit in certain situations. This treatment is known generally as the **dual transportation problem** because it is the converse to the primal outlined in the previous sections. (The terms are used analogously to those in chapter 8.)

Consider the case of a small grocery company with three retail shops. In a given week it can purchase a certain type of fruit in four markets at a cost per box of $0.8, $0.9, $0.9 and $1 respectively.

Transport, cleaning and packing costs per box (in $) purchased from each market for each shop are given in the following table:

Shops

		I	II	III
	I	0.7	0.5	0.7
Markets	II	0.5	0.6	0.6
	III	0.6	0.4	0.5
	IV	0.3	0.6	0.6

The company proposes to sell the fruit in each of its three shops at a price equivalent to $2 per box.

The company has an option to purchase 60, 70, 60 and 30 boxes respectively from each market and the demands from the managers of its three shops are respectively 80, 50 and 70 boxes.

The problem is to determine how the shops should be supplied from each market to maximize the profit during that week on that line of fruit.

The first stage is to formulate the problem. We do this by preparing a **profits tableau** (similar to a costs tableau, except that the cells contain profit figures instead of cost figures) and an O/D tableau. Because the total capacity exceeds the total requirement, an additional column is allowed for a dummy destination, in the manner described in section H.

In the profits tableau shown below, the profits at the dummy destinations are $0 from each source; for all the other cells the profit figures are arrived at by the following formula:

profit/box = selling price − transport and other costs − purchase cost.

For example, in the case of route (2,3) profit/box = 2.0 − 0.6 − 0.9 = $0.5.

Profits tableau ($):

0.5	0.7	0.5	0.0
0.6	0.5	0.5	0.0
0.5	0.7	0.6	0.0
0.7	0.4	0.4	0.0

In this example, by contrast with those in the earlier sections of this chapter, we are seeking to maximize a profit rather than to minimize a cost. To be able to use the same algorithm that we have used in the previous examples, we can convert the profits tableau into the equivalent of a costs tableau by first multiplying all the cells in the profit tableau by -1 then adding on the minimum quantity required to make all entries in the new tableau $\geqslant 0$. This process is illustrated below. Since the largest negative quantity in any of the cells of the intermediate tableau [diagram (ii)] is -0.7, this means that 0.7 is the minimum quantity which has to be added to all the cells to make them $\geqslant 0$. The resulting costs tableau is shown in diagram (iii).

(i) Profits tableau   (ii) Intermediate tableau   (iii) Costs tableau

0.5	0.7	0.5	0.0
0.6	0.5	0.5	0.0
0.5	0.7	0.6	0.0
0.7	0.4	0.4	0.0

$\xrightarrow{\times -1}$

-0.5	-0.7	-0.5	0.0
-0.6	-0.5	-0.5	0.0
-0.5	-0.7	-0.6	0.0
-0.7	-0.4	-0.4	0.0

$\xrightarrow{+0.7}$

0.2	0.0	0.2	0.7
0.1	0.2	0.2	0.7
0.2	0.0	0.1	0.7
0.0	0.3	0.3	0.7

We can now set about solving the problem by seeking to allocate loads such that total costs are minimized. The optimal routes in this situation will also be the optimal routes in the profit maximization situation. An optimal solution is given as follows:

	80	50	70	20
60		50		10
70	50		10	10
60			60	
30	30			

This tableau allocates ten boxes each from markets I and II to the dummy destination, meaning in practice that these are not purchased. The distribution of actual purchases and allocation is shown by the first three columns of the table only: i.e.

shop I needs 80 boxes of which 50 come from market II and 30 from market IV;

shop II needs 50 boxes and gets them all from market I;

shop III needs 70 boxes of which 10 come from market II and 60 from market III.

By valuing the quantities shown in the optimal O/D tableau in terms of the profits given in the corresponding cells of the profits tableau, we arrive

at a total estimated profit on this line for the week of $127, as calculated
in the following table:

(1) Cell no.	(2) No. of boxes purchased	(3) Profit per box ($)	(4) Profit per cell ($) (2) × (3)
(1,2)	50	0.7	35.0
(2,1)	50	0.6	30.0
(2,3)	10	0.5	5.0
(3,3)	60	0.6	36.0
(4,1)	30	0.7	21.0
Total boxes:	200	Total profit:	127.0

Questions

9.1 An oil company has 3 deposits which supply 4 distribution centers. The
distances from depot 1 to the 4 distribution centers are 20, 40, 80 and 90
miles respectively, those from depot II are 20, 30, 50 and 50 miles, and
those from depot III 30, 20, 30 and 20 miles. Tabluate this information
in the manner demonstrated in section A and prepare a tableau of costs/
tanker load from each depot to each distribution center, if the cost of
transportation is 20 cents/tanker mile. Keep your costs tableau for use in
subsequent questions.

9.2 Consider the data for question 1. In a given week the supply from the
3 depots is 500, 600 and 200 tanker loads and the demand from the 4
distribution centres is 200, 100, 600 and 400 loads respectively. The
problem is to decide the number of tanker loads to be despatched from
each depot to each distribution center. Formulate the problem in the
manner demonstrated in section B. Save your results for use in subsequent
questions.

9.3 Apply Vogel's Rule to the problem formulated in question 2, so as to
arrive at an initial basic feasible solution. Keep your results for questions
following.

9.4 Taking the basic feasible solution arrived at in the answer to question
3, calculate the dual values for the sources and destinations of the costs
tableau. Keep a note of your answer for use in question 5.

9.5 Now determine whether or not the initial basic feasible solution arrived
at in the answer to question 3 is optimal.

9.6 Now calculate the total transportation cost for the week based on the
figures given in the costs and O/D tableaux of the earlier questions.

9.7 In question 5 we found that the initial basic feasible solution arrived
at by Vogel's Rule was in fact optimal, so that the problem could be
considered solved with no further operations required. Let us now take
the same O/D tableau (provided below) but assume that the costs tableau
is slightly different and that, in testing whether an optimal solution is
achieved, cell (3,2) shows a positive profit.

	200	100	600	400
500	200	100	200	
600			400	200
200				200

Apply the procedure described in section E to determine what additional number of tanker loads could be carried by route (3,2) and, if this were done, what other alterations would be required to the tableau to bring it back into balance. Keep your answer for question 8.

9.8 (i) Can the problem of question 7 now be considered solved? (ii) If not, what remains to be done?

9.9 A soft drinks company manufactures its products in 4 factories and distributes to warehouses in 3 locations. The transport costs tableau (in pence per carton of bottles) and the daily O/D requirements tableau (in cartons) are given below.

Costs tableau:

12	19	10
12	7	16
28	17	5
15	35	28

O/D tableau:

	4500	7500	4000
6000			
2500			
3000			
4500			

(i) How many routes must be listed in the basic feasible solution?
(ii) Use Vogel's Rule to determine an initial basic feasible solution.

At what stage does a choice have to be made between different courses of action, and what is the effect of having to make this choice?

9.10 Use Vogel's rule to determine a basic feasible solution for the problem with costs and O/D requirements tableaux given below:

Costs tableau:

9	12	9	7	9
7	3	8	7	5
6	5	10	4	13
5	9	6	3	2

O/D tableau:

	4	4	6	2	4
5					
4					
2					
9					

When different choices arise, take the following actions to ensure that your answer is the same as the answer provided at the end of this book: (a) when cell (2,2) is filled with 4 units, eliminate row 2; (b) when both cells (3,1) and (3,4) can be filled with 2 units use route (3,1). Save your answer for use in question 11.

9.11 Test the solution arrived at in the answer to question 10, to find out whether it is optimal.

You should find, in fact, that it is not optimal and that you now have to make a choice between two courses of action. What are they, and what should you do? Note your results for use in question 12.

9.12 The answer to question 11 indicates that one of two routes has to be introduced into the solution, and the choice between them is to be made arbitrarily. If the decision is to introduce route (4,1), what changes have to be made to the O/D tableau?

Test the new solution to establish whether it is optimal. If not, what is the next step in this particular example? Save your results for use in question 13.

9.13 We decide to introduce route (4,4) into the solution of question 12 which is now in fact optimal. Go through these operations yourself so as to compare your results with those in the printed answer to this question. Do you notice anything else about the result? If so, what conclusions can you draw?

9.14 In the following tableaux we display a situation where there is an excess of capacity over demand. (It is, in fact, a variation of question 2, with the week's capacity of depot III increased by 100 tanker loads.)

Costs tableau: O/D tableau:

4	8	16	18
4	6	10	10
6	4	6	4

	200	100	600	400
500				
600				
300				

How should you modify the tableaux so as to be able to determine the optimal allocation from sources to destinations in this situation of over-capacity? Save your answer for use in question 15.

9.15 Now calculate an optimal allocation policy using the tableaux written out in the answer to question 14.

9.16 In the following tableaux we display a situation where total requirement exceeds total capacity. (This is in fact a further variation of the example of question 2, with the week's requirement from distribution center II increased by 200 tanker loads.)

Costs tableau: O/D tableau:

                                     200   300   600   400

4	8	16	18
4	6	10	10
6	4	6	4

500				
600				
200				

Determine an optimal allocation policy for this situation. [To enable your result to coincide with the answer given, when applying Vogel's Rule eliminate column 3 when filling cell (2,3) with 400 units.]

9.17 Consider again the costs tableau of question 9, where the costs are given in cents per carton of soft drinks transported from each of four factories to each of three warehouses. Assuming that there are reasons why route (3,3) must not be used and route (2,1) must be used, amend the costs tableau so as to ensure that these requirements are met. Save your tableau for use in question 18.

9.18 Use the tableau given in the answer to question 17 in conjunction with the O/D tableau of question 9 to calculate an optimal allocation policy for this situation. What will be the total transport cost for the day?

9.19 An agricultural merchant buys a certain type of fodder from three sources to supply his four outlets in different towns. Considering purchase and transportation costs against selling price, the profit in $/ton that he makes at each outlet from the fodder he buys from each source can be tabulated as follows:

		Outlets		
	I	II	III	IV
Sources I	2.8	3.5	4.3	2.3
Sources II	3.0	3.1	4.5	1.7
Sources III	2.5	3.5	2.0	4.8

Convert this profits tableau into a costs tableau in the manner shown in section K. Keep a note of your answer for question 20.

9.20 In a given month the merchant of question 19 requires 175, 100, 75 and 50 tons of fodder respectively at his four outlets and can obtain 100, 200 and 100 tons respectively from the three sources.

(i) Lay out the O/D tableau beside the costs tableau calculated in the answer to question 19 and determine the optimal method of allocating the fodder from the 3 sources to the 4 outlets.

(ii) Calculate the merchant's profit for the month from the total transaction.

Appendix — The Use of Computers

In the introduction to this chapter we pointed out that the transportation problem is a special case of linear programming. In practice, however, although the techniques described in this chapter allow reasonably complex problems to be handled without a computer, it is usually far simpler, quicker and more accurate to use one.

To illustrate the use of the computer in the solution of a transportation problem the same interactive linear programming package LPCU described in some detail in the computer appendix to chapter 8 will be employed to solve the basic example used in this chapter, formulated in section B. In this the objective is to determine the best way to transport different quantities of an identical product manufactured in three factories located in different parts of the country to four warehouses situated in other towns at minimum cost.

The problem is reproduced below with the entries in the tableau representing the costs of transporting one ton of product from each origin to each destination.

Destination

		I	II	III	IV
Origin	tons	300	400	250	200
I	500	3.6	8.0	8.4	9.6
II	250	3.6	4.8	14.8	3.2
III	400	3.2	6.4	8.8	9.6

To use the LPCU package it is necessary to express the data for the problem in an appropriate form. Here there are 12 variables — the amounts in tons carried on each route, although as was pointed out in the chapter only 6 (number of origins + number of destinations − 1) will actually carry goods in the optimal solution. Let us label these variables as indicated below with x_1 indicating the amount carried from origin I to destination I, x_7 the amount carried from origin II to destination III and so on as indicated in the following table:

Destination

Origin	I	II	III	IV
I	x_1	x_2	x_3	x_4
II	x_5	x_6	x_7	x_8
III	x_9	x_{10}	x_{11}	x_{12}

The problem can then be formulated as follows:

Minimize $3.6x_1 + 8.0x_2 + 8.4x_3 + 9.6x_4 + 3.6x_5 + 4.8x_6 + 14.8x_7 +$

$$3.2x_8 + 3.2x_9 + 6.4x_{10} + 8.8x_{11} + 9.6x_{12}$$

Subject to

$$
\begin{array}{ll}
x_1 + x_2 + x_3 + x_4 & = 500 \\
\quad x_5 + x_6 + x_7 + x_8 & = 250 \\
\quad\quad x_9 + x_{10} + x_{11} + x_{12} & = 400 \\
x_1 \qquad + x_5 \qquad + x_9 & = 300 \\
\quad x_2 \qquad + x_6 \qquad + x_{10} & = 400 \\
\quad\quad x_3 \qquad + x_7 \qquad + x_{11} & = 250 \\
\quad\quad\quad x_4 \qquad + x_8 \qquad + x_{12} & = 200
\end{array}
$$

and the usual non-negativity constraints i.e. $x_1, x_2, \ldots x_{12} \geqslant 0$.

In this formulation the objective function denotes the sum of the costs of transporting x_1 tons of the product at \$3.6/ton + x_2 tons at \$8.0/ton + ..., etc., the first three equality constraints indicate the amounts carried from each origin and the last four the totals supplied to each destination. The constraints are laid out in this form so that their relationship with the tabulation of the data in the manner below, which is appropriate for input into the computer package, can be seen.

Constraint	\multicolumn{12}{c}{Route}	Relation-ship	tons

Constraint	1	2	3	4	5	6	7	8	9	10	11	12	Relation-ship	tons
Origin I	1	1	1	1	0	0	0	0	0	0	0	0	=	500
Origin II	0	0	0	0	1	1	1	1	0	0	0	0	=	250
Origin III	0	0	0	0	0	0	0	0	1	1	1	1	=	400
Destination I	1	0	0	0	1	0	0	0	1	0	0	0	=	300
Destination II	0	1	0	0	0	1	0	0	0	1	0	0	=	400
Destination III	0	0	1	0	0	0	1	0	0	0	1	0	=	250
Destination IV	0	0	0	1	0	0	0	1	0	0	0	1	=	200
Cost (\$/ton)	3.6	8.0	8.4	9.6	3.6	4.8	14.8	3.2	3.2	6.4	8.8	9.6		

The programme LPCU is then run as follows in a similar manner to chapter 8 and it will be noted that the answer is identical with that of the text. The printout is only briefly annotated here, as a full description and interpretation was provided for the fertilizer example of chapter 8. Since this is a minimization problem, the coefficients of the objective function are not reversed as they were in the fertilizer maximization problem.

```
TYPE JOB NUMBER← MGA182

TYPE PASSWORD
%▒▒▒▒
DATE:   14/03/78   CHANNEL: 3
19-27-31←LPCU
***INTERACTIVE SOLUTION OF LINEAR PROGRAMMING PROBLEMS
VERSION OF 04/02/78
AVAILABLE OPTIONS (FIRST 4 CHARACTERS SIGNIFICANT)
INPUTDATA   LISTDATA    CHANGEDATA   STOREDATA   HELP    SOLVEPROBLEM
INVBASIS    CSENSITIVITY RSENSITIVITY   PICTURE       FINISH  ALLRESULTS


OPTION?←INPUTDATA
IS DATA FROM A SUBFILE?←NO
TYPE NUMBER OF VARIABLES
←12
TYPE NUMBER OF CONSTRAINTS
←7


ENTER MATRIX ROW BY ROW TYPING EVERY ELEMENT SEPARATED BY SPACES
TYPE ROW  1
← 1 1 1 1 0 0 0 0 0 0 0 0
TYPE ROW 2
← 0 0 0 0 1 1 1 1 0 0 0 0
TYPE ROW 3
← 0 0 0 0 0 0 0 0 1 1 1 1
TYPE ROW 4
← 1 0 0 0 1 0 0 0 1 0 0 0
TYPE ROW 5
← 0 1 0 0 0 1 0 0 0 1 0 0
TYPE ROW 6
← 0 0 1 0 0 0 1 0 0 0 1 0
TYPE ROW 7
← 0 0 0 1 0 0 0 1 0 0 0 1
TYPE THE R.H.S.(S) OF CONSTRAINT EQUATIONS
← 500   250   400   300   400   250   200
TYPE CONSTRAINT TYPES, L FOR <=, E FOR =, G FOR > = FOR EACH ROW
← E E E E E E E

TYPE THE COEFFICIENTS OF THE OBJECTIVE FUNCTION.
← 3.6   8.0   8.4   9.6   3.6   4.8   14.8 3.2   3.2   6.4   8.8   9.6
```

OPTION?←<u>PICTURE</u>

Comment
This command tabulates
the data of the problem.

	1	2	3	4	5	6	7	8	9	10	11	12		B
1	1	1	1	1									=	500.0000
2					1	1	1	1					=	250.0000
3									1	1	1	1	=	400.0000
4	1				1				1				=	300.0000
5		1				1				1			=	400.0000
6			1				1				1		=	250.0000
7				1				1				1	=	200.0000

C   • • • • • • • • • • ⑂ •

LIST OF * VALUES:

C(1)	3.6000	C(2)	8.0000	C(3)	8.4000	C(4)	9.6000
C(5)	3.6000	C(6)	4.8000	C(7)	14.8000	C(8)	3.2000
C(9)	3.2000	C(10)	6.4000	C(11)	8.8000	C(12)	9.6000

OPTION?←<u>SOLVEPROBLEM</u>
SOLUTION IS

X1	=	250.000
X3	=	250.000
X15	=	0.000
X9	=	50.000
X8	=	200.000
X6	=	50.000
X10	=	350.000

Comment
X15 is a slack variable required
by the Revised Simplex method
and is ignored, leaving 6 routes used.

OPTIMUM VALUE = 6280.000
DUAL VALUES (SHADOW PRICES) ARE

0.400	=
−1.600	=
0.000	=
3.200	=
6.400	=
8.000	=
4.800	=

OPTION?←<u>FINISH</u>

19-38-16←<u>LOGOUT</u>

CONNECTED FOR	11 MINS
MILL TIME USED	9 SECS
SESSION COST	1.98

Further Reading

The principles of the transportation method were quite fully described in this chapter. Further reading such as chapter 11 of 'Quantitative Approaches to Management' by R.I. Levin and C.A. Kirkpatrick, McGraw-Hill 1978 or chapter 5 of 'Introduction to Management Science', by Cook and Russell, Prentice-Hall, 1981, are probably more useful in providing a slightly different slant than in developing the technique further. An article by D. Klingman and F. Glover entitled 'Network Application in Industry and Government', *AIIE Transactions,* Vol. I, No. 4 (1977), discusses some of the applications of the technique in industry and government.

Both Levin and Kirkpatrick and Cook and Russell discuss a special case of the transportation problem known as the **assignment problem**, which has some applications in practice. As its name implies the technique can be used in such allocation situations as the assignment of salesmen to territories where the aim is to maximize overall sales and estimates of the potential success of each salesman in each territory are available.

ANSWERS TO QUESTIONS

Chapter 2

2.1 $319.1. **2.2** $311.4.

2.3 $i = 8.4471\%$ [Rearrange the formula $A = P(1+i)^n$ to make $(1+i)$ the subject: $(1+i) = \sqrt[n]{(A/P)}$.]

2.4 $163.7. **2.5** $6108.8

2.6

Year	Payment
1	700
2	300
3	200

2.7 (i)

Year	Payment	Discount factor $i = 8\%$	Present value
1	700	0.9259	648.1
2	300	0.8573	257.2
3	200	0.7938	158.8
			1064.1

   (ii) Yes. For a payment of $1000 you are obtaining something which has an equivalent preset value, to you, of $1064.1.

2.8 (i)

Year	Payment	Discount factor $i = 8\%$	Present value
1	200	0.9259	185.2
2	300	0.8573	257.2
3	700	0.7938	555.7
			998.1

PV = $998.1.

   (ii) The difference arises because the cash sums have accrued in a different sequence and hence their present values are different.

2.9 (i) $100 × 6.1446 = $614.46. (ii) The discount rate would be only about 5½%, i.e. about half way between the factor for 5% (7.7217) and that for 6% (7.3601). (iii) It would be good policy to sell, bad policy to buy.

2.10 (i) $300 × (4.3295 − 0.9524) = $300 × 3.3771 = $1013.1
(ii) $300 × (6.4632 − 3.5460) = $300 × 2.9172 = $875.2
(iii) $300 × (8.3064 − 5.7864) = $300 × 2.52 = $756

2.11 (i) The flow of payments of cash and receipts of cash in defined amounts and at defined times. (ii) It should be ignored as irrelevant to a cash flow forecast. Entries made against depreciation in the financial accounts are not payments made in cash. A cash flow statement shows the amount paid for the machine when it is purchased, any operating, maintenance and repair costs during its life and the amount (if any) received for it when it is sold; together with the times when these payments are actually made or received in cash.

2.12

Time	0	1	2	3	4
Initial cost	−10000				
Running expenses		−5000	−5000	−5000	−5000
Cash receipts		+3000	+5000	+7000	+9000
NCF	−10000	−2000	0	+2000	+4000

2.13   (i)

(1)	(2)	(3)	(4)
0	−1500	1.0000	−1500.0
1	+ 600	0.9346	560.8
2	+ 300	0.8734	262.0
3	+ 800	0.8163	653.0
	+ 200		− 24.2

(ii) It is negative.   (iii) He should not accept.

2.14

Time (in years)	Net cash flow in $
0	−25000
1	+10000
2	+ 7000
3	+ 7000
4	+ 7000

2.15   (i)

Year	NCF in $	Discount factor $i = 10\%$	Present value in $
0	−25000	1.0000	−25000
1	+10000	0.9091	+ 9091
2	+ 7000 ⎫	3.1699	
3	+ 7000 ⎬	−0.9091	
4	+ 7000 ⎭	2.2608	+15825.6
Total	+ 6000	NPV = −	83.4

(ii) On this forecast the investment is unprofitable as the NPV is negative (therefore the rate of return is less than the cost of capital).

2.16

Time	0	1	2	3	4
Training etc.	−65				
Salaries		−40	−40	−40	−40
Commissions		−12.5	−25	−25	−25
Cost of goods		−50	−100	−100	−100
Sales income		+100	+200	+200	+200
NCF (in $'000)	−65	−2.5	+ 35	+ 35	+ 35

2.17

Year	NCF in $	Discount factor $i = 12\%$	Present value in $
0	−65000	1.0000	−65000
1	−2500	0.8929	−2232.3
2	+35000⎫	3.0374	
3	+35000⎬	−0.8929	
4	+35000⎭	2.1445	75057.5
		NPV =	+ 7825.2

The NPV is positive, so on this estimate the project will be profitable if it lasts 4 years.

2.18

(1)	(2)	(3)	(4)
1	−0.5	0.9009	−0.45045
2	−0.4	0.8116	−0.32464
3	+1.2	0.7312	+0.87744
	+0.3		+0.10235

NPV = $102,350 and is positive. On these estimates the project will be profitable.

2.19

Time	0	0.5	1	1.5	2	2.5
NCF	+3000	−1200		−1200		−1200

2.20
$$NPV = 3000 - \frac{1200}{1.12^{0.5}} - \frac{1200}{1.12^{1.5}} - \frac{1200}{1.12^{2.5}}$$

$$= 3000 - \frac{1}{1.12^{0.5}}\left[1200 - \frac{1200}{1.12} - \frac{1200}{1.12^2}\right]$$

$$= 3000 - \frac{3228.1}{1.12^{0.5}} = -\$50.3$$

As NPV is negative, the rate of interest the man would be paying if he accepted the offer is greater than 12%. Thus he would be better off borrowing from his bank.

Chapter 3

3.1 Zero. **3.2** (ii) $i = 10\%$. Because, when discounted at 10%, the NPV of the project = $0.

3.3
$$d = -a_0/a' = 2.0/0.6 = 3.3333$$

3.4 (i) $i_1 = 15\%$ and $i_2 = 16\%$ ($d = 3.3333$ and the period of the annuity is 5 years. In table 2, column 5, we find the factors 3.3522 in row 15 and 3.2743 in row 16.) (ii) They are the two rates which straddle the actual DCF rate of the investment. In the problem under review, this means that the DCF rate is greater than 15% but less than 16%.

3.5 DCF rate = 15.2%. (IRR $= 15 + \frac{3.3522 - 3.3333}{3.3522 - 3.2743} = 15 + \frac{0.0189}{0.0779}$

$$= 15 + 0.243 = 15.243\%)$$

3.6   12.72% (The investment represents an annuity of $1.2 million/annum, for a period of 5 years. $d = 4.25/1.2 = 3.5417$. $i_1 = 12\%$. $d_1 = 3.6048$. $i_2 = 13\%$. $d_2 = 3.5172$).

3.7 $4,435,000 (to nearest thousand). The board of company B could therefore have obtained a further $185,000 on the price that they were asking. (Let x be the sum in $m that company A was prepared to pay. The discount factor for a 5-year annuity at 11% is given by the tables as 3.6959. Thus, $x - (1.2 \times 3.6959) = 0$ i.e. $x = 1.2 \times 3.6959 = 4.435$)

3.8   (i)

Time	0	1	2	3
NCF	−1500	300	800	600

(ii) 6% or 7%. (average annual return $= \dfrac{300 + 800 + 600}{3} = \dfrac{1700}{3}$

$$= 566.7$$

Therefore $d = 1500/566.7 = 2.647$

In table 2, column 3, the figure in row 6 is 2.6730, that in row 7 is 2.6243. Either 6% or 7% would serve as a starting rate).

· 3.9   IRR = 5.96%. (With $i_1 = 6\%$, $NPV_1 = -\$1.22$. IRR is, clearly, very slightly less than 6%. With $i_2 = 5\%$, $NPV_2 = +\$29.60$. Applying formula 2, for $i_1 > i_2$, we arrive at IRR $= 5 + 29.60/30.82 = 5.96\%$.)

3.10   (i)

Time (in years)	0	1	2	3	4
NCF (in $'000)	−120	30	40	50	60

(ii) 18% would be a good starting rate.

3.11   16.3% (With $i_1 = 18\%$, $NPV_1 = -\$4469$. With $i_2 = 16\%$, $NPV_2 = +\$764$. Using formula 2, IRR $= 16 + 1528/5233 = 16.292$)

3.12   (i)

Time (in years)	0	1	2	3	4
NCF (in $m)	−2.0	0.2	0.9	0.9	1.2

(ii)   22% would be good starting rate.

3.13   17.8% (With $i_1 = 22\%$, $NPV_1 = -\$0.1940$. With $i_2 = 16\%$, $NPV_2 = +\$0.0807$. Using formula 2, IRR $= 16 + 6 \times 0.0807/0.2747 = 17.763$)

3.14

Time	0	1	2	3	4
NCF	−0.5	0	0	0.037	0.8

$(a_3 = 0.4 - [0.2 \times (1.12)^2] - [0.1 \times (1.12)] = 0.4 - 0.251 - 0.112 = 0.037)$

3.15   IRR = 13.9%

3.16   (i)

Time in years	0	0.5	1	1.5	2	2.5
NCF in $	−30000	5000		10000		20000

(ii) 8.4% (with $i_1 = 10\%$, $NPV_1 = -30000 + 30619/1.049 = -\$811$. With $i_2 = 8\%$, $NPV_2 = -30000 + 31405/1.039 = \$226$. IRR $= 8 + 2 \times 226/1037 = 8.4359$)

3.17

Time	0	0.5	1.5	2.5	3.5
NCF	−6000	+2000	+2000	+2000	+2000

3.18   (i) Yes. With $i = 12\%$, NPV $= -6000 + \dfrac{1}{(1.12)^{0.5}}[2000 + (2000 \times 2.4018)]$ $= \$428.8$. As this is positive, IRR must exceed 12%. (ii) 16.4% (with $i_2 = 18\%$, $NPV_2 = -\$155.6$).

3.19   Project B has a higher IRR than project A because its return is earned at an initially higher rate. However the duration of project B is less. Although project A is not earning at such a high rate as project B, its total profit over the life of the project is greater because it continues for longer.

3.20   The shop-building project is not acceptable because both the IRR and the

NPV are lower for this project than for either of the other two. As between the office-building and the house-building projects, the former has a higher NPV because it is generally a larger project involving the investment of greater sums of money, though its rate of return on this money is less than it would be for house-building.

Chapter 4

4.1 For outright purchase, NPV $= -\$10{,}000$. The proposed leasing arrangement may be compared to a 10 year annuity of $-\$1500$/annum with $i = 10\%$/annum. NPV $= -1500 \times 6.1446 = -\$9217$. On this basis, it is less costly to lease than to buy outright.

4.2 In this case the NPV of the leasing arrangement would be $-[1500 + (1500 \times 5.7590)] = -\$10139$. In these conditions it would be more costly to lease than to buy outright.

4.3

Time in years	0	1	2	3	4
Costs in $					
(i) Purchase	−10000				+2000
(ii) HP	− 4000	−3500	−3500		+2000
(iii) Lease	− 2400	−2400	−2400	−2400	

4.4 (i) NPV $= -10000 + (2000 \times 0.6355) = -10000 + 1271 = -\$8729$. (ii) NPV $= -4000 - (3500 \times 1.6901) + (2000 \times 0.6355) = -4000 - 5915 + 1271 = -\$8644$. (iii) NPV $= 2400 (2400 \times 2.4018) = 2400 - 5764 = -\$8164$. On this analysis, leasing is the cheapest method of financing.

4.5

Time in years	0	0.5	1	1.5	2	2.5	3	3.5	4
Costs in $'000									
(i) Purchase	490		−10		−10		−10		+120
Lease		−120		−120		−120		−120	

4.6 (i) NPV $= -490000 - (10000 \times 2.5313) + (120000 \times 0.7084) = -490000 - 25313 + 85008 = -\$430{,}305$
(ii)

$$NPV = -120000 \left[\frac{1}{(1.09)^{0.5}} + \frac{1}{(1.09)^{1.5}} + \frac{1}{(1.09)^{2.5}} + \frac{1}{(1.09)^{3.5}} \right]$$

$$= -\frac{120000}{(1.09)^{0.5}} (1 + 2.5313) = -\$405885$$

Leasing is the more economical alternative in PV terms.

4.7 If $i = 11\%$/annum, the case to the shipping company for the sale and leaseback agreement is as follows: NPV $= 600000 - (100000 \times 5.8892) = \$11080$. With no sale and leaseback (presuming that the shipping company can raise its cash requirements in some other way at 11%/annum), NPV $= 50000 \times 0.3522 = \$17{,}610$. This is the present value of the $50,000 that the ship would be worth to the company at the end of the 10 year period if it retained ownership. In the circumstances, sale and leaseback would be a more expensive method of raising cash.

4.8

Time in years	0	1	2	3	4	5
NCF in $'000	−600	+ 100	+ 100	+100	+100	+100

Time in years	6	7	8	9	10
NCF in $'000	+100	+ 100	+ 100	+100	+150

DCF rate = 11.26%

4.9

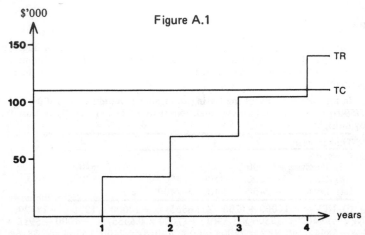

Figure A.1

4.10   Yes.   **4.11**   NPV = − $3691. In fact the DCF rate of this project, if it lasts 4 years, is about 10.4%. If the company's cost of capital is 12% it will lose money.

4.12

Time	0	0.5	1.5	2.5	3.5	4.5
Shopfitting costs in $'000	−16					
Staff etc. costs in $'000		−8	−10	−10	−10	−10
Direct costs in $'000		−24	−28	−32	−36	−40
Total costs in $'000	−16	−32	−38	−42	−46	−50
Revenues in $'000		36	42	48	54	60
NCF in $'000	−16	4	4	6	8	10

4.13   The project will not be accepted as the pay-back period is greater than three years.

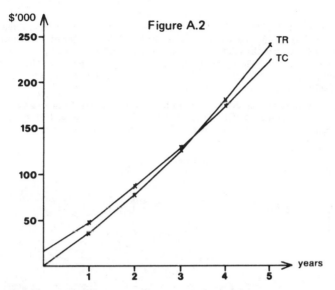

Figure A.2

4.14 $4000.   This indicates that, if the forecast figures are accurate, the project would be profitable even at the high cost of capital required in the question. The result, it is interesting to note, differs from that obtained by application of the pay-back method.

4.15   Break-even chart sketched herewith for guidance. TR = total revenue. TC = total costs. TCC = total craftsman costs. TDC = total direct costs. OH = overhead costs.

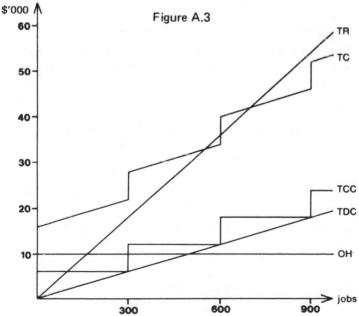

Figure A.3

4.16 (i) Two, at (550,33) and (700,42) respectively. (ii) Two at the first, three at the second. (iii) 550 and 700. The operation is profitable if the number of jobs/annum is greater than 550 but less than 600, after which a third craftsman has to be engaged to handle the extra work. The operation again becomes profitable when the number of jobs/annum exceeds 700. (iv) Costs = revenues = $33,000 at the first break-even point, $42,000 at the second break-even point.

4.17 Break-even point is achieved with production of 500 transformers a year. Graph sketched for guidance. TR = total revenues. TC = total costs. TMC = total material costs. TLC = total labour costs. OH = overheads and machines.

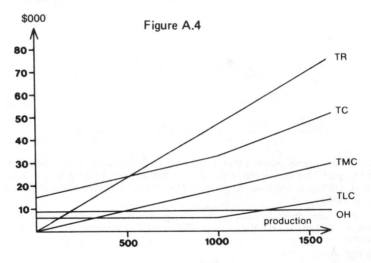

Figure A.4

4.18 (i) Loss of $6,000. (ii) Profit of $12,000. (iii) Profit of $24,000.

4.19 New break-even point is at production level of $833\frac{1}{3}$ transformers/annum.

4.20 3000 units (i.e. total annual costs $96,000 ÷ profit/order gained of $32).

Chapter 5

5.1 In this context the 'optimal life' of an asset is that period of ownership from the time the asset is acquired to the time it should be replaced by another identical asset that results in least costs to the owner.

Time in years	1	2	3	4	5	6	7
Operating costs ($)	200	300	600	1000	1500	2000	3500
Depreciation ($)	5000	1000	1000	1000	500	500	0
Net costs flow ($)	5200	1300	1600	2000	2000	2500	3500

5.3

(1) Year	(2) Costs flow in $	(3) Total costs in $	(4) Av. annual cost (3) ÷ (1)
1	5200	5200	5200
2	1300	6500	3250
3	1600	8100	2700
4	2000	10100	2525
5	2000	12100	2420
6	2500	14600	2433
7	3500	(calculations unnecessary after year 6)	

The optimal life of this type of lathe with this costs flow is 5 years, when annual costs average $2420.

5.4

Time in years	Costs flow in $	Discount factor $i = 10\%$	PV in $	Total PV in $	Repl. factor $i = 10\%$	NPV of repl. cycle in $
1	5200	0.9091	4727.3	4727.3	11.0000	52000.3
2	1300	0.8264	1074.3	5801.6	5.7619	33428.2
3	1600	0.7513	1202.1	7003.7	4.0211	28162.6
4	2000	0.6830	1366.0	8369.7	3.1547	26403.9
5	2000	0.6209	1241.8	9611.5	2.6380	25355.1
6	2500	0.5645	1411.2	11022.7	2.2961	25309.2
7	3500	0.5132	1796.2	12818.9	2.0541	26331.3

By this method the optimal life is found to be 6 years. (In question 3, with no discounting, it was 5 years.)

5.5 (i) It represents the NPV of the infinite chain of replacements: namely, the sum of money that would have to be invested now (at the appropriate rate of return = cost of capital) to meet all depreciation and operating costs of this asset and its replacements, assuming it is always replaced at equal intervals of time by the same type of asset having the same costs flow.

(ii) The result obtained by the method of section A is simply the average cost/annum, ignoring the time value of money, when the asset is used for a given number of years before replacement.

5.6

Year	Costs flow in $	Discount factor $i = 10\%$	PV in $	Total PV in $	Replacement factor	NPV of repl. cycle in $
1	5500	0.9091	5000.1	5000.1	11.0000	55001.1
2	1800	0.8264	1487.5	6487.6	5.7619	37380.9
3	1200	0.7513	901.6	7389.2	4.0211	29712.7
4	800	0.6830	546.4	7935.6	3.1547	25034.4
5	1500	0.6209	931.4	8867.0	2.6380	23391.1
6	2500	0.5645	1411.3	10278.3	2.2961	23600.0

The most economical replacement cycle for the type B lathe is 5 years and its NPV is $23,391 which makes it cheaper than type A (6 years but $25,309).

5.7

(1)	(2)	(3)	(4)	(5)	(6)	(7)	(8)
1	1300	0.9091	1181.8	1181.8	23391.1	21264.9	22446.7
2	1600	0.8264	1322.2	2504.0	23391.1	19330.4	21834.4
3	2000	0.7513	1502.6	4006.6	23391.1	17573.7	21580.3
4	2000	0.6830	1366.0	5372.6	23391.1	15976.1	21348.7
5	2500	0.6209	1522.3	6924.9	23391.1	14523.5	21448.4

The company should continue to operate its existing lathe for another 4 years.

5.8

(1)	(2)	(3)	(4)	(5)	(6)	(7)	(8)
1	2000	0.9091	1818.2	1818.2	23391.1	21264.9	23083.1
2	2000	0.8264	1652.8	3471.0	23391.1	19330.4	22801.4
3	2500	0.7513	1878.3	5349.3	23391.1	17573.7	22923.0

The existing lathe should be retained for a further two years.

5.9

(1)	(2)	(3)	(4)	(5)	(6)	(7)
1	1600	0.8929	1428.6	1428.6	9.3333	13333.6
2	200	0.7972	159.4	1588.0	4.9308	7830.1
3	300	0.7118	213.5	1801.5	3.4696	6250.5
4	400	0.6355	254.2	2055.8	2.7436	5640.3
5	600	0.5674	340.4	2396.1	2.3117	5539.1
6	1000	0.5066	506.6	2902.7	2.0269	5883.5

A new well should therefore be drilled every five years, when minimum NPV is $5,539,100.

5.10 The replacement cycle calculation shows that on the new site an oilwell should be drilled every 4 years, when minimum NPV is $2,232,500. However, if the company is to move now it will have to pay an additional $1,500,000 + 500,000/1.12 in PV terms. Thus the total NPV of moving to the new site is 2,232,500 + 1,500,000 + 446,500 = $4,179,000. This is less than the NPV of the replacement chain if operations are to be continued in the existing oilfield, so the move is worthwhile.

5.11

(1)	(2)	(3)	(4)	(5)	(6)	(7)	(8)
1	300	0.8929	267.9	267.9	4179.0	3731.4	3999.3
2	400	0.7972	318.9	586.8	4179.0	3331.5	3918.3
3	600	0.7118	427.1	1013.9	4179.0	2974.6	3988.5

It can be seen from the table that it is cheapest for the company to continue working the existing field for a further two years.

5.12 month $1 = 30$
month $2 = 48$ $(45 + 3)$
month $3 = 84.3$ $(75 + 4.5 + 4.8)$
month $4 = 128.1$ $(105 + 7.5 + 7.2 + 8.4)$
month $5 = 92.9$ $(45 + 10.5 + 12 + 12.6 + 12.8)$
month $6 = 70.9$ $(4.5 + 16.8 + 21.1 + 19.2 + 9.3)$

5.13 (i) 3.3 months. (ii) $\bar{u}$. In this case $\bar{u} = (1 \times 0.1) + (2 \times 0.15) + (3 \times 0.25) + (4 \times 0.35) + (5 \times 0.15) = 0.1 + 0.3 + 0.75 + 1.4 + 0.75 = 3.3$

5.14 (i) At the start the number of components requiring replacement fluctuates from one time period to the next but these fluctuations diminish over time until finally a stage is reached, called the 'steady state', in which the number requiring replacement is the same in each time period.
(ii)   91. $(u_0/\bar{u} = 300/3.3 = 90.9)$

5.15   (i) A policy of replacing each individual component at the time when it fails.
(ii) $636.4 (i.e. 300/3.3 × 7)

5.16   (i) A policy of replacing all components together, whether they have failed
or not.   (ii) 300 × 4 = $1200

5.17   (i) A policy of replacing all components in groups, with individual replacement
of any that fail between group replacements.
(ii)

Cycle length in months	Average cost/cycle
1	1200
2	705
3	582
4	584

(iii) The average cost of the optimal mixed strategy, with cycle length 3 months, is
$582 per month. This compares with a cost of $636 per month, as calculated in
question 15, for a strategy of individual replacement.

5.18   (i) Average tire life = (0.15 × 10,000) + (0.25 × 20,000) + (0.4 × 30,000) +
(0.2 × 40,000) = 26,500 miles.
(ii) Average cost/tire-mile = 200/26,500 = $0.00755.
(iii) Average cost/truck-mile = 0.00755 × 16 = $0.1208.

5.19   Mileage   Expected number of tire failures
          10000   2.4   (16 × 0.15)
          20000   4.36   (16 × 0.25 + 2.4 × 0.15)
          30000   7.654   (16 × 0.4 + 2.4 × 0.25 + 4.36 × 0.15)
          40000   6.3981 (16 × 0.2 + 2.4 × 0.4 + 4.36 × 0.25 + 7.654 ×0.15)
          50000   5.0972 (2.4 × 0.2 + 4.36 × 0.4 +7.654 × 0.25 + 6.3981 × 0.15)

5.20   Average replacement cost/10000 mile unit for a mixed strategy is shown in the
following table for replacement cycles of different lengths.

Replacement cycle (miles)	Average cost/cycle $	Average cost/ truck-mile $
10000	1600	0.16
20000	1040	0.104
30000	984	0.0984
40000	1120.7	0.112

'Optimal t' for a mixed replacement strategy is at 30000 miles and its average cost/
truck-mile of $0.0984 compares with an average cost/truck-mile of $0.121 for an
individual replacement strategy: a saving of $0.0224/truck-mile.

Chapter 6

6.1   (i) Economic order quantity.   (ii) 1. Demand for the commodity is constant,
continuous and known. 2. There is instantaneous replenishment of stocks.
3. Inventory holding cost per item is proportional to the number of items in stock
and the time for which they are held in stock.

6.2   (i) μ (which in this example represents a rate of issue of 25 units/month).
(ii) 25 × 8 = 200

6.3   100 units.

6.4   (1) In the classical EOQ model the cost/reordering cycle has two elements:
set-up costs (e.g. paperwork, setting up for production run etc.) which are
independent of the size of the order, and stock-holding costs (storage space, interest
on money tied up in stock etc.) which vary with the quantity and value of the goods

held in stock and the time for which they are held in stock.   (ii) It is divided by the number of time periods in the replenishment cycle.

6.5   (i) \$4. (ii) \$180 ($b = 3/12 = 1/4, q = 240, t = 240/40 = 6$ where the basic unit of time = 1 month. Inventory holding cost/cycle $= \tfrac{1}{2}bqt = \tfrac{1}{2} \times \tfrac{1}{4} \times 240 \times 6$). (iii) \$184 (set-up cost + inventory holding cost).

(iv) \$30.67 $\left(\dfrac{\text{total inventory cost/reordering cycle}}{\text{duration of cycle}} \right)$

6.6   At intervals of one thirtieth of a year (i.e. 1.6 weeks if a working year is taken as 50 weeks). ($a = 600, b = 900, \mu = 1200$. By formula (C1),

$$T = \sqrt{\frac{2a}{b\mu}} = \sqrt{\left(\frac{2 \times 600}{900 \times 1200}\right)} = \sqrt{\frac{1}{900}} = \frac{1}{30}$$

6.7   40 units. $Q = \mu T = 1200/30$. Cross-checking applying formula (C2),

$$Q = \sqrt{\left(\frac{2a\mu}{b}\right)} = \sqrt{\left(\frac{2 \times 600 \times 1200}{900}\right)} = \sqrt{1600}$$

6.8   \$36,000/annum. By formula (C1), $C = \sqrt{2ab\mu} = \sqrt{(2 \times 600 \times 900 \times 1200)}$ Cross-checking applying formula (B1),

$$C = \frac{a}{T} + \tfrac{1}{2}b\mu T = (600 \times 30) + \frac{900 \times 1200}{2 \times 30}$$

6.9 $\mu = 27$ million/annum = 2.25 million/month. $l = 1$ month. $Q' = l\mu = 2\,250\,000$.

6.10 $Q = 1\,500\,000$. $T = Q/\mu = \tfrac{2}{3}$ month (20 days). At the time each order is initiated there has to be 30 days' supply (Q') in stock or in the pipeline. But the optimal reordering quantity (Q) is sufficient for only 20 days. Therefore $Q' > Q$. What this means in practice is that at the time each new order is placed there must be 10 days' stock in hand and a previous order already 20 days in the pipeline.

6.11   (i) $t' = q/k = 1800/300 = 6$ hours.
          (ii) $\mu = 2400/48 = 50$ (in items/hour).
               $q' = t'(k - \mu) = 6(300 - 50) = 1500$ items.
          (iii) $t = q/\mu = 1800/50 = 36$ hours.

6.12   \$10.4 [$a = 5$ (in \$), $b = 0.005$ (in \$/item/week), $k = 300 \times 48$ (in items/week), $\mu = 2400$ (in items/week), $t = 3/4$ (in weeks). Then proceed by formula (E3)].

6.13 $Q = 2400$ [by formula (E5)]. $C = \$10$ [by formula (E6)] (as compared with \$10.4 for the existing strategy.

6.14 $a = 140$ (in \$), $b = 14$ (in \$/car/week), $\mu = 150$ (in cars/week), $z = 6$ (in \$1 car out of stock/week). Therefore $Q = 100$ [by formula (F4)].

6.15 $C = \$420$/week [by formula (F5)] = \$21,000/annum.

6.16 $a = 8$ (in \$), $b = 0.05$ (in \$/bottle/day), $\mu = 25$ (in bottles/day), $z = 0.2$ (in \$/bottle out of stock/day). Therefore $Q = 100$, $S = 80$ [by formulae (F4) and (F6)]. Therefore the maximum number out of stock in each regular cycle ($Q - S$) is 20.

6.17 $T = Q/\mu = 100/25 = 4$ days. The duration of the stockout is $(Q - S)/\mu = 20/25 = 4/5$ day.

6.18 $Q = 1200$

6.19   The respective calculations are as follows: $Q = 1200$, $C = \$1600$, $q_1 = 2500$,

c_1 = \$1584.5, q_2 = 5000, c_2 = \$1561, q_3 = 10,000, c_3 = \$1,968. It is definitely not worth his while to manufacture in larger batches than 5000. There is a saving of about \$40/annum in his total inventory costs if he manufactures in batches of 5000: whether it is worth committing himself to 50 months' stock to obtain such a relatively small saving, is another matter.

6.20   Minimum acceptable discount is 12½%, corresponding to a maximum price per tire of \$7⅞. (With his present reordering policy on this size of tire the retailer's total purchase and inventory cost/month is \$280. If he orders in batches of 112 tires every 4 months the maximum price/tire he should pay will be that sum which gives him the same total monthly cost as at present. Thus applying formula (G1), the *maximum* value for p_1 is given by

$$280 = \frac{14 \times 28}{112} + \frac{1 \times 112}{2} + 28p_1$$

whence p_1 = 7⅞.)

Chapter 7

7.1   (i) (a) Activities A, B, C and E are sequential, activities A, D, E are sequential, activity D is concurrent with the two sequential activities B and C. (b) Activity A is labelled (1, 2), activity C is labelled (3, 4) and activity D is labelled (2, 4). (ii) An event has no duration. It is the moment in time when an activity begins or ends.

7.2   (i)

Activity	IPA
A	–
B	A
C	B
D	B
E	A
F	E
G	C,F
H	D,G

(ii) After completion of activity A, activities B and E can begin. Activities C and D both depend on the completion of activity B; activity F on that of activity E. Activity G depends on the completion of both activities C and F, activity H on that of activities D and G. Activity A commences the network and activity H completes it but the network itself does not specify whether these are real or artificial activities.

7.3

Activity	Description	IPA
A	Drive into garage	–
B	Fill tank	A
C	Check oil	A
D	Check oil	C
E	Adjust tire pressures	A
F	Pay for gas and oil	B,D
G	Drive off	E,F

7.4

Figure A.5

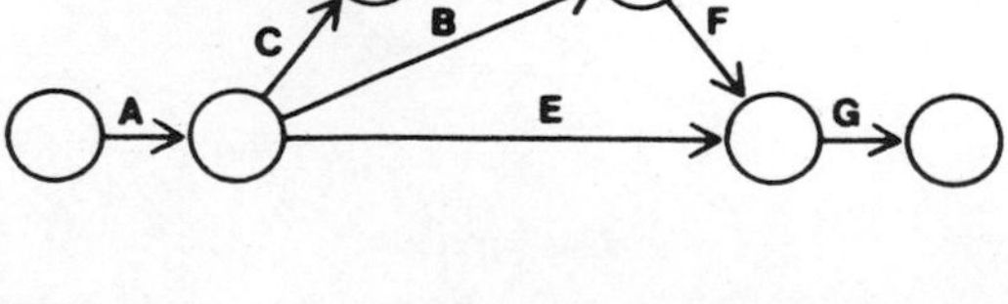

7.5   (i) Activity E occurs twice, at (4,5) and (8,3). (ii) Activities H and K are
danglers. (iii) Activities I, E and G form a loop. In these respects the network has to
be replanned. Further; (iv) In the case of activity F the head of the arrow should be
to the right of its tail and the number of the head event greater than that of the tail
event. However, in this case there is no *planning* error, merely a *drawing* error. The
relevant part of the network should have been drawn thus:

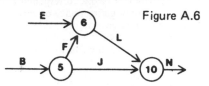

Figure A.6

7.6

Activity	Description	IPA
A	Fill kettle and bring to boil	–
B	Place tea in teapot	–
C	Pour boiling water on tea in teapot and stir	A,B
D	Pour milk in cup	–
E	Pour tea on milk in cup	C,D
F	Put sugar in tea and stir	E

Activities C and E may require dummies because they have more than one IPA. None
of the others will need a dummy, though a lead activity will be needed as an IPA to A,
B and D.

7.7

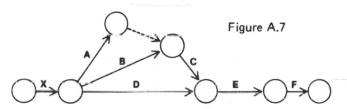

Figure A.7

Note: There are other equally correct ways to draw this network.

7.8   (i) Friday. (ii) May 10. (iii) There is no corresponding project day. May 13 is
a Saturday and the numbering of this project calendar implies that Saturday is not
normally a working day in the project.

7.9   Completion of the project requires 29 units of project time. (In this question
we did not specify what these units are e.g. minutes, hours, days, weeks etc. – nor
how they relate to calendar time.)

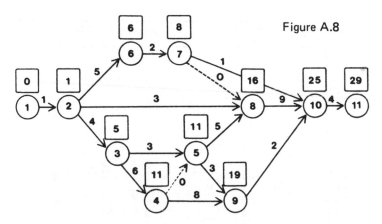

Figure A.8

7.10

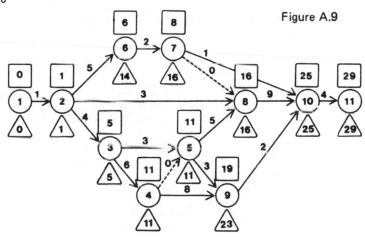

Figure A.9

7.11 Total float of $(6,7) = 16 - 6 - 2 = 8$
Total float of $(3,4) = 11 - 5 - 6 = 0$
Total float of $(3,5) = 11 - 5 - 3 = 3$
Total float of $(8,10) = 25 - 16 - 9 = 0$
All answers are given in units of project time.

7.12

Activity	Earliest starting time	Duration	Total float
(1,2)	0	1	0
(2,3)	1	4	0
(2,6)	1	5	8
(2,8)	1	3	12
(3,4)	5	6	0
(3,5)	5	3	3
(4,5)	11	0	0
(4,9)	11	8	4
(5,8)	11	5	0
(5,9)	11	3	9
(6,7)	6	2	8
(7,8)	8	0	8
(7,10)	8	1	16
(8,10)	16	9	0
(9,10)	19	2	4
(10,11)	25	4	0

7.13   The activities which lie on the critical path are: (1,2) (2,3) (3,4) (4,5) (5,8) (8,10) (10,11)

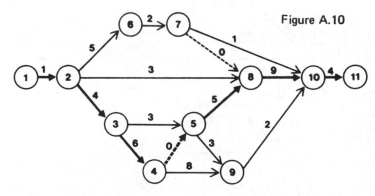

Figure A.10

7.14   A model answer should have stressed the following three points: (i) That the time taken to execute the sequential activities on the critical path is the minimum time in which the project can be completed. (ii) That any delay in completing the total chain of sequential activities which constitute the critical path will represent a corresponding delay in the completion of the project as a whole. (iii) That the time required for the project as a whole can only be reduced by shortening the duration of those activities which lie on its critical path.

7.15   (i) Free float is defined as the maximum time that completion of an activity can be delayed, without delaying the start of any subsequent activity on the same path. (ii) not necessarily. Delay in completing such an activity is likely to lead to corresponding delays in the completion of all subsequent activities on the same path (unless the time lost can be recovered by completing them more quickly) but, if that path is not the critical path, it need not delay the completion of the project as a whole.

7.16

Activity	Free float
(1,2)	0
(2,3)	0
(2,6)	0
(2,8)	12
(3,4)	0
(3,5)	3
(4,5)	0
(4,9)	0
(5,8)	0
(5,9)	5
(6,7)	0
(7,8)	8
(7,10)	16
(8,10)	0
(9,10)	4
(10,11)	0

7.17 You should have begun by working out EET's, LET's and floats so as to arrive at the following result.

Table of floats

Activity	Duration	TF	FF
(1,2)	2	0	0
(2,3)	4	0	0
(2,4)	7	2	0
(3,4)	3	2	0
(3,5)	8	0	0
(4,5)	3	2	2
(5,6)	5	0	0

Figure A.11

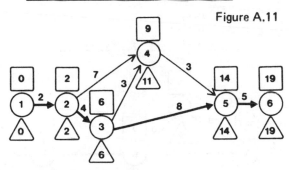

The answers to the specific questions are: (i) no change; (ii) no change; (iii) the start of activity (4,5) is delayed by 1 week but there is no effect on its sequential activity, on the line of the critical path or on the completion date of the project as a whole; (iv) starting date of activity (5,6) and completion of project brought forward by 1 week, but no change in line of critical path.

7.18   As the original network had only one critical path, and this activity was on it, the completion date of the project as a whole would also be reduced: but not by the full 3 weeks. The new position is as shown below. All activities except (3,5) are now critical and total duration has been reduced from 19 to 17 weeks.

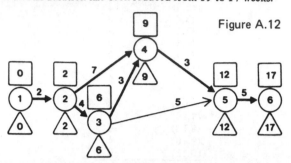

Figure A.12

7.19   This alteration involves a change in logic which means, in this case, that the network has to be redrawn. The effect is that the duration of the project as a whole is unchanged at 17 weeks, but the activities formerly known as (2,3) and (3,4) are no longer on the critical path. The network itself can, of course, be redrawn and renumbered in various ways. One version and its corresponding float table are shown below.

Activity				
Now	Formerly	Duration	TF	FF
(1,2)	(1,2)	2	0	0
(2,3)	(3,4)	3	4	0
(2,4)	(2,3)	4	1	0
(2,5)	(2,4)	7	0	0
(3,5)	–	0	4	4
(4,6)	(3,5)	5	1	1
(5,6)	(4,5)	3	0	0
(6,7)	(5,6)	5	0	0

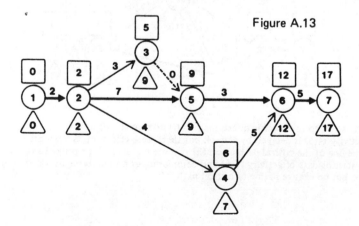

Figure A.13

7.20   **Figure A.14**

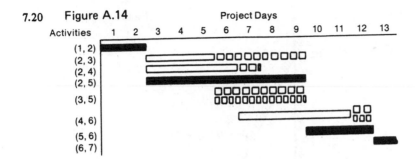

Chapter 8

8.1

Cloth	Material used in metres		Material available in metres
	Design 1	Design 2	
Silk	2	1	32
Cotton	3	4	60
Wool	1½	5	60

8.2   1. The silk constraint: $2x + y \leqslant 32$. 2. The cotton constraint: $3x + 4y \leqslant 60$. 3. The wool constraint: $1\frac{1}{2}x + 5y \leqslant 60$. 4. The non-negativity constraints: $x \geqslant 0$ and $y \geqslant 0$.

8.3   (1) Vitamin A constraint: $15x + 15y \geqslant 5$
        (2) Vitamin B constraint: $14x + 28y \geqslant 7$
        (3) Vitamin C constraint: $50x + 20y \geqslant 10$
Notice that for (1) to (3) the sign is $\geqslant$, not $\leqslant$.
The non-negativity constraints: (4) $x \geqslant 0$ and (5) $y \geqslant 0$.

8.4   (i) The feasible region is that area of the graph that satisfies all the constraints of the problem. All points that are inside it or on its boundaries represent possible solutions of the problem: no point outside its boundaries is a possible solution.
(ii)

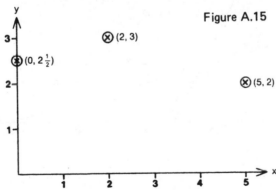

Figure A.15

8.5   (i) $2x + y = 32$. (ii) For $x = 0$, $y \doteqdot 32$. (iii) For $y = 0$, $x = 16$.

8.5(iv)

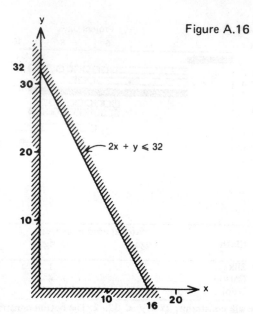

Figure A.16

8.6

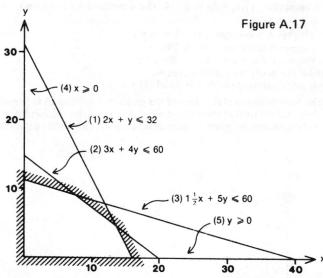

Figure A.17

8.7

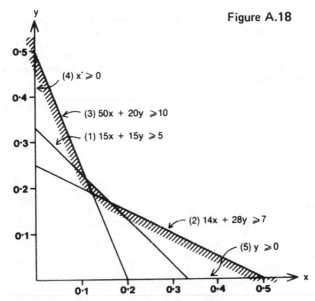

Figure A.18

8.8   (i) OF = x + y. (ii) OF = 5x + 3y. (iii) In each case the OF is to be maximized. (iv) In both cases the tailor is limited (constrained) by the quantities of the different types of cloth that he has in stock. Within those constraints his objective, in the first case, is simply to make as many dresses as he can, whereas in the second case his objective is to make that combination of dresses which (out of all possible combinations) gives him the greatest profit.

8.9   Each point on this graph (if we are prepared to assume that a part-completed dress yields a proportional profit. see last two paragraphs of section C on page 144) shows one combination of the quantities of each design of dress that would yield a total profit of $60. Graphs of the OF corresponding to progressively greater profits than $60 would be parallel to this and progressively further away from the origin.

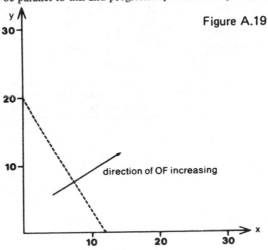

Figure A.19

direction of OF increasing

8.10 The optimal extreme point is D at the intersection of the limits of the silk and cotton constraints with coordinates $(13\tfrac{3}{5}, 4\tfrac{4}{5})$. Rounding this down, we have 13 dresses of design 1 and 4 of design 2, yielding a total profit of $77. (Note: in fact a greater profit ($80) can be made by producing 16 of design 1 and 0 of design 2 (point E). This illustrates the drawback of rounding down in certain problems and the need for a method of integer programming.)

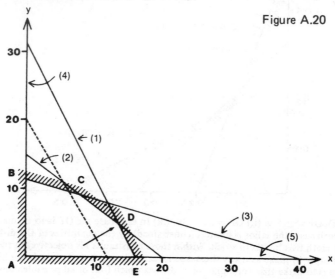

Figure A.20

8.11
(i)

Vitamin	mg/cc of each vitamin Concentrate		Min. requirement of each vitamin in mg/cc of health-drink
	X	Y	
A	15	15	5
B	14	28	7
C	50	20	10
Cost in cents/cc	0.5	0.4	

(ii) OF $=0.5x + 0.4y$ and is to be minimized.

8.12 (i) The optimal extreme point is at the intersection of the boundaries of the vitamin A constraint (1) and the vitamin C constraint (3). This represents the combination which exactly meets the minimum specification for those two vitamins in the final product. The vitamin B content will exceed the minimum specification.

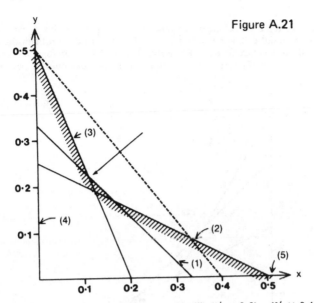

Figure A.21

(ii) $\frac{1}{9}$ cc of concentrate X; $\frac{2}{9}$ cc of concentrate Y. (iii) ($\frac{1}{9}$ × 0.5) + ($\frac{2}{9}$ × 0.4) = 0.1444 cents/cc.

8.13   A sketch shows that the OF is minimized at the extreme point represented by the intersection of the limits of constraints (2) and (3), i.e. $\frac{1}{3} x + \frac{1}{5} y = 2$ and $x + y = 8$. Therefore $x = 3$; $y = 5$; and OF = 15 + 20 = 35.

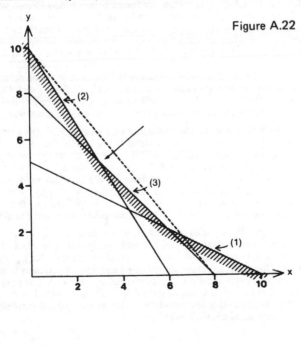

Figure A.22

8.14   See sketch for labelling of extreme points. At point A, $x = 0$, $y = 10$, and the OF = 40. At point C, $x = 6$ $y = 2$ and the OF = 38. (In this problem the OF is to be minimized, so the extreme point B is optimal as the OF is less for the coordinates (values) of x and y at point B than for those at the two neighboring points A and C.)

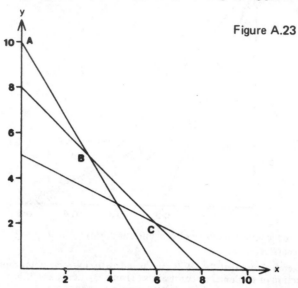

Figure A.23

8.15 (i) The optimal solution was originally found to be at the extreme point represented by the intersection of the silk and cotton constraints, where $x = 13^3/_5$, $y = 4^4/_5$, and we have now assumed that the tailor can make a profit on these fractions. The relevant shadow prices are therefore: (a) for silk, $(14.4 - 13.6) \times 5 + (4.2 - 4.8) \times 3 = \$2.2/\text{meter}$. (b) For cotton, $(13.4 - 13.6) \times 5 + (5.2 - 4.8) \times 3 = \$0.2/\text{meter}$.
(ii) The shadow price for wool is zero because the optimal extreme point is within the boundary of the wool constraint: i.e. if $13^3/_5$ of dress 1 and $4^4/_5$ of dress 2 are made, all the silk and cotton will be used up but there will still be some wool left over, so there would be nothing to gain from buying more wool.

8.16   The tailor would want to buy enough cotton so as to shift the cotton constraint to the right until it met the intersection of the boundaries of constraints (1) and (3)..This point would then become the optimal extreme point. It occurs on the graph (approximately) at (11.8, 8.5). Hence: (i) the tailor would produce 11.8 dresses of design 1 and 8.5 dresses of design 2, (ii) the total profit would then become $(5 \times 11.8) + (3 \times 8.4) = \$84.2$; (iii) where x = 11.8, y = 8.4, the total consumption of cotton is $(3 \times 11.8) + (4 \times 8.4) = 69$ meters. Therefore, as the tailor already has 60 meters in stock, he should purchase an additional 9 meters.

8.17   (i) See sketch. The optimal extreme point would now be at the intersection of the boundaries of constraints (2) and (3), and the optimal quantities of the two concentrates in each cc of tonic would be: $^1/_8$ cc of concentrate X; $^3/_{16}$ cc of concentrate Y. This gives the minimum specified amounts of vitamins B and C and an excess of the minimum specification for vitamin A. Cost/cc of the concentrates in this case = 0.1375 cents, a saving of 0.0069/cc. (ii) There would be no change in the optimal purchasing policy and associated costs, as the optimal extreme point is still at the intersection of constraints (1) and (3).

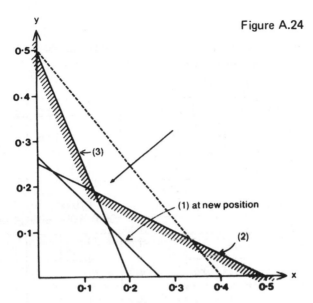

Figure A.24

8.18 The primal problem can be tabulated as follows:

	a	b	c	
x	10	3	6	80
y	3	10	5	50
	80	80	60	

From this, the dual problem can be formulated as:

Maximize $80x + 50y$

subject to $10x + 3y \leqslant 80 \ldots (1)$

$3x + 10y \leqslant 80 \ldots (2)$

$6x + 5y \leqslant 60 \ldots (3)$

$x, y \geqslant 0$

8.19 The optimal extreme point is at the intersection of the boundaries of constraints (1) and (3). For $10x + 3y = 80$; $6x + 5y = 60$; $x = 6\frac{7}{8}$, $y = 3\frac{3}{4}$, and the optimal value of the OF = 737½

8.20 If the RHS of (1) in the dual problem is increased by 1, the new extreme point is $(7\frac{1}{32}, 3\frac{9}{16})$; i.e. the increase in the objective function is $(7\frac{1}{32} - 6\frac{7}{8}) \times 80 + (3\frac{9}{16} - 3\frac{3}{4}) \times 50 = 3\frac{1}{8}$. If the RHS of (3) in the dual problem is increased by 1. the new extreme point is $(6\frac{25}{32}, 4\frac{1}{16})$; i.e. the increase in the objective function is $(6\frac{25}{32} - 6\frac{7}{8}) \times 80 + (4\frac{1}{16} - 3\frac{3}{4}) \times 50 = 8\frac{1}{8}$. Therefore, in the primal problem $a = 3\frac{1}{8}$, $b = 0$, $c = 8\frac{1}{8}$.

Chapter 9

9.1   (i) Table of distances (in miles)   (ii) Costs tableau (in $)
                Distribution centers

		I	II	III	IV
	I	20	40	80	90
Depots	II	20	30	50	50
	III	30	20	30	20

4	8	16	18
4	6	10	10
6	4	6	4

9.2

Costs tableau:

4	8	16	18
4	6	10	10
6	4	6	4

O/D tableau:

	200	100	600	400
500				
600				
200				

9.3

Costs tableau:

4	8	16	18
4	6	10	10
6	4	6	4

O/D tableau:

	200	100	600	400
500	200	100	200	
600			400	200
200				200

9.4

Costs tableau:

	4	8	16	16
0	④	⑧	⑯	18
6	4	6	⑩	⑩
12	6	4	6	④

Note: In this case we started by assigning 0 to source I as its fictitious cost and proceeded from there. If you started by assigning 0 to a different source you should have arrived at fictitious costs for the other sources and destinations which are different from those we have shown, but with the same *relative* differences in each case. Thus, the relative price of one tanker load delivered from source III should be $6 greater than that of one delivered from source II, the relative cost of a tanker load received at destination I should be $12 less than that of one received at destination IV, and so on.

9.5 The initial basic feasible solution is in fact optimal, since the profits are negative on all the unused routes, as shown in the following costs tableau.

Costs tableau:

	4	**8**	**16**	**16**
0	(0) ④	(0) ⑧	(0) ⑯	(−2) 18
6	(−6) 4	(−4) 6	(0) ⑩	(0) ⑩
12	(−14) 6	(−8) 4	(−2) 6	(0) ④

9.6 Total transportation cost for the week is $11,600.

Cell no.	Tanker loads by this route	Transportation cost per tanker load ($)	Total Transportation cost ($)
(1,1)	200	4	800
(1,2)	100	8	800
(1,3)	200	16	3200
(2,3)	400	10	4000
(2,4)	200	10	2000
(3,4)	200	4	800
		Total:	11600

9.7 Inserting $+\theta$ in cell (3,2) we have to adjust the other cells as follows to keep the tableau in balance:

	200	**100**	**600**	**400**
500	200	$100 - \theta$	$200 + \theta$	
600			$400 - \theta$	$200 + \theta$
200		$+\theta$		$200 - \theta$

Not more than 100 tanker loads can be taken from route (1,2) so this is the maximum additional number that can be transferred to route (3,2). The O/D tableau can then be rewritten as follows:

	200	**100**	**600**	**400**
500	200		300	
600			300	300
200		100		100

9.8   (i) No; we have merely achieved an alternative basic feasible solution, which may or may not be optimal. (ii) The next stage is to conduct a test on the costs tableau to establish whether or not this particular basic feasible solution is optimal. If it is not, the whole process must be repeated through as many successive stages as are necessary until a basic feasible solution is found which is optimal.

9.9   (i) 6 routes must be listed ($m + n - 1 = 6$). (ii) When cell (4,1) is filled with 4500, either column 1 or row 4 must be eliminated (not both). Depending on which choice is made, the two possible initial feasible solutions are shown as follows:

	5000	1000
	2500	
		3000
4500	0	

0	5000	1000
	2500	
		3000
4500		

In this case the two versions are essentially the same in respect of loads actually carried: the difference is only in the route which carries zero load. Both solutions are in fact optimal.

9.10   If the instructions given with this question are followed, the initial basic feasible solution is as given below:

Costs tableau:

9	12	9	7	9
7	3	8	7	5
6	5	10	4	13
5	9	6	3	2

O/D tableau:

	4	4	6	2	4
5	2		1	2	
4		4			
2	2	0			
9			5		4

9.11

Costs tableau:

	9	8	9	7	5
0	(9)	12	(9)	(7)	9
5	7	(3)	8	7	5
3	(6)	(5)	10	4	13
3	5	9	(6)	3	(2)

O/D tableau:

	4	4	6	2	4
5	2		1	2	
4		4			
2	2	0			
9			5		4

Two of the routes, (4,1) and (4,4), show a positive profit which is the same on both routes. A decision has to be made to introduce one or other route into the solution. The choice has to be made arbitrarily.

9.12 The amended O/D tableau is shown below, together with the test to determine whether it is optimal.

Costs tableau:

	8	7	9	7	5
0	9	12	(9)	(7)	9
4	7	(3)	8	7	5
2	(6)	(5)	10	4	13
3	(5)	9	(6)	3	(2)

O/D tableau:

	4	4	6	2	4
5			3	2	
4		4			
2	2	0			
9	2		3		4

This solution is shown to be not optimal, and an arbitrary choice has to be made as to whether to introduce route (3,4) or route (4,4) into the solution.

9.13

Costs tableau:

	8	7	9	6	5
0	9	12	(9)	7	9
4	7	(3)	8	7	5
2	(6)	(5)	10	4	13
3	(5)	9	(6)	(3)	(2)

O/D tableau:

	4	4	6	2	4
5			5		
4		4			
2	2	0			
9	2		1	2	4

Notice the existence of degeneracy in that the optimal solution contains one route (3,2) which carries zero load. Furthermore, the unused route (3,4) has zero profit. This means that there exists a situation of multiple optima.

9.14 The tableaux should be modified by introducing a dummy destination with zero transport cost from each source and a demand exactly equal to the excess capacity, so that total demand and total capacity are in balance. The effect should be as shown below:

Costs tableau:

4	8	16	18	0
4	6	10	10	0
6	4	6	4	0

O/D tableau:

	200	100	600	400	100
500					
600					
300					

9.15 The initial basic feasible solution calculated by Vogel's rule and given below is in fact optimal.

	200	100	600	400	100
500	200	100	100		100
600			500	100	
300				300	

This means that source I is required to supply 100 units (i.e. tanker loads in the week, if we treat this as a variation of the example in question 2) less than its capacity. This is the quantity that was allocated to the dummy destination on route (1,5).

9.16   After introducing a fourth dummy source with a capacity of 200 units (i.e. tanker loads in the week, if we treat this as a variation of the example in question 2) we arrive by Vogel's Rule at the following initial basic feasible solution:

Costs tableau: O/D tableau:

4	8	16	18
4	6	10	10
6	4	6	4
0	0	0	0

	200	300	600	400
500	200	300		
600		0	400	200
200				200
200			200	

When tested, this is found to be an optimal solution. The capacity of 200 units from the dummy source IV is allocated to route (4,3), which means that destination III can receive only 400 units out of its total requirement of 600. Note that this is another example of a multiple optima situation.

9.17   If an artificial cost of, say, 100 cents/carton is applied to route (3,3) to ensure that it is not used in the solution, and an artificial cost of, say, −100 cents/ carton is applied to route (2,1) (of which the real cost is 23 cents/carton) to ensure that it is as fully used as the constraints of the problem permit, the amended costs tableau will appear as follows:

12	19	10
−100	7	16
28	17	100
15	35	28

9.18   In the following tables we show the initial basic feasible solution derived by Vogel's Rule which is found also to be optimal, and the calculation of total transport cost for the day, which is found to be $3040.

O/D tableau:

	4500	7500	4000
6000		2000	4000
2500	2500		
3000		3000	
4500	2000	˙2500	

Total Cost calculation:

route no.	Quantity transported (cartons)	Cost per carton (p)	Total cost ($)
(1,2)	2000	19	380
(1,3)	4000	10	400
(2,1)	2500	23	575
(3,2)	3000	17	510
(4,1)	2000	15	300
(4,2)	2500	35	875
			3040

If the choice of route had been completely free the cost of an optimal solution would have been $2050/day. The additional cost in this case results from the requirement not to use route (3,3) and to make the fullest possible use of route (2,1).

9.19

−2.8	−3.5	−4.3	−2.3
−3.0	−3.1	−4.5	−1.7
−2.5	−3.5	−2.0	−4.8

Intermediate tableau
(profits tableau × −1)

2.0	1.3	0.5	2.5
1.8	1.7	0.3	3.1
2.3	1.3	2.8	0.0

Costs tableau
(achieved by adding 4.8 to all cells of inter-mediate tableau)

9.20

(i)   Costs tableau

2.0	1.3	0.5	2.5
1.8	1.7	0.3	3.1
2.3	1.3	2.8	0.0

O/D tableau:

	175	100	75	50
100				
200				
100				

An initial basic feasible solution calculated by Vogel's Rule, and which is also optimal, is shown as follows:

	175	100	75	50
100	50	50		
200	125		75	
100		50		50

(ii) The total profit for the month is found by $(50 \times 2.8) + (50 \times 3.5) + (125 \times 3.0) + (75 \times 4.5) + (50 \times 3.5) + (50 \times 4.8) = \$1442.5$

TABLES

TABLE 1 — Present Value Factors — Individual Payments

Time Periods	1	2	3	4	5	6	7	8
1%	0.9901	0.9803	0.9706	0.9610	0.9515	0.9420	0.9327	0.9235
2%	0.9804	0.9612	0.9423	0.9238	0.9057	0.8880	0.8706	0.8535
3%	0.9709	0.9426	0.9151	0.8885	0.8626	0.8375	0.8131	0.7894
4%	0.9615	0.9246	0.8890	0.8548	0.8219	0.7903	0.7599	0.7307
5%	0.9524	0.9070	0.8638	0.8227	0.7835	0.7462	0.7107	0.6768
6%	0.9434	0.8900	0.8396	0.7921	0.7473	0.7050	0.6651	0.6274
7%	0.9346	0.8734	0.8163	0.7629	0.7130	0.6663	0.6228	0.5820
8%	0.9259	0.8573	0.7938	0.7350	0.6806	0.6302	0.5835	0.5403
9%	0.9174	0.8417	0.7722	0.7084	0.6499	0.5963	0.5470	0.5019
10%	0.9091	0.8264	0.7513	0.6830	0.6209	0.5645	0.5132	0.4665
11%	0.9009	0.8116	0.7312	0.6587	0.5935	0.5346	0.4817	0.4339
12%	0.8929	0.7972	0.7118	0.6355	0.5674	0.5066	0.4523	0.4039
13%	0.8850	0.7831	0.6931	0.6133	0.5428	0.4803	0.4251	0.3762
14%	0.8772	0.7695	0.6750	0.5921	0.5194	0.4556	0.3996	0.3506
15%	0.8696	0.7561	0.6575	0.5718	0.4972	0.4323	0.3759	0.3269
16%	0.8621	0.7432	0.6407	0.5523	0.4761	0.4104	0.3538	0.3050
17%	0.8547	0.7305	0.6244	0.5337	0.4561	0.3898	0.3332	0.2848
18%	0.8475	0.7182	0.6086	0.5158	0.4371	0.3704	0.3139	0.2660
19%	0.8403	0.7062	0.5934	0.4987	0.4190	0.3521	0.2959	0.2487
20%	0.8333	0.6944	0.5787	0.4823	0.4019	0.3349	0.2791	0.2326
21%	0.8264	0.6830	0.5645	0.4665	0.3855	0.3186	0.2633	0.2176
22%	0.8197	0.6719	0.5507	0.4514	0.3700	0.3033	0.2486	0.2038
23%	0.8130	0.6610	0.5374	0.4369	0.3552	0.2888	0.2348	0.1909
24%	0.8065	0.6504	0.5245	0.4230	0.3411	0.2751	0.2218	0.1789
25%	0.8000	0.6400	0.5120	0.4096	0.3277	0.2621	0.2097	0.1678

Time Periods	9	10	11	12	13	14	15	16
1%	0.9143	0.9053	0.8963	0.8874	0.8787	0.8700	0.8613	0.8528
2%	0.8368	0.8203	0.8043	0.7885	0.7730	0.7579	0.7430	0.7284
3%	0.7664	0.7441	0.7224	0.7014	0.6810	0.6611	0.6419	0.6232
4%	0.7026	0.6756	0.6496	0.6246	0.6006	0.5775	0.5553	0.5339
5%	0.6446	0.6139	0.5847	0.5568	0.5303	0.5051	0.4810	0.4581
6%	0.5919	0.5584	0.5268	0.4970	0.4688	0.4423	0.4173	0.3936
7%	0.5439	0.5083	0.4751	0.4440	0.4150	0.3878	0.3624	0.3387
8%	0.5002	0.4632	0.4289	0.3971	0.3677	0.3405	0.3152	0.2919
9%	0.4604	0.4224	0.3875	0.3555	0.3262	0.2992	0.2745	0.2519
10%	0.4241	0.3855	0.3505	0.3186	0.2897	0.2633	0.2394	0.2176
11%	0.3909	0.3522	0.3173	0.2858	0.2575	0.2320	0.2090	0.1883
12%	0.3606	0.3220	0.2875	0.2567	0.2292	0.2046	0.1827	0.1631
13%	0.3329	0.2946	0.2607	0.2307	0.2042	0.1807	0.1599	0.1415
14%	0.3075	0.2697	0.2366	0.2076	0.1821	0.1597	0.1401	0.1229
15%	0.2843	0.2472	0.2149	0.1869	0.1625	0.1413	0.1229	0.1069
16%	0.2630	0.2267	0.1954	0.1685	0.1452	0.1252	0.1079	0.0930
17%	0.2434	0.2080	0.1778	0.1520	0.1299	0.1110	0.0949	0.0811
18%	0.2255	0.1911	0.1619	0.1372	0.1163	0.0985	0.0835	0.0708
19%	0.2090	0.1756	0.1476	0.1240	0.1042	0.0876	0.0736	0.0618
20%	0.1938	0.1615	0.1346	0.1122	0.0935	0.0779	0.0649	0.0541
21%	0.1799	0.1486	0.1228	0.1015	0.0839	0.0693	0.0573	0.0474
22%	0.1670	0.1369	0.1122	0.0920	0.0754	0.0618	0.0507	0.0415
23%	0.1552	0.1262	0.1026	0.0834	0.0678	0.0551	0.0448	0.0364
24%	0.1443	0.1164	0.0938	0.0757	0.0610	0.0492	0.0397	0.0320
25%	0.1342	0.1074	0.0859	0.0687	0.0550	0.0440	0.0352	0.0281

TABLE 2 — Present Value Factors — Annuities

Time Periods	1	2	3	4	5	6	7	8
1%	0.9901	1.9704	2.9410	3.9020	4.8534	5.7955	6.7282	7.6517
2%	0.9804	1.9416	2.8839	3.8077	4.7135	5.6014	6.4720	7.3255
3%	0.9709	1.9135	2.8286	3.7171	4.5797	5.4172	6.2303	7.0197
4%	0.9615	1.8861	2.7751	3.6299	4.4518	5.2421	6.0021	6.7327
5%	0.9524	1.8594	2.7233	3.5460	4.3295	5.0757	5.7864	6.4632
6%	0.9434	1.8334	2.6730	3.4651	4.2124	4.9173	5.5824	6.2098
7%	0.9346	1.8080	2.6243	3.3872	4.1002	4.7665	5.3893	5.9713
8%	0.9259	1.7833	2.5771	3.3121	3.9927	4.6229	5.2064	5.7466
9%	0.9174	1.7591	2.5313	3.2397	3.8897	4.4859	5.0330	5.5348
10%	0.9091	1.7355	2.4869	3.1699	3.7908	4.3553	4.8684	5.3349
11%	0.9010	1.7125	2.4437	3.1025	3.6959	4.2305	4.7122	5.1461
12%	0.8929	1.6901	2.4018	3.0374	3.6048	4.1114	4.5638	4.9676
13%	0.8850	1.6681	2.3612	2.9745	3.5172	3.9976	4.4226	4.7988
14%	0.8772	1.6467	2.3216	2.9137	3.4331	3.8887	4.2883	4.6389
15%	0.8696	1.6257	2.2832	2.8550	3.3522	3.7845	4.1604	4.4873
16%	0.8621	1.6052	2.2459	2.7982	3.2743	3.6847	4.0386	4.3436
17%	0.8547	1.5852	2.2096	2.7432	3.1994	3.5892	3.9224	4.2072
18%	0.8475	1.5656	2.1743	2.6901	3.1272	3.4976	3.8115	4.0776
19%	0.8403	1.5465	2.1399	2.6386	3.0576	3.4098	3.7057	3.9544
20%	0.8333	1.5278	2.1065	2.5887	2.9906	3.3255	3.6046	3.8372
21%	0.8264	1.5095	2.0739	2.5404	2.9260	3.2446	3.5080	3.7256
22%	0.8197	1.4915	2.0422	2.4936	2.8636	3.1669	3.4155	3.6193
23%	0.8130	1.4740	2.0114	2.4483	2.8035	3.0923	3.3270	3.5179
24%	0.8065	1.4568	1.9813	2.4043	2.7454	3.0205	3.2423	3.4212
25%	0.8000	1.4400	1.9520	2.3616	2.6893	2.9514	3.1611	3.3289

Time Periods	9	10	11	12	13	14	15	16
1%	8.5660	9.4713	10.3676	11.2551	12.1337	13.0037	13.8651	14.7179
2%	8.1622	8.9826	9.7869	10.5753	11.3484	12.1062	12.8493	13.5777
3%	7.7861	8.5302	9.2526	9.9540	10.6350	11.2961	11.9379	12.5611
4%	7.4353	8.1109	8.7605	9.3851	9.9857	10.5631	11.1184	11.6523
5%	7.1078	7.7217	8.3064	8.8633	9.3936	9.8986	10.3797	10.8378
6%	6.8017	7.3601	7.8869	8.3838	8.8527	9.2950	9.7123	10.1059
7%	6.5152	7.0236	7.4987	7.9427	8.3577	8.7456	9.1079	9.4467
8%	6.2469	6.7101	7.1390	7.5361	7.9038	8.2442	8.5595	8.8514
9%	5.9953	6.4177	6.8052	7.1607	7.4869	7.7862	8.0607	8.3126
10%	5.7590	6.1446	6.4951	6.8137	7.1034	7.3670	7.6061	7.8237
11%	5.5371	5.8892	6.2065	6.4924	6.7499	6.9819	7.1909	7.3792
12%	5.3283	5.6502	5.9377	6.1944	6.4236	6.6282	6.8109	6.9740
13%	5.1317	5.4262	5.6869	5.9177	6.1218	6.3025	6.4624	6.6039
14%	4.9464	5.2161	5.4527	5.6603	5.8424	6.0021	6.1422	6.2651
15%	4.7716	5.0188	5.2337	5.4206	5.5832	5.7245	5.8474	5.9542
16%	4.6065	4.8332	5.0286	5.1971	5.3423	5.4675	5.5755	5.6685
17%	4.4506	4.6586	4.8364	4.9884	5.1183	5.2293	5.3242	5.4053
18%	4.3030	4.4941	4.6560	4.7932	4.9095	5.0081	5.0916	5.1624
19%	4.1633	4.3389	4.4865	4.6105	4.7147	4.8023	4.8759	4.9377
20%	4.0310	4.1925	4.3271	4.4392	4.5327	4.6106	4.6755	4.7296
21%	3.9054	4.0541	4.1769	4.2785	4.3624	4.4317	4.4890	4.5364
22%	3.7863	3.9232	4.0354	4.1274	4.2028	4.2646	4.3152	4.3567
23%	3.6731	3.7993	3.9019	3.9852	4.0530	4.1082	4.1530	4.1894
24%	3.5655	3.6819	3.7757	3.8514	3.9124	3.9616	4.0013	4.0333
25%	3.4631	3.5705	3.6564	3.7251	3.7801	3.8241	3.8593	3.8874

TABLE 3 — Replacement Factors

Time Periods	1	2	3	4	5	6	7	8
1%	101.0000	50.7512	34.0022	25.6281	20.6040	17.2548	14.8628	13.0690
2%	51.0000	25.7525	17.3377	13.1312	10.6079	8.9263	7.7256	6.8255
3%	34.3333	17.4204	11.7843	8.9676	7.2785	6.1533	5.3502	4.7485
4%	26.0000	13.2549	9.0087	6.8873	5.6157	4.7690	4.1652	3.7132
5%	21.0000	10.7561	7.3442	5.6402	4.6195	3.9403	3.4564	3.0944
6%	17.6667	9.0906	6.2352	4.8099	3.9566	3.3894	2.9856	2.6839
7%	15.2857	7.9013	5.4436	4.2175	3.4842	2.9971	2.6508	2.3924
8%	13.5000	7.0096	4.8504	3.7740	3.1307	2.7039	2.4009	2.1752
9%	12.1111	6.3163	4.3895	3.4297	2.8566	2.4769	2.2077	2.0075
10%	11.0000	5.7619	4.0211	3.1547	2.6380	2.2961	2.0541	1.8744
11%	10.0909	5.3085	3.7201	2.9302	2.4597	2.1489	2.9292	1.7666
12%	9.3333	4.9308	3.4696	2.7436	2.3117	2.0269	2.8260	1.6775
13%	8.6923	4.6114	3.2579	2.5861	2.1870	1.9243	1.7393	1.6030
14%	8.1429	4.3378	3.0767	2.4515	2.0806	1.8368	1.6657	1.5398
15%	7.6667	4.1008	2.9198	2.3351	1.9888	1.7616	1.6024	1.4857
16%	7.2500	3.8935	2.7829	2.2336	1.9088	1.6962	1.5476	1.4389
17%	6.8824	3.7108	2.6622	2.1443	1.8386	1.6389	1.4997	1.3982
18%	6.5556	3.5484	2.5551	2.0652	1.7765	1.5884	1.4576	1.3625
19%	6.2632	3.4033	2.4595	1.9947	1.7213	1.5435	1.4203	1.3310
20%	6.0000	3.2727	2.3736	1.9314	1.6719	1.5035	1.3871	1.3030
21%	5.7619	3.1547	2.2961	1.8744	1.6275	1.4676	1.3575	1.2782
22%	5.5455	3.0475	2.2257	1.8228	1.5873	1.4353	1.3308	1.2559
23%	5.3478	2.9497	2.1616	1.7759	1.5509	1.4060	1.3068	1.2359
24%	5.1667	2.8601	2.1030	1.7330	1.5177	1.3795	1.2851	1.2179
25%	5.0000	2.7778	2.0492	1.6938	1.4874	1.3553	1.2654	1.2016

INDEX